Finding
Mr Right

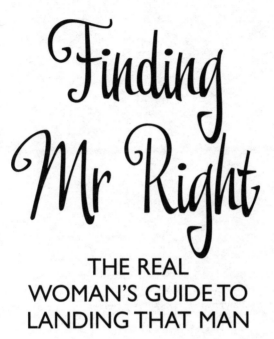

Finding Mr Right

THE REAL WOMAN'S GUIDE TO LANDING THAT MAN

Annie Harrison

BOOKS

First published in Great Britain in 2009 by
JR Books, 10 Greenland Street, London NW1 0ND
www.jrbooks.com

A catalogue record for this book is available from the British Library.

ISBN 978-1-906779-13-9

1 3 5 7 9 10 8 6 4 2

Printed by MPG Books, Bodmin, Cornwall

Every effort has been made to contact contributors. If you have any queries, please contact JR Books.

To the three men in my life:
Stephen, Daniel and Louis

Contents

Cautionary tales

Baby, I want you

Overcoming a single state of mind

Late love: pulling all the pieces together

his is a secret book and it's secret in two ways: first, it's just for you, to be read in private. Don't leave it around on your coffee table for anyone to see and don't read it on the train going into work. Take time to read it in a quiet place by yourself. Second, although I'm not making any promises here, these pages might just hold the key to changing your mindset and circumstances to create fresh opportunities for finding your life partner.

Finding Mr Right: The Real Woman's Guide to Landing That Man is aimed at the woman of a certain age who for various reasons hasn't yet found her man and settled down. Whatever her personal story, it's for the single woman who wants another chance at love and feels uncomfortable facing the future alone. I compiled this book because I felt so strongly about the fate (and I use the word wisely) of single women in their thirties and forties who are desperate to marry and in some cases have babies. I was one of those women. For years, I wasted time in the hands of a serial monogamist and I came on much too strong to any man I met. I made bad decisions and wept for the children I thought I might never have. As the years trundled on, my options on all sides seemed to be narrowing. The late thirties and early forties can be tumultuous, emotional and scary for single women as time and ageing suddenly speed up.

During this time, some of us find ourselves playing a game of brinkmanship – enjoying our hard-earned independence and financial freedom while waiting for that big biological alarm clock to go off and spoil the fun. The stakes are high and the questions 'Why me, what I have done wrong?', 'Where is he?' or even 'Will I ever have a child?' churn round and round in one's mind. It was this fear of being forever alone, followed by my relief and utter joy at finally becoming a wife and mother that prompted me to write this book. *Finding Mr Right* was to be my mission and passion, and the more I wrote, the more I discovered and wanted to share.

In compiling *Finding Mr Right*, I am grateful for the many invaluable contributions that I've received from journalists, friends, psychologists, academics, doctors, matchmakers, acquaintances, outspoken individuals and those willing to share their experiences, both men and women. The response to the questions posed on my research website has been phenomenal and an eye-opener.

Although I myself walked down the aisle a couple of months before my 39th birthday and gave birth to our first son just days before turning 40, this book is not the sum total of my experiences. These events inspired me to compile this anthology, but I am indebted to hundreds of people who sent me emails, written accounts, called me or have given me the threads from which I could pull this book together. It's my hope that this collection of experiences and observations examining the state of reluctant singledom will provide inspiration and encouragement to those who feel left behind. In assimilating the different perspectives, I decided to take a no-holds barred approach so the copy is sometimes shocking, upfront and personal. Where possible, I have attempted to veer away from the patronising preaching of the 'smug-married' and provide a non-judgemental look at all the issues from different standpoints.

The first part of *Finding Mr Right* recounts a number of success stories and takes an optimistic stance on the state of the single woman in her thirties and forties, including 'how-it-all-went-right' stories. It's important to present balance, however, so the second part comprises a collection of cautionary tales (including some contributions from men) highlighting the very real perils facing single women who navigate a course through this precarious life chapter (a sort of 'how-it-can-all-go-horribly-wrong' section). Take note. The third part concerns the 'b' word: babies. This section dips into the issues relating to having them, or not as the case may be. For many women, the topic of babies is emotive and pressing. Men may come and go but there is something 'last-chance saloon' about motherhood. I have attempted to present all the topics, especially the chapters on babies, as objectively as possible. This doesn't mean that I support all the views expressed – I am merely sharing collective experiences and presenting the issues from different perspectives.

Finally, I have done my best to ensure that *Finding Mr Right* ends on upbeat and constructive notes. There *is* a way forward, through a change in attitude and fundamental shifts of certain rigid mindsets and beliefs. Hopefully, this book will offer you ways in which you can 'overcome' being single in the way most appropriate for you.

We're all different so not every page of this book will be relevant to everyone who reads it. Saying this, you may well recognise yourself in one or more of the chapters and find yourself thinking, 'Hey, that's me. I've been in that situation!' And as you read on, you'll come across insights, anecdotes and tales to which you can relate and from which you can take heed. And also encouragement, lots of it.

There is no magic formula or instant solution common to our great personal diversity. However, during the compilation of this book, I noticed many recurring themes, whether they were from men who'd had bad experiences, women feeling the pressure of their age or those who'd eventually found contentment in the arms of their life partner. If so many different takes on a single subject shout out the same messages, they must hold the key to ultimate success in finding, attracting and leading a happy life with a life partner and/or having a baby.

I can't tell you what to do but I hope the testimonies in this book will help you on your path to self-fulfilment. The trial and error is all here and everyone I have interviewed or who has contributed truly speaks from the heart. I have loved writing it and sharing what I've learned.

All the best for your future,
Annie Harrison

It's Never Too Late

Take stock of your present situation and lay down the foundations for the future. Here, women reveal their perspectives on the single life and leaving it behind.

'To love is to risk not being loved in return. To hope is to risk pain. To try is to risk failure, but risk must be taken because the greatest hazard in life is to risk nothing.' Anon.

1.

'It must be so hard starting from scratch at your age'

eard any of these before? This list ranges from the infuriating, to the tactless, insulting, laughable and 'meant to be helpful' that mothers, ex-boyfriends, friends and the world at large seem to say to single women, reminding them of their single status.

'Have you met "the one" yet?'

'I can't understand it – you're lovely, attractive, smart and successful. Why haven't you been snapped up?'

From an acquaintance: 'I absolutely must introduce you to John. He's so sweet and like you, he's been single forever. I'm going to get you both round for dinner.'

'Are you a lesbian?'

At a social gathering: 'Hello there! You must be Mum!'

At a wedding: 'We've put all the singles together on an odds and ends table.'

From your mother: 'When, oh when, am I going to get some grandchildren?'

Also: 'I read an article the other day which said that by their late thirties, women's fertility plunges to such an extent that only five per cent can actually get pregnant. You'd better get a move on finding a husband.'

Or even: 'It's such a pity that you didn't marry Paul. He was so charming. Didn't he get married to Sarah – that really beautiful girl? Do you still see him in your circle of friends?'

From your best friend: 'Guess what? We're engaged! Look at my ring!'

Also: 'I'm pregnant! We're going to have a baby!'

From your last serious boyfriend: 'Although Saskia and I have only known each other for a couple of months, I thought it only fair to tell you. I have asked her to marry me.'

From your employer: 'The board has requested all single members of staff to provide skeleton cover in the office between Christmas and New Year as other staff members have family commitments.'

From the holiday company: 'Children go free. Forty per cent surcharge for single room occupancy.'

From the estate agent at a viewing: 'And in here we have the nursery . . . You could make this into a study or office.'

From a married woman with children: 'You're so wise not to have married and had kids. I tell you, every second of my life is taken up with family stuff – husband, children, school – you've got the right idea. Don't go there.'

And we read it everywhere too:

Mini Christmas Pudding: Serves 1.

On lots of forms: Circle appropriate Married Living With Partner Divorced Single

Spouse's/partner's details . . .

Number of children . . .

On a wedding invitation: (Name) plus guest

On a Christmas card: To Jane, Merry Christmas and a Happy New Year, Lots of love from Camilla, Rupert, Naomi, Charlie, Toby, Anouska . . . and the bump!

Invitation: St Margaret's School 1982 Reunion. Bring husbands and children. See you there!

2.

An older girl's guide to husband hunting

Shane Watson

It is odd that in 2007 someone wrote a book about withholding sex to bag a husband (*Not Tonight, Mr Right*). Odder still that it should sell so well, as if it actually held the key to finding a man.

Then again, there is one subject that unattached females will never tire of: how not to end up single. If you are uncomfortably alone, you're desperate for clues. If you are comfortably single, you're still curious – lest you should ever start to panic.

The point is that women, especially those for whom time is running out in the procreation sense, are extremely vulnerable to this stuff. I should know. Having got married for the first time in my forties, I am officially the most interesting person among my own sex. At parties, I am constantly hauled over to meet single women, expressly to impart the details of my miraculous, last-minute sprint across the line. I am a freak of nature, living proof that nubile doesn't necessarily always get the bloke. People long for a hidden secret: something I did that I hadn't done before; a deciding factor that tipped the balance.

So ladies, here are my personal tips on how to get a man to marry you in your forties.

Don't obsess about waxed legs and so on

It's wrong to think you have to be a perfect size 10 before anything can happen – that way lies the shiny stiffness that men don't like. There is a myth that confidence is about being buffed and tweaked to within an inch of your life, but actually that just creates expectation. You want to be thinking, 'Hellooo, who are you?' not, 'Will you notice the effort I have made, thank you?'

There is an argument that supergrooming gives you an added determination – nobody wants to waste an all-over body exfoliation and seaweed wrap – but I found that just enough is better than the works. You still feel like you, and you don't have that pinched 'someone had better make this worthwhile' look.

Where to find him

The big problem for older singles is choosing what not to go to. There is nothing so dispiriting as the dinner party where you are being set up with the short-limbed biologist (apart from the dinner party where you are sitting next to two temporarily husbandless women). These experiences can drain your precious supply of positive energy – the single girl's number-one asset, after a healthy bank account – and you have a duty to protect this at all costs.

The secret is to view your social life in three categories: slob time with friends, possible-meeting-men time, but probably not and good-chance-of-meeting-men occasions. The first and the last you do automatically, the uncertain category is the one to avoid. On the good-chance occasions (a party, in my case), the trick is to assume, well before you even get there, that this is The Night. It generates a mix of adrenaline and pheromones that people have been trying to bottle since the beginning of time. If you go to a party in your second-hottest dress because you're saving the other one, and you're a bit, 'I can always leave after ten minutes', The One will look in your direction and think: 'Hmm . . . Downer.'

Where are all the men?

They are there, but you are scaring them away by looking so grumpy and hard to please. Or you never get round to meeting them because you are too busy hanging out at the bar with your old mates. Or they know about The List. They haven't actually seen The List, but they have picked up on the fact that you are strictly interested in artistic types/Spaniards/whatever, so they don't bother to make the effort. Or that you are automatically discounting them, either because of The List or because they are married. (So? They have friends. And brothers. And cousins. And work colleagues.)

Keep an open mind. The One is never going to present himself as The One. He is going to be The One You Least Expect. (This is a fact. And he won't live anywhere near you. And he will be wearing a shirt that you don't like.)

Abandon The List

You know The List: hate men who wear black shirts, hate men who wear hair products, hate men who play golf. The List is probably the No. 1 reason why people stay single. You are expecting him to arrive in the precise package you ordered when actually, if you're lucky, he will tick one of the boxes.

Put The List out of your head and deal with what is in front of you. Not your type? Right. And that's been such a success for you to date, has it?

Do something differently

For example, on The Night, I didn't go for my standard fall-back (white jeans, wedges), I went for a girlie dress and flat sandals, just for a change. This might have made the difference because if you always project the same image a) you become like wallpaper to the people who already know you – and don't discount them – and b) you bore yourself and therefore never project the right crackle and pop. Part of the game (after a period of being overlooked) is believing that you are worth the effort, not just passable in a low-lit environment.

Also, it might just be me, but shorter is more conducive to meeting The One. Heels are sexy, but they can make you look a bit intimidating (especially if you are tipping 6ft). In the flat sandals that I almost never wear, I felt a bit skippy and flighty. Just a thought.

Avoid your friends

They will cramp your style. You need to be able to flirt outrageously and reinvent yourself slightly if you are to attract The One. In addition, if something does happen when your mates are around, they will panic and put you on edge, gawp open-mouthed or start popping up behind sofas, sniggering. So, don't always go to a party with a girlfriend or rush to find the people you've known all your life. The fact that I went unchaperoned on The Night meant that I was free, in need of a lift home and nobody was watching – crucial.

Don't be too cool

Finding a man does not involve sophisticated game-playing. It turns out that it's not so tricky, providing you – the single girl – show enthusiastic interest. And I recommend trebling what you would describe as enthusiastic. You may think you are being friendly, but single girls have a subconscious fear of looking eager – aka desperate – so there's a good chance that you are actually coming over a bit Morticia.

Note: it's a mistake to think grown-up men are all superconfident. They need stupid amounts of encouragement – you might as well still be at the school bus stop when it comes to fear of rejection. Tell him you love how tall he is – unless he isn't, but do lay it on a bit.

Be 40 flirty

Fortysomethings have one thing going for them that their younger competitors do not: we can do life alone, and probably quite well, what with all the practice we've had. This is quite appealing, in the busy, busy 'so-not-desperate-for-you-to-look-after-me-and-pay-for-everything' sense. Be slightly elusive though obviously keen. (You have a life. You are having so much fun. You can't cancel your trip to Morocco . . .) With other age groups this can be interpreted as too independent to get involved but with the fortysomething, it is normal and reassuring.

Don't get drunk

Well, obviously get wonderfully drunk, but not insensible. Men are terrified of bad drunks, especially when they are too old to sling over their shoulders. Never get drunk and dial. It's a bad look. They will pretend that they thought it was sweet and funny, but actually they will be planning to chuck you.

Go for it, girls! I'm living proof that it can be done.

Shane Watson is a columnist for the Sunday Times Style *magazine and author of* How To Meet a Man after Forty and Other Midlife Dilemmas Solved.

3.

Finding love in your forties

Mariella Frostrup

There are many nasty phrases used about women approaching 40. 'Desperate', 'over-eager' and 'past their sell-by date' are three of the most popular. I can't say that I felt any of those things when a life that might be lived without a family and maybe even a long-term partner began to seem a possibility. I was resigned, perhaps curious, as to how a woman so committed to the idea of a family could end up alone. I was even a little excited about what this entirely unimagined life would be like, so when a charity trek in Nepal for *Marie Claire* led to me meeting the man who made my life's original ambitions seem possible again, it came as a complete surprise.

It wasn't love at first sight; in fact we bickered for the entire week in sibling fashion. But when we returned and met up for a drink to look over holiday photos, he reached out and held my hand and it felt like a perfect fit. A year later, he chose the idyllic setting of the Banyan Tree resort in the Seychelles to propose to me at midnight on the eve of my 40th birthday. It's probably his being a lawyer that made him orchestrate a scenario that virtually guaranteed him a positive response.

So why did it take so long for an intelligent, attractive and capable woman to find the thing she most desired? Perhaps it wasn't until I hit 40 that I realised that I boasted any of those virtues. Instead, I had cast myself as the unappealing, unattractive and wholly hopeless victim of a series of bounders who took advantage of me. It never occurred to me that I was myopically focused on men who were quite clearly offering the polar opposite of what I had my heart set on – which were, in order of importance, lasting love, security and, hopefully, kids.

If you meet a man on a drunken night out, judge a 3am offer of sex to be the guaranteed precursor to dating, then feel betrayed when he fails to fight his way through the fog of his hangover to call the next day, the only person responsible for the perceived deception is yourself. Then again, if you employ the opposite approach and interview prospective partners to ascertain their ambitions in love, it's considered equally off-putting. Men seem to take exception to the idea that, at a certain point (sadly all too often dictated by biological clock rather than increasing self-esteem), women take their destiny into their own hands, refusing to leap blindfolded into relationships that don't offer them what they need.

If there is an identifiable difference in expectation in our fifth decade, it's a simple one: when we contemplate a Smart Car, we don't expect it to turn into a Range Rover over time. Even so, although my drug of choice was twinkling men who commanded an audience, and whose romantic history didn't suggest stability, it wasn't as if they were in the minority. In fact, if my husband's ex-girlfriends were asked to describe the guy they dated prior to his meeting me, they would no doubt come up with a similar description for the man who has been my anchor since we met on that Himalayan trek. There's definitely that unpredictable element of timing involved for both parties in order to stumble across each other at the right moment.

Now I can't help thinking that hindsight is overrated. It offers no real window to the future, only the annoying potential to make past mistakes look avoidable. I'm not convinced that anything I could have done would have led to me meeting my husband earlier, but there is plenty I could have done to reduce my level of emotional suffering in the intervening years. I used to have a postcard stuck on my cooker hood that read, 'Oops, I forgot to have children.' It was one of those Fifties-styled, post-modern pieces of propaganda attempting to inject a note of humour into a battle for basic human rights that we christened feminism. At best, it was blackly comic. The vote, the Pill and the Equal Pay Act had led women relentlessly forward into a brave new world where we were expected to work, have babies, run homes, enjoy casual sex, deny our expectations of long-term relationships and, in our spare time, nurture our partners and relieve them of the burden of being the sole earner. It may sound like an excuse, but it's no wonder that trying to live up to all those expectations proved too daunting.

The other day, as I bathed my two babies, both miraculously conceived a long time after we're expected to embark on motherhood, and certainly not because of a positive choice to sacrifice family for career in the intervening years, I found myself wondering where that card had got to. I don't recall the moment that I decided it was no longer funny or simply in bad taste, but at some mystery point in my late thirties it must have hit the bin. It had been an emblem of bravado through my late twenties and thirties: not so much alone as naively hopeful of each new relationship, refusing to believe that the hopeless choices I was making were anything other than bad luck.

It's easy to say that from my current vantage point I can look back and see how complicit I was in the behaviour that kept me single. Easy, but not necessarily true. But it is just possible that the day that postcard and the false face it put on my endeavours to find lasting happiness hit the bin was the day I faced up to what really mattered. I decided just in time to accept nothing less than respect, kindness, decency and some engagement with the future from the next man I allowed to engage my passion.

Mariella Frostrup is a prolific and opinion-forming journalist, arts critic, and radio and television presenter.

4.

If I could change one thing in my life . . . Getting unstuck from your rut and moving on

Hindsight is a wonderful thing and there cannot be a soul on this planet who hasn't had a few regrets about something in his or her past. Incidents and missed opportunities occur in everyone's lives, and become woven into the rich fabric that goes into making us who we are. It's the law of cause and effect. As any Buddhist will tell you, 'You make your choices, and you bear the results.' We are the sum total of our life's experiences. Where we are now and how we feel are a direct result of everything that has happened to us from birth right through to this very minute. So to be single against your will in your late thirties isn't necessarily anyone's fault, it just happened.

Thinking back over your life there will have been certain key points which had a dramatic effect on the linked sequence of events across the years. Much of what happens to us we can put down to fate, although we may have engineered or accelerated certain life events – getting a particular job, buying a property, meeting someone on holiday. As in the film *Sliding Doors*, moments and decisions occur that can transform our lives completely.

And in a fateful way much of our lives is determined by others. We don't ask to be born, but in the biggest race of our life we fight biological odds of

400 million to one to be created and arrive kicking and screaming into this world.

Once born, we cannot choose our siblings, where we live or who our classmates are. Having grown up, we can accept a job, but can't necessarily select colleagues or clients. Other things beyond our control can affect us – traffic accidents, strikes, a lottery win, the economy, war or acts of God. We can determine our own destiny up to a point, we can pursue certain dreams and set our own goals, but fate has a powerful hand to play in the way our lives unfold.

And this is why so many single women reach their late thirties and are puzzled and concerned about their predicament. Obviously there are a few exceptions, but most of us don't have a life plan which includes, 'I want to succeed in my career, own property, lead a great social life, pursue my interests in x, y, z. Oh, and by the way, I *must* be single by the time I am 39.'

Many women allow themselves to be dragged down by guilt and bewilderment. 'I haven't been a bad person; I am attractive, popular, smart; I'm kind, feminine and funny. I've known some lovely guys in the past. OK, I've made a few mistakes along the way, but how can it be that fate conspired to leave me single? How did other women, some with lesser qualities than me, bag all the decent men?'

During the 1990s there was a play and later a film entitled *Six Degrees of Separation*. The premise is that if a person is one step or link away from each person she knows and two steps away from each person who is known by one of the people she knows, then everyone is no more than six steps away from anyone on this planet. This means that all of us are only separated by six links from Prince William or Barack Obama, or anyone else we choose to name on Planet Earth.

Ergo, you are also only a maximum of six steps away from your perfect lifelong partner. Six steps. All you have to do is find those steps and take them.

But to get back to the title of this chapter . . . Just supposing you could change one thing in your life, then the knock-on effect would alter everything that follows. You would not be sitting where you are now, reading this. Many of us muse over our lives and look at 'what if' scenarios that would have changed things dramatically. How many of us have not had a misspent youth at some point? How many of us dated the wrong person, or didn't get the job that we were so sure was ours by rights? How many of us have been gazumped or denied a dream home, only to find something better later? Good and bad things happen to everyone, even those who seem to have it all. Life is full of swings and roundabouts, ups and downs.

Shit happens, but so does happiness. And if your life has ended up in a way that leaves you discontent, then you must change it.

Many people get stuck: you need a job to pay the mortgage; there are not enough hours in the day to fit in work *and* play; it's pointless, difficult (and expensive) just to move for the sake of it; changing jobs is risky. Or they repeat a pattern of mistakes whereby they are attracted to the wrong kind of partner every time.

So, the routine and the humdrum you have carved out for yourself continues, while all around you other people are changing their lives – getting married, switching jobs, moving on, having fun and having babies. They aren't doing anything radical, just getting on with their lives, while you are left stuck in neutral, seemingly forever.

But don't run away from it. Change it. *If you are stuck, get yourself unstuck.* Just as key events or pivotal points in your life have lead you down different paths, you just need to change one or a few aspects of how you live now to ease you from your rut and set you on your journey to emotional fulfilment.

If the desire to be loved, loving someone and having a permanent relationship is leaving you feeling trapped by your present circumstances, then look carefully at the patterns and processes in your life, together with who you are. Create a sea change in your attitudes and things in your life that you can alter without major upheaval – where you go on holiday, how you spend your weekends, how you do your hair . . . Take up new hobbies and pursuits, broaden your horizons by doing something new or different or challenging. Write down your values and aspirations and take a long hard look at yourself. Something needs to change to create a catalyst effect. What is it?

Don't be afraid to get some help. Sign up to a reputable dating agency or join the online dating world – you will be heartened by the response. Sometimes we need a little bit of nurturing, encouragement or mental tinkering to set us straight. A carefully selected therapist, hypnotist or life coach can really help to ease the stalemate.

There *is* someone out there for you. Believe this, and you will find him.

5.

Pearls of wisdom from ladies who know

The following is a collection of anecdotes and insights from women whose lives changed when they eventually met their partners. Read on and be inspired.

Fateful attraction

Cheryl met Roger at 42 and is now mother to Emily and Rory, and step-mother to four.

'In my late twenties and thirties I was always a great believer in serendipity. Whenever I met a man, invariably I felt the hand of fate pushing me towards him. Our meeting might have been by chance, but this was "meant to be". Consequently, everyone I met was "the one" and I threw myself headlong into relationships determined to make them work. As I got older, my friends became exasperated – I was known for saying on several occasions, "I have just met the most wonderful, perfect man. We sat up talking till 4am, putting the world to rights. We've mapped out our future and we're moving in together . . ."

'Early on in a relationship, most of us are in the thrall of new love. As we progress through our thirties, some of us close our ears, eyes and minds to any warning signs that might call for us to reign in on our enthusiasm for a new man and acknowledge any unpleasant truths. I know I did!

'I refused to see faults, impracticalities, bad signals and straightforward incompatibility. I was caught up in serendipity every time – and I always got it wrong. I was prepared to compromise on everything, just so I could feel good about "having a relationship". I believe I had a low sense of self-esteem, stemming from childhood. I was not a high achiever and in my family we had an ethos of "making do" – not a great neighbourhood, not a good school, selfish parents . . .

'By the time I reached 40, I woke up to the fact that hurling myself at a man 'because it was fate' was not the answer. I realised that I was trying to fit a square peg in a round hole. It wasn't fate at all – it was desperation. My blinkered determination was so strong that I dreamed of being able to prove everyone wrong and say, "I told you so!"

'I had always hoped for a family, but by the time I was 40 and still single, I had resigned myself to singledom and certain childlessness. I put all my effort into my job and some charity fundraising and got a cat. Plainly, relationships were not for me.

'I met Roger on a cookery holiday in Italy. He was the only man there – and at 57, the oldest too. Because I wasn't under any fateful (or fatal) pressure to "get a relationship", I was far more natural. We cooked some wonderful food together, explored the heavenly Tuscan countryside and sat talking, drinking wine and watching the sunset over the sunflower fields and vineyards. Now, *that* was romantic! We met up after the holiday to share photographs over a home-cooked Italian meal and took it from there. As a widower, Roger was reluctant to begin another relationship too quickly. My hesitancy also helped us to take it just one step at a time.

'We married when I was 42 and I found out that I was expecting twins. I had given up on relationships and on the prospect of having a child. Now I have both in spades, plus an unexpected, and sometimes challenging role as a stepmother.'

Cheryl's advice: 'You cannot force fate – fate will work for you when you least expect it. Don't go looking for it: let it come to you. Don't be blinded by love or compromise totally when you meet someone. Take note of the warning signals and never resolve to change someone to suit you, or change yourself to suit them. There is someone out there for you. Relax, chill out and look the other way. If fate determines it, he will tap on your shoulder and say, "I have been looking for you."'

Desperate and delusional

Sophie, 42, is a consultant oncologist, now married to Nick, who runs a printing business. She has just had baby Joshua and has been married almost a year and half. Here, Sophie recalls (with horror) her delusions and inability in the past to accept when a relationship had ended.

'Professionally, I have always been smart – I *have* to be, but I cringe when I think of how dreadfully inept and pathetic I was on the dating front. I have spent most of my adult life studying and working in hospitals. With very few exceptions, I always dated men from the medical profession. I was once compared to the crazy hospital administrator, Joanna Clore, from Channel 4's *The Green Wing*. I had many problems on the man front – I tried too hard, dated people too close to home (professionally speaking) and I was generally full on.

'My one big problem was that I found the ending of a relationship impossible to accept, even if I'd instigated it – I always wanted to remain friends. The usual chain of events meant that me and my ex would meet for an occasional drink, I would invite him over for dinner and one thing would lead to another. In my mind I had cured myself of being a former girlfriend and had instead tempted him back into my life again. A relationship that had been off was quickly converted back to one that was on again. I didn't do this just once but over the years, more times than I care to admit. My friends all castigated and lectured me about "over meaning over, and when you're dumped, find someone else," but it was like a kind of addiction to me. Finally, at the age of 38, one incident terminated once and for all my delusional aspirations to inveigle my way back in to a relationship that had irretrievably broken down.

'I had been going out with Callum, a doctor junior to me in age and rank, for about six months. We'd had a lot of fun and the relationship was quite relaxed. I admit, I'd even been mentally "making plans" for the future so I was devastated when he announced that he'd met someone else and that we were finished. I found it impossible to accept and began my "let's be good friends routine". Callum seemed to accept this, and it wasn't long before we were occasionally falling back into bed with each other, although he was adamant we were not a couple.

'One morning over breakfast at my apartment, Callum asked if I could lend him £3,000. He said he still had loans that needed paying off but he was expecting some money from his grandmother's legacy soon. Naturally, I was delighted to help, and felt that this financial arrangement bound us even closer together. So I paid up. About a week later a colleague took me to one side after surgery and told me that Callum had used the £3,000 I'd loaned him to buy a diamond engagement ring for the "someone else" he'd alluded to! And no, of course I didn't get the money back. In one fell swoop I had been dumped (again), humiliated, conned and passed over for a younger nurse. Furthermore these details about my personal life were all public knowledge within the hospital, from the porters up to the chief executive. Oh, the shame!

'When I met Nick a year later he found my reticence and caution quite alluring. And he bought me an engagement ring with his own money.'

Sophie says: 'My advice to anyone suffering from delusions about relationships, similar to mine, is never, ever, ever go back – even if it's just for an old times' sake fling. If he wants you back, he would have to beg on his knees and do everything in his power to win you over again. And still you must say no. Men enjoy the hunt and the chase. If you're presenting yourself on a plate, even for a new relationship, there will be no challenge. And never, ever, lend money to an ex-boyfriend.'

A *clean start*

Charlotte was 37 when she met Craig (after a lifetime of disastrous dating, of which the longest relationship was four months). She's now married and mother to Eliza.

'In recent years the word "toxic" has been used to describe the poisoning of emotions and relationships. It is a powerful word and as a writer, I feel that it's an apt description of my life prior to meeting Craig. A lake filled with toxic chemicals kills living things and causes stagnation, and I believe the same is true of emotions. Bad experiences, like battle scars, are left behind and take a long time to heal. If we move from one bad relationship without purging the toxicity left behind or allowing the wounds to heal then we are just creating more pollution with which to taint and destroy the next.

'For reasons I won't go into here, I had a catalogue of bad dating and relationship experiences going right back to my teens. By my mid-thirties, I was such a cynical and resentful individual that one man walked out of a restaurant via the kitchens on our first date!

'I took the advice of a friend and started seeing a therapist, who helped me to clear the dross from my past. Together we wiped my slate clean and erased all the one-night stands, arguments, bad experiences and feelings of low self-esteem. We swept away all the poison and worked on my self-image. I was also encouraged to help others in order to avoid becoming too self-absorbed, so I helped out at a hostel for the homeless. I saw for myself the effects bad experiences had on others, physically and mentally.

'Away from my therapist I rewrote my "rules" for dating men and resolved to be in control of my destiny. I was a lake, pure and fresh, and would not allow myself or anyone else to pollute its clear waters. I know it sounds weird but visualisation is a great therapy and good way to achieve goals.

'I met Craig while skiing in Austria. He found me "enigmatic and mysterious". I didn't harp on about all the bad relationships I'd had or put him off with a twisted attitude to men – I was the new me and a better person for it. A good relationship had been so difficult in the past. Now, it seemed straightforward, natural and totally uplifting. Having Eliza completed the picture.'

Charlotte says: 'My advice would be: If you have had bad relationships or still have issues to work through, take a break from looking for a man and sort yourself out. Get help, if you need it. Try and find someone who can help you visualise the breaking of ties and the removal of bad or harmful things that might be holding you back now. When you are ready, start afresh and keep some form of spiritual or religious insight in your head every day and commune with it.'

Irritatingly independent

Mary met Peter at 38 and married at 40. She had Poppy at 42, and another baby is due a month after her 45th birthday.

'My problem was that I was unbelievably independent. I was a commercial lawyer and thought most men were beneath me – intellectually, financially and in the way they presented themselves. This was a good excuse but in reality, I was completely married to my career and my success.

'One morning I woke up and decided the emphasis in my life had to change: I had a nasty habit of scaring men off with my power dressing, power thinking, female empowerment and supersonic-lawyer-thing. It all became abundantly clear when I took a good look at myself in a full-length mirror. I was dressed in my dark tailored business suit and observed my neat bleached hair and bright red lipstick. Standing tall in my heels and black stockings, I resembled a dominatrix. All that was missing was the whip! I realised then that I was coming across as threatening. Men need to feel they are protecting women, that *they* are the hunter-gatherers.

'I discussed this one evening with a male colleague who clarified the situation for me. He said that men like to compete with other men, not with women. Outside the work environment, high-powered women are scary to just about all men. They're definitely not a turn-on. Men have a basic need to be needed. Without being superior, they want to be able to do things that women can't. The guys want someone with whom they can grow, who can teach them how to be more sensitive.

'I met Peter when I went to stay with some married friends, John and Minty, at their farmhouse. Peter was John's brother, and was a fruit farmer. Not my type at all! But during that winter weekend, he impressed me. I had a puncture on my BMW convertible, and he changed the wheel in the pouring rain and fixed a faulty electric window. He then came in, dripping wet, and prepared a magnificent roast for twelve people, single-handedly. Later, he iced a Christmas cake for the village raffle. Not only was he manly, practical, resilient, kind and a good cook; over dinner I found him witty, intriguing and attractive. He was also six years younger than me. I softened in his company and he was able to bring out an inner gentleness I never knew I possessed.

'After a successful career I was fortunate to have my family late in life, without any problems. I almost feel that I don't deserve this. Peter's humility, contentment, kindness and energy made me see how hardened I had become. I was humbled and deeply honoured to marry him and have his children.'

Mary advises: 'Don't let your job or career dominate you. Switch off the power woman thing if you meet a good man. Don't compete with men – they can do that with other men. Men want someone they can grow with, someone they feel they can protect. If he feels you can fend for yourself, then he may be redundant and leave. Don't make him feel inferior to you. Men are not that difficult to figure out. He will have lots to offer. Make sure you don't trump him at every turn and that you can offer a contrasting feminine side. You don't have to give up your career – just tone down its dominance on you and your lives together.'

Escape the 'single girl syndrome'

Cara, 43, married Simon when they were both 40. Over 20 years, Cara had had 12 'steady' relationships, but was always looking out for someone better. After ten months on her own, she met Simon at the funeral of a work colleague.

'I suffered from what the Americans call "single girl syndrome". I was so busy having fun and could never find anyone right for me. Consequently, I was never in a "real" relationship. I always found faults – he wasn't the handsomest man in the room, he wasn't quite tall enough, he wasn't as successful as I would like, he wasn't fit enough – the list was never-ending.

'Whenever the initial romance in a relationship began to transform into attachment, I felt it was curbing my lifestyle. Snuggling down on the sofa with my man to watch a TV drama series or ironing his shirts just wasn't what I had in mind when it came to relationships. I would far rather be out clubbing, having a good time with my girlfriends or be down at the gym getting toned. One relationship also really hurt me and it took years to shake off the pain. I visited a psychologist who revealed that I had a problem loving myself and had barriers to break down before I could love anyone else. I also realised that I had never in my whole life been in a relationship with someone who loved me. No one had ever said, "I love you". I never stayed long enough for love to grow.

'I met Simon when I was at a very low ebb and I think that for the first time I was able to be the real me. Neither of us intended for our meeting to turn into friendship, and for friendship to blossom into love and marriage, but it did. Loving someone and being loved is the best feeling in the world. Or maybe it's having two babies to love when I thought my time was up. Both are utterly wonderful.'

Cara says: 'My advice to women in their thirties would be don't flit about and act like you are still in your twenties. Grow up and get in touch with your own feelings (or lack of them). In a man, see if his good qualities outweigh the bad. At the same time, take a close look at yourself and do the same exercise. Don't fear attachment to someone, embrace it. And improve your sense of self-esteem: if you can't respect yourself, how can you expect someone else to?'

Dismiss the Hollywood image of 'Mr Right'. Go and find 'Mr Right for you'

Nita, 45, married Rick when she was 39. They have two children, Felix and Barney.

'Ever since I was a small girl, I was captivated by films and entertainment and was fortunate enough to work as a make-up artist. I came into contact with A-list celebrities and spent most of my working life off set transforming people's faces. Not surprisingly, I began to confuse my real world with the unattainable heights of beauty, romance and love portrayed in the movies. Again, unsurprisingly, my target for Mr Right was exceedingly high – I wanted a dashingly handsome, ruggedly strong, powerhouse of lust and romance. George Clooney would have been ideal! Hardly surprising then that he didn't live in my neck of the woods.

'I think a lot of women have become brainwashed by the media and the culture of celebrity. Most men are normal, and so are most women. I also learned that things are never what they seem and the Hollywood ending is so utterly unlikely that it would never, ever happen, let alone to me. It would make sense to give a regular guy a chance. So that's what I did.

'Rick would kill me for describing him as a regular guy, but he is a million miles from the Tom Cruise Action Man type I had envisaged. He is nice looking (not a lot of hair, mind), smiles a lot, is handy about the house with his Black & Decker, makes me laugh and is completely ensconced in the responsibilities of fatherhood. And he loves me, and I love him. Rick works in films too, and our paths had crossed for years. It was only when we shared a car travelling to a film shoot on a Scottish mountain that we really got talking. I knew within ten minutes that we were right for each other. I was 38 and Rick was my Mr Right.'

Nita says: 'My advice would be stop looking for Mr Right – he doesn't exist. Instead, dispense with any ideal you hold in your head. You will have been influenced by all different kinds of things, including your friends, the media and other role models in your life (what about your father?). Instead, be very open-minded. Have no preconceptions. Are you a Hollywood goddess? No? I'm not saying lower your standards: just accept that most men are average, everyday people just like you. You don't have to settle for the first man that comes along, so be prepared to kiss a few frogs along the way. Come down from fantasyland and be prepared to take a chance. Remember, you won't find Mr Right, but you might just find Mr Right For You.'

Just be yourself

Vicky was 38 when she met Nigel. She was still 38 when they got married.

'I have spent most of my adult life pretending. I have always tried to fit into groups or cliques by being like the people in them, although I am naturally more solitary by nature. I just wanted to be liked. I used to boast a lot about my achievements and even made things up to impress people. During my twenties, if I was ever on my own, I was miserable in my own company. I mellowed as I went through my thirties, but I realised that I was copying my friends or people I admired. I copied people's clothes and even entered a career I didn't particularly like, just so I could be like my friends. I bought a particular model of car because my friend had one; I went on holidays I didn't enjoy because that's what the group had decided, and I even went out with someone because he was a friend of my friend's boyfriend. (It really depresses me writing this when I think back to what I was like!)

'I didn't really decide to be me – it just happened. I was sent to work in France for a couple of months, although my French was very shaky. While there I met Nigel, who was also British. We soon teamed up socially as we couldn't get along in French. At first neither of us was physically attracted to each other (after all, he didn't fit my friends' "ideal types"), but we developed a sparking fusion on a completely new level – it was all in the head and so exciting and stimulating! I was also away from home in a different environment so I had to be myself, not some invention.

'Nigel was the complete opposite of the stereotypes I had always gone for in the past, just to fit in. With him, I also found a new me – someone who could express an independent view, develop her style and taste. We realised the sheer depth of our feelings for each other when his assignment ended and he returned from Paris to London. We ached to be together and for the first time in my life I knew what love was.

'It was great being able to plan my wedding all by myself. My two closest friends were surprised not be invited to be bridesmaids (I didn't have any) and I loved being able to do things my way.'

Vicky's advice: 'Just be yourself. Don't do things to please others or earn respectability. A man will love you for being you, not some kind of other person impressionist.'

Choose normal, not someone you want to change to fit your ideal

Kathryn was 39 when she met Martin. Now 42, they have two children together.

'After years of disastrous dating I met Martin. I had always been attracted to the wrong kind of men for me. I probably had a self-destruct button when it came to man selection. I learned nothing from my disasters and kept believing I could mould or even "cure" men to suit me. I think it stemmed from a low sense of self-esteem, with throwbacks to my relationships with my parents and being bullied at boarding school.

'I met Martin through mysinglefriend.com. My sister, Elspeth, thought I needed a fresh approach to dating and put my details forward. After some initial reticence, I became hooked. It seemed such an obvious way to meet people and it was great fun. I came into cyber contact with some interesting men, and found the whole process intriguing and inspirational. I was drawn to Martin and we began a relationship over the phone, because he lived 150 miles away. We discussed everything, and I couldn't wait until the allotted time every night when we would speak. The anticipation and nerves before our first date were huge. I wanted it all to work out and for me not to mess it up. I also hoped he wouldn't find me too old looking.

'Martin was the first normal man I think I had ever met. He runs a successful mail order company, and he wanted to settle down and have a family. He is practical, popular, kind, friendly and funny. I was blown away by how he fell in love with me – he was completely smitten. He told a friend of mine that he would do ANYTHING, absolutely ANYTHING to get me. I found my reserved attitude to commitment eradicated by his unashamed love, and reciprocated fully. I had finally stopped wishing for, or trying to change a man to fit in with my preconceptions. Because we were unable to spend a lot of time together, we made the absolute most of our weekends. As they say, 'absence really does make the heart grow fonder.' He wasn't what I had envisaged but he was perfect and I didn't want to change him one jot.'

Kathryn says: 'Give the guys a break! Men are just as confused about women as women are about men. Don't try and change someone because he doesn't suit you. Accept it: he doesn't suit you. Internet dating is a great way to widen your potential market. There *are* lots of men out there and there is someone right for you. Go with the flow, relax and be yourself.'

Be the hunted, not the hunter

Olivia, 43, has been living with Alastair for the last four years.

'Right across the animal kingdom, and in all cultures and civilisations since man inhabited the planet, in courtship the male of the species has chased and caught the female. True, there might be a few exceptions to this rule but by and large, it's the boys pursuing the girls.

'So I don't know why I wasted about five years of my adult life pursuing any man who took my fancy and then bemoaned the fact that I couldn't meet a man who was right for me. At the age of 35 I decided that I would "take action" and become a "dating activist". I answered adverts in the paper, tried to pick up men up in pubs and at clubs. I flirted outrageously with colleagues and pursued relentlessly those who didn't appear to be returning my affections. I had a lot going for me – I was attractive and bright, with a good sense of humour. I had travelled throughout the world in my job as an IT consultant, and I had a nice home and a zippy car.

'Looking back on the way I behaved, I am appalled. Men were like prey and I hunted them down. It all became about the capture and making a conquest. I didn't know what I wanted once I had them, so moved on to the next one.

'I am ashamed to admit it, but the turning point came one morning in the office. The night before, I had slept with a man I had met while out with colleagues after work. He was rather gorgeous, but hadn't asked if he could see me again so I deliberately left one of my rings on his bedside table, using it as the perfect excuse to engineer another meeting.

'I found his office number in the phone book and rang him at work. I told him that I had left my grandmother's engagement ring at his house and asked if I could come over and pick it up. He said that he had it with him at his office and would arrange for a courier to deliver it to my workplace. When it arrived, there was a slip of paper in the envelope saying, "You are a slut and your grandfather was obviously a cheapskate." Harsh words when you are desperate to find someone to love and be loved by.

'You should always expect the unexpected, but forget all this "seek and ye shall find" mullarky because it just doesn't apply to lifelong partners. Yes, you can throw your heart and soul into finding the right house, job, car and outfit, but the harder you look for the perfect man the more he will elude you.

'So, I laid off the hunting and chasing, and explored more cultural interests. I went to literary festivals and art galleries and began attending a wine appreciation class, where I met Alastair, a fellow oenophilist. Each week we sat next to each other. After class, we started going out for dinner at a nearby restaurant and over an extended period of time became friends, soul mates and then lovers.'

Olivia's advice would be: 'Let the men come to you. Men prefer to do the chasing – they will be put off by a woman who is too keen and relentless in her pursuit. I've even heard men discussing women who try to corner them, describing them as mad, unstable, desperate or aggressive. Difficult it may seem, but try to play a bit hard-to-get. It adds a bit of mystery. Be your own person: independent and confident. This is far more attractive to the male of the species than being a determined predator.'

Desperate cows' lives

And now for a male perspective . . . Patrick was 39 when he met Nicky (then 37), two years ago.

'I met and married Nicky very quickly, finally, after a long and generally unsuccessful series of romances. I found that as I got older, the women I was attracted to were also older. But the older they were, the more desperate they appeared to be. In many cases, I was surprised by how much crap they took in a relationship. I admit, I could be a real tosser and utterly selfish with it.

'I had a girlfriend a couple of years back who was a year older than me, and desperate to "make it work." I behaved appallingly because I knew I didn't want to spend the rest of my life with her. I was always late and sometimes didn't show up at all. I openly flirted with other women, "forgot" my wallet on several occasions and although I could, never shopped, cooked, put the washing machine on or did any other domestic chores. She did it all for me. Even though she enjoyed a drink, she always stayed sober to drive me home after parties. That was great! The worse I behaved, the more of a doormat she became. I even tried to end the relationship, but she always came back accepting the blame and grovelling for me to stay.

'When I met Nicky, she was not desperate at all. She felt important, had high standards and a strong sense of self-worth. She was so sexy, too – she just oozed head-turning sex appeal and confidence. I had to chase her and impress her to get her to notice me. She was a prize definitely worth working for and the more elusive she appeared, the more I wanted her. I was stunned when she went on a holiday with a girlfriend to Italy and when she began considering a job offer in the States. I knew that if I wasn't careful then she would slip out of my hands, so I proposed. She is the only woman I have ever loved and even now we are married her energy, originality, sexiness and independence ensure that I am in a constant "keen-as-mustard" state.'

Patrick says: 'Don't think or act in a desperate way. Think what you want out of life and go and get it! If you compromise your life to accommodate a love interest, he won't thank you for it. Men enjoy the thrill of pursuit and always want something they can't have. Have high standards – you wouldn't accept bad behaviour from your friends or colleagues. Don't put up with being given the run-around by a dickhead who's never going to commit!'

6.

Being the ideal woman

*Y*ou can tell a lot about a man by the way he handles lost luggage and tangled Christmas tree lights. But foreign travel and domestic yuletide bliss usually come further down the line in a relationship.

Whilst women might have some idea about the kind of man they are attracted to, I thought it only right that we should hear from the fellas their views on the female traits they find most alluring.

In the course of research for this book, I asked over 60 men what they liked about women, and what was important to them when choosing a partner. I also asked them what they found off-putting, particularly in women over 35. The following is a distillation of their thoughts and opinions.

This may sound startlingly obvious, but men prefer 'real' women. Of course before he finally settles down, every red-blooded male conjures up notions of his ideal partner. In almost comic-book fantasy he might imagine a half-Swedish, half-Thai, permanently 25-year-old Lara Croft clone with a penchant for stilettos and expensive, slutty cocktail dresses. Plus she would be gifted with super intelligence but would prefer to resolve a fierce debate on the world economic crisis by tumbling into bed for rampant sex.

But men know they won't end up with this fantasy figure. Inside they are seeking someone who can complement their personality, with whom they connect on an intellectual level and with whom they can carve out a happy and fulfilled life. Their wish list of the ideal woman doesn't really exist in a serious capacity – a man wants someone who can look in a drawer and find his socks, even 'though they aren't there'. He wants someone by his side to support him over the years through good and bad times.

Men use an innate homing technique to find their life partner. After travelling through their love life, most men who are now married eventually stopped and thought, 'Yes, she's the one.'

When men and women are in their teens and twenties, their desires are more basic. Relationships come and go, and there tends to be a more carefree approach to romance and commitment but as they get older, the stakes are raised dramatically – more so for women. There is a perception that time is running out and they no longer wish to invest so much emotion and energy in a relationship that might, ultimately, fail. While there exists an imperative on the part of women, for men, clocking up years in their late thirties doesn't seem to bother them so much. They don't share the same agenda as women and they don't have a deadline for marriage.

Against an egg-timer backdrop of diminishing time, sadly, some women appear to self-destruct as they reach the end of their thirties – the pressure they put on themselves being all too much. A lot of men out there report off-putting experiences when dating women of a certain age. One can assume most of these women enjoyed normal and generally happy relationships during their twenties, but the years have notched up and they are still single and unhappy about it. However impossible it may sound, I would urge women feeling rising panic about their domestic and emotional future to mask their insecurities and find out what men want. Possessing understanding, empathy and enigma while toning down the verbal, visual and physical assault all make getting to a second date and beyond a better prospect.

We each have our own individual aspirations, identities and tastes, and in researching this book the same messages have been repeated over and over. From this united chorus, which is not research-based, I can only conclude that while a man is attracted by a woman's unique characteristics and personality, many common similarities are sought when dating 'women of a certain age'.

So, putting specifics to one side and just concentrating on generalisations, what qualities do men look for in their ideal woman? There follows a number of points, in no particular order, embellished with comments and emails received from men, offering their opinions on their likes and dislikes of thirtysomething women.

✱ Slim, but not emaciated

It's women, not men, who drive themselves crazy with their obsessions about their weight. What kind of man insists that his size 12 girlfriend, who is physically just right, should go on a diet until she reaches size 00?

'Women who diet too much look older and gnarled: the idea of snuggling up to a skeleton and having no one to enjoy the pleasures of good food with is a real turn-off.'

Miles, 36

'Stick-thin women are unattractive because they are too bony and don't look healthy, fecund or motherly.'

Hamish, 37

✴ Well presented, but not a fashion victim

OK guys, who gives a monkeys whether a handbag costs £20 or £600? (Unless you're paying for it.) Again, it would seem that in their bid to catch the eye of a potential suitor some women go to extraordinary lengths to impress men. Unless they work in fashion or retail, most men are unlikely to know or care whether a frock is Chanel, the shoes are Ferragamo or the bag is Prada or M&S's own brand. Yes, they tend to like women who are smart and stylish, but there's really no need to go overboard financially to impress. Certain female celebrities are actually trying to impress women, not men, and imprint a look or style (including malnourished).

'If you asked the players coming off the rugby pitch what they think will be the hottest women's styles this spring, then you're not going to get a straight (or printable) answer.'

Brad, 32

'I like women to be well dressed – it indicates that they take care of themselves and highlights their femininity. This is something that a woman should take care of herself. As a man, I can only ever undress a woman. I couldn't dress her – I have no idea about colours or styles.'

Mick, 37

✴ In control, not under the influence

Unless a man has a drink and/or drugs problem himself, he is unlikely to select a woman as a life partner (and maybe mother to his children) if she is snorting cocaine or drinking to excess. Blotting out one's angst with chemical dependency isn't the fast-track to a stable, happy relationship. And a falling-down, gushing, aggressive or morose drunk isn't an attractive prospect either. At this stage in a woman's life, she should know how much drink she can handle and manage unconscionable behaviour.

'Have you ever been on the receiving end of a sniffy, self-obsessed, babbling woman who has to keep nipping off to the toilet or to meet shadowy figures on street corners to get her next fix? I have. Don't go there!'

Jonty, 36

'Lisa was lovely, but she keep having to drown her sorrows with alcohol. Since I was going out with her, her need to obliterate herself from her daily life started to become insulting. Was I so bad that she had to be pissed to enjoy my company? I found somebody else.'

Niall, 35

✳ Babies and children – show, not tell

The broody, hormonal and pressing desire to have a baby can be very strong. If you're clocking up birthdays on the wrong side of 35, feelings can be overwhelming. Being emotional, tearful, urgent and desperate with your current beau will destroy the relationship. Men don't display these outward signs of weakness and for the most part, they don't understand them. They don't like them either. Outbursts of female baby desire put a huge and invariably unsustainable pressure on relationships, which can end up being destroyed – and no baby either.

'She asked me, hypothetically, of course, whether I would prefer to have boys or girls, and what I would call them. That question ruined what would otherwise have been an enjoyable first date. I had no wish to see her again after that.'

Michael, 35

'I first saw Renee playing with her friend's two boys at a barbecue. They were having such fun, and I immediately saw something nurturing and unselfish in her. This was the first time I ever looked for or saw mothering qualities in someone I later dated. We now have two boys of our own.'

Leo, 37

✳ Be unique

Don't be or say what you think people want. Be yourself. Men like women who conform to the womanly image but are different, individual, original and quirky. Variety is the spice of life, or so they say. Men like their women to be independent financially (in an uncompetitive way) and independent in their thinking. Be clear about your style, identity, opinions, ideas, beliefs, creativity and passions.

'Rafaela has an elegant 1950s speedboat and arranges weekend summer house parties at her cottage with cruises on the Norfolk broads – singles, couples, children and dogs all welcome. She had a wonderful style about her – her personal brand is very strong and she's a popular lass; everyone likes her. I couldn't believe no one had snapped her up, so I did.'

Toby, 39

'I'd never met anyone like Eve before. Everything about her is forthright and stylish, from her signature lipstick colour to her zany house décor. She has her own views and sticks to them without trying to change the way other people think. She exudes prodigious creative energy when she enters a room and has a way of turning heads. Eve always stands out from the crowd. Despite her sometimes irritating perfectionism I love her because she is so different and modest with it. Her unusualness makes her very attractive. The more I get to know her, the more I discover and it just gets better.'

Robbie, 33

✳ Let men be the hunters

If a man is attracted to a woman, then he will set out on a quest to win her attentions. There is a childlike quality that affects most of us: we want something more if we can't have it. Dating someone is not just about getting along and having things in common; there are more subtle factors, which due to the urgency that some women feel are sometimes discarded. Men like to be intrigued; they like women to be a bit mysterious. If he likes you, he will pursue you. If you offer yourself up on a platter, ready for marriage and reproduction, you will deny him a male rite of passage, whatever his age.

At some point in our lives we've all been pursued by someone we didn't fancy. Remember how the more we avoided him, the more he chased? It might seem a risky thing to do, but playing hard-to-get can be exciting for both parties and it makes the prize worth having. And how many potential marrying kinds have been turned off by a woman's voracious appetite for sex on the first night?

'I avoid women in their late thirties. They are obsessed with settling down and having babies. I don't want to be interrogated about my life intentions when I start going out with someone. It's a real turn-off.'

Greg, 41

'I shagged my way through my twenties without a care, as did most of the women I bedded. I toned this down in my thirties and began having steady, monogamous relationships. But what is it with women 35+ who leap into bed on the first date? It looks as if they are a) desperate, b) have no self-respect or c) think that this will guarantee them a second date. I find it disappointing and sad. It's not a way to find love.'

Arif, 38

'It took me three weeks to get a second date with Hannah. We talked a lot on the phone and she seemed keen, but getting to spend any time with her was tough. She went on holiday on her own, had a close clique of friends and was always busy with her horses. I slogged away, and the more I chased, the more I had to have her. I eventually persuaded her to marry me. She's still very busy, but I do see (a bit) more of her now.'

Steve, 38 when he proposed to Hannah, who was 37

'Following a 15-year casual attitude to relationships, I met Ellie and was immediately smitten. This was the first time in my life I had ever felt anything like this – I ached with a need to be with her and pursued her relentlessly. I sent her flowers, called her all the time, whisked her away for romantic weekends and declared my love. Ellie's so enigmatic, but she was coy and overwhelmed with all my attentions. She eluded me a lot of the time – not answering her phone, not being available, working late and having "other things" to do. It was hard work, but I would have done whatever it took to get her. Just when I thought I was being a complete twat and losing her, she turned round and grabbed me. She had just needed some time to get used to the idea of being a couple.'

Kelvin, 36 on Mary also 36

✶ Get over your ex, and shut up about your job!

Hands up, guys, how many of you want to spend the evening hearing all about the many shortcomings of your date's ex? Hmm . . . OK, what about the complexities of her well paid, but not very exciting job? No?

Don't carry around your emotional baggage and offload it onto a new man. It just creates a bad impression. Do you want to come across as any of the following: work-obsessed, nasty, hard-done-by, hard-nosed, crazy, nagging, doormat-like, bitter, boring, competitive or angry? Leave your ex and office politics out of conversations with a new man until he enquires about them later on.

'There were three of us in this relationship: me, Michelle and her ex-boyfriend Julian. Everywhere we went as a couple, Julian in the form of angst came along too. I got heartily sick of being compared, albeit positively, with this apparition-like legacy of her former lover. Julian wasn't going to leave – so I did!'

Jim, 38

'That's the problem with divorced women. They are inextricably linked, financially and emotionally, to the bastard who married them, and if they've got kids, and you haven't, then you're just going to have to put up or shut up.'

Jerry, 36

'I was intrigued by Stella. On our first evening together we talked exclusively about books, films, theatre, music and places we'd visited. It was like The South Bank Show. I kissed her goodbye and she waved at me from the back of her cab. I realised I knew everything and yet nothing about her. I needed to see her again to find out more about this mysterious woman. Four years down the line, I know her pretty well. At 38, Stella had a strategy for dating: she made a conscious decision not to talk about herself. She would only disclose information if asked, never volunteer it, and even then she was enigmatic. She was like a puzzle I had to solve. As a strategy for luring a man in, it worked.'

Matt, 41

'What is it with women that they have to be so insecure about their achievements and so one-dimensional by talking about work all the time? I work hard and have a good career but I'm really not interested on a first or second date in hearing about corporate wranglings, difficult markets, diminishing bonuses or opportunities for promotion. It's so boring!'

Giles, 37

'I've dated a number of women in their mid-thirties and just about every one has pitched herself as a confident go-getter, who's ambitious, outgoing, self-assured and sex-mad. Women might think that men are turned on by these attributes but they just come across as too in-your-face. If I'm going to get close to someone, I want someone softer, more feminine and mysterious. The reality of these über-dynamic women is that they rarely possess any of their self-styled characteristics and gush at you full-throttle. I'm talking about PRs, actresses, accountants, lawyers and teachers all behaving badly on a first date. Meanwhile, we guys are invariably pigeon-holed as either Superman ready to save them from their fabulous careers, or as cold-hearted bastards for walking off into the night, vowing never to return.'

George, 35

✳ Go easy on the money and power

In this age of equality with women in increasing numbers striving for and achieving great careers, it's a sad fact that men seem to prefer women to earn less than them. Nothing undermines a man more than a high-achieving woman with a bigger salary. Maybe it's a kind of emasculation, or perhaps it's because there's more to lose if she gives up work to have a baby later on. Perhaps good old-fashioned chivalry is under threat. Not all men think and feel this way, but it should be borne in mind that despite the obvious rewards, men don't like to feel financially inferior.

'A guy doesn't really know a woman until he's come up against her in court. My ex-wife took me to the cleaners in the divorce courts. The wealth I had built up over 30 years was plundered by her lawyer and my assets were stripped. Consequently, now I would only date a woman who was a high earner, rich in her own right and 100 per cent financially independent.'

Hamish, 50

'I have changed my views on this completely. Having always worked hard and been successful in my career, I deeply resented the fact that my girlfriend (now my wife) earned a lot more than me. It was always an underlying issue in our relationship about "who paid for what", and for me being made to feel increasingly dependent on her. However, when we had children that all changed and when I lost my job it was humbling, but a salvation too. I think this financial inferiority thing is something men need to get over. The current economic climate has eradicated pride and levelled the playing field. As an individual, as a couple, as a family, people should be grateful for any income, whoever earned it.'

Jean-Luc, 43

'Initially, I was impressed with Nicole, a women I'd met through an introductions agency. She seemed perfect – pretty, intelligent, successful and obviously wealthy. She spoiled it all by gloating and seeming to enjoy the fact that she had just made a 20-strong workforce redundant in her organisation. She felt nothing for these people. Nicole then appeared genuinely upset because the strap on her Rolex snapped during dinner. At that point I realised this woman had lost touch with reality.'

Duncan, 36

By and large, like women, men don't want to be alone. So what qualities do they look for in a life partner? Here are few non-physical traits from their wish lists:

Feminine, maternal, independent, original, stylish, kind, gentle, good cook/home maker, sociable, challenging, attractive, sexy, compassionate, spontaneous, pretty, witty, funny, intelligent, calm, trustworthy, mysterious, enigmatic, happy, nurturing, empathetic, supportive and optimistic. Plus they want someone who will commit to them.

. . . and finally, a few less attractive qualities to set off their hazard lights:
Hung up about career, babies, commitment, ex-partner; boring, too available, desperate, angry, unhappy, bitter, self-obsessed, over-emotional, too upfront, sexually rapacious, predatory, pessimistic, dependent in all senses of the word and lacking in humour.

Many thanks to all the men who assisted me in my research by emailing in their thoughts, opinions, likes and dislikes – and to those hapless guys of my acquaintance that I've collared for views at every opportunity.

7.

The farmer wants a wife

The farmhouse is an impressive, rambling home on the edge of a valley. It is part of a large working arable farm and is now home to Hugh and Emma S. and their four children. The garden comprises an expanse of lawn with roses in borders and a large section is given over to swings, a climbing frame and goal posts – a true family home. But for Hugh, fatherhood came to him rapidly at the age of 49, and he is only 52 now. Literally overnight, he found himself father to Elizabeth, 9, Henry, 7, and Ben, 2. He was a single parent with no partner or wife.

Hugh is a genial gentleman farmer. Formerly a confirmed bachelor, he channelled his energies into running his farm and commanding weekend warriors on manoeuvres with the Territorial Army. He recalls, 'Marriage didn't have any appeal – I just wasn't the marrying kind. I'd had a few girlfriends over the years, nobody permanent, but I was very self-sufficient and enjoyed my work. There is a good sense of community around here and I didn't feel the need to have a family.'

The farm has been in his family for over 100 years. After a short stint in the army and a couple of years at agricultural college he inherited the business from his father, who died several years after retiring.

Hugh's only sibling, Jennifer, was his complete opposite. After a short career in public relations in London, she married Richard, a stockbroker. They had three children and moved to leafy Surrey. One weekend about 12 years ago, eagerly awaiting the arrival of their first child, Jennifer and Richard descended on Hugh, brandishing various documents. As Richard was the only child of ancient parents, the couple wanted to nominate Hugh as guardian to their child, and any other children they might have. He agreed and signed.

Several years later, the unexpected and horrific happened when Jennifer and Richard were killed together in a motorway crash. And so it came to pass that three orphaned, devastated and bereaved children (Ben, still in nappies) came to live with their guardian, Uncle Hugh, in a chaotic, dusty and cluttered farmhouse, miles from their home, school and friends.

'Obviously, it was a great shock to all of us. I had no idea how to look after children. We had a fantastic social worker Nicky, who helped us in the first few months and the children received bereavement counselling from our local hospice. All these things were a real help. I tried to get a permanent nanny, but no one would stay – the children were all traumatised and unhappy, the house was a mess and I hadn't got a clue how to be a parent. We had a series of agency nannies and I finally got a cleaner. It wasn't hard for my friends to convince me that what I really needed was a wife.'

Hugh admits this sounds chauvinistic and that his reasons for wanting a wife were practical rather than emotional, but the house, the children and now he too needed a good woman to take charge. But a wife doesn't 'apply' for a job for life, so how would an old-timer with three adopted children ever meet and court the right woman with such a calamitous situation at home in the rural West Country?

Friends suggested he contact three introduction agencies in London. Although a little reticent, one of the agencies took him on. In his favour, Hugh was nice looking, intelligent, fun to be with and comfortably well off – it was just his needs that were a little unconventional. He had a succession of dates with women in their early thirties. Most of them liked him but were deterred by his obvious desire for domestic help. Just at the point when he was about to give up on 'this contrived way of dating', he met Emma – not through the introduction agency, but at a country show to which he had taken his new family.

Emma was 39, single and 'empty inside' about her childless state. She is attractive, witty and Amazonian in stature, being over 6ft tall. Her parents were farmers in Lincolnshire, and she owned and ran a successful events company. She recalls: 'I saw this attractive man come into the flower marquee with three beautiful children, the youngest in a pushchair. I had a kind of pang – what a lovely Daddy, what a lucky woman, wherever she is – to be married to such a nice man with kind eyes. Why couldn't that have happened to me?

'He came over to talk to my colleague and I noticed that the eldest boy called him Hugh. Hugh and I were introduced and we got talking. In the space of just five minutes we got on so well, it was as if we had known each other for ages. I asked him about the children and he said, "I'm their guardian, not their real father. They live with me now. I don't have a wife, but I really need one now!" Jokingly, he added, "If you're single, would you like to marry me?" Do you know, a little voice in my head said, "Yes, yes, yes!" but I just laughed.

'We started seeing each other, and I used my management skills on sorting out his house and making it more child-friendly. I organised some family outings during the holidays and we went away for a week to France. I moved in shortly after that.

'Hugh proposed apologetically and obscenely quickly, and I accepted on the condition that we had a child (or children) of our own – immediately. So that's what we did. I went from being a single girl on her own to being a pregnant stepmother of three with a huge renovation and homemaking project to undertake. Plus, of course, wife to a gorgeous man who I cannot believe wasn't snapped up years ago!'

So how is everything shaping up for the couple now, two years down the line? Hugh admits, 'Inevitably it was tough at first but the children are brilliant. We have all adapted to our new roles and have grown as people. I adore being a family man and we have added young Rufus to the clan. All the children call me Hugh – I'll never really be "Daddy". But they call Emma "Emma Mum" and there is a feeling of completion and optimism for the future. I couldn't have done this without Emma. The two older children still miss their parents and the special love they had between them, and always will. Emma and I will never replace what they had but we have all made the best of what was a really difficult situation to begin with.'

Emma says: 'In the space of one year my life turned around so dramatically. It's what I always wanted – a loving husband and a big family home filled with kids. It wasn't always easy. We all had to do a lot of accepting of each other, and when Rufus was born, it very nearly all became too much. But we all needed each other, and love overcame all the adversities we faced. We are a happy family. Because the children had lost their own mother, I don't believe I was ever the "wicked stepmother" figure that some women become. They were very welcoming in that respect.

'I feel as if I have caught up on my "lost decades". Although I am a confident person in a professional capacity I had a complete lack of confidence in myself and my hitherto disastrous relationships with men. Becoming an overnight wife and mother was a baptism of fire but I relish the role of stepmother to the kids – I love seeing their achievements and development. Attending school events and meeting other parents restored my confidence and has greatly enriched my life. And I still pinch myself to make sure it is true that I really am married to such a wonderful man. Am I sounding like a smug-married?'

8.

Free again

Frances Manwaring

Whatever the reasons my former partner provided for ending our relationship of many years, the net effect was to create a seething mix of incredulity, disbelief, incomprehension and denial that churned in my head like a washing machine stuck in mid-cycle.

Song lyrics, forgotten since the highs and lows of adolescence, haunted me. 'Baby, there's no easy way to hear the words I'm sorry I don't love you . . .' But the one that took up and kept headspace for longest was an old Barbra Streisand song, 'Free Again'. To the accompaniment of uplifting soundtracks, I kept replaying our movie trying to produce a different ending and only achieving countless sleepless nights. The pain was excruciating, as was the desolation and sense of loss. Amputees describe experiencing itches where their severed limb used to be. Losing a love is similar – despite the fact that they've gone from your life, the memory of what once was lingers on often for years, sometimes for ever. Heartless though this may sound, I think it would have been easier to cope, had he died.

Divorce or separation affects life on every level, particularly in terms of your self-confidence and sense of who you are. You quickly discover who your friends are, or not – that's a real eye-opener. Then there's the hideousness of being single again, especially if it's not your choice, and that's a book in itself. There's also the embarrassment factor – where does *that* come from? You avoid seeing people you know because somehow it seems so shameful to have had the bad taste to have been dumped, closing the opportunity to set the record straight and explain why.

You spend many wide-awake nights howling at the moon, worrying about money and practicalities like where and how you will live. In my case, we didn't have children to complicate things further, although there was the whole gritty issue of how to deal with children that weren't mine of whom I'd grown fond.

Then there are all the intangibles like loss of social status. Before, I was attached to a very successful man and so I had to come to terms with no longer being on the A-list in my area. Life as a single (not young) woman is a totally different beast from that as Mrs Somebody and I had a rude awakening when I discovered how precarious my status was without him, another body blow to the already wobbling self-esteem. Invitations dried up instantly, and moving out of the 'palace' to a more modest house was tough – everything looked like a slum in comparison. Ultimately I bought a beautiful house with my sister that I loved, and which provided much-needed sanctuary for several years.

Then the fear factor grabs hold – the fear that you're on the shelf, the realisation that heads don't turn as they used to when you walk into a room and that most men, even the most unlikely, who happen to be available, have hooked up with women at least ten years younger than you are. I suddenly understood the feeling of invisibility described by many middle-aged women.

And then there's the dismal knowledge that if there is another person in your life they're likely to be as fucked up as you are. Oh, and the men your friends think of as suitable future dates are likely to cause you to double the Valium dosage! Most of your married friends see you as someone to go out with on girls' nights out. Heaven forbid that you should mess up numbers at dinner or have an opportunity to prey on their men! Sometimes, though, they graciously invite you to bigger parties where the risk is diluted.

The relationship with your body moves to a whole new low. Any detailed inventory should be avoided like the plague, particularly in full daylight, if sanity is to remain part of the repertoire. Almost inevitably women go backwards when a relationship ends. Their style of commitment is so different from men's. That's not to say that all men are bastards – I gave up that once-fashionable posture a long time ago. It's just that I think women mourn the passing of love in a protracted, drawn-out way that sets us apart from men. It's not that men don't experience very deep emotions, they just manifest differently, from what I've observed, enabling them to move on more readily than we do.

Going backwards includes financial loss – I don't know too many women who benefited financially from their partnerships, although I know some must. Certainly, I myself lost out initially, big-time, although I admit some of this was through my own stupidity.

The list goes on and on, and the desolation of a break-up is almost indescribable. Long after the superficial scars are gone, despair lurks inside you like an ugly, malevolent troll under a bridge waiting for the opportunity to attack whenever hope tries tentatively to cross that bridge and liberate you from the barren, devastated place on the other side. Many people say that work is their lifeline at such times, and so it was for me. Somehow, in among the emotional mayhem, my sister and I launched a satirical magazine. That was an inspired move. We had a mad couple of years of energy and creativity, and it was exhilarating and amazing fun.

While the magazine didn't survive, it was effectively my 'transitional relationship' and quite likely prevented me from launching into an ill-starred rebound affair with some unsuitable man. My sister and I did some of our best work during that time. And while you can't predict which door will open when the one in front of you closes, every action has a reaction and another door always does open. Creating the magazine changed both our lives in ways we are only beginning to understand and we are about to venture forth again with a less ambitious, but probably more likely to succeed electronic version, using the great brand and all the intellectual property developed during our creative frenzy.

Probably for the first time in my life, the break-up galvanised me to put a value on myself and what I am capable of. I have forged a new career that I love, which gives me the deep sense of the self-worth that I had struggled to achieve previously. Up until then I had spent so much of my life defining myself by the men I have loved that there was very little room for the person I should have been to blossom. This was probably, and indirectly, the predominant reason why this relationship and a previous one failed.

Now I know exactly who I am and I know that my happiness is in my own gift, not someone else's. I finally get the Kahlil Gibran° thing about walking side by side. Despite this, I had to fight not to feel hard done by – the 'poor me's' kicked in too easily and it took a conscious act of will to take control this or those negative feelings might have consumed me.

°No human relation gives one possession in another – every two souls are absolutely different. In friendship or in love, the two side by side raise hands together to find what one cannot reach alone. Kahlil Gibran's words from Mary Haskell's journal (8 June 1924).

It wasn't all gloom. Life, as they say, does go on and there have been some truly entertaining moments. In addition to the roller-coaster ride that was creating the magazine, at one point I started writing terrible poetry, something I've never felt the slightest urge to do before or since. Six months after we'd broken up, I was fortunate enough to be able to indulge in some spectacular retail therapy. I managed to sell my flat in London at a time when the exchange rate was favourable. I bought a couple of expensive items that I knew he'd really hate – the satisfaction in that was immense!

Women are extremely good at giving themselves away when they become involved with a man. Nurture or nature, I'm not sure. All I know is that in my life I have been exceptionally good at this. Thankfully, at the bottom of my personal trough, I finally took ownership of my role amid all the misery and promised myself that I would never reprise it. In all seriousness, I knew I couldn't survive another shredding. I have spent years rebuilding my own power base and I will not lose that again to any man, however dear he might be to me. Having made that decision, it's made a heap of other decisions flow. I embrace wholeheartedly the proposition that the definition of insanity is doing the same thing repeatedly and expecting a different outcome.

Recently I met a wonderful man, with whom I had a relationship for more than a year that was at times stormy and full of volatility, something I saw as being tremendously healthy – in my mid-forties I finally discovered that the world didn't stop if I fought my corner. We worked our way through some big issues, not least of which was that being with him caused me to pick the scabs off some old wounds. This relationship had an honesty that I can now see the previous ones lacked. It wasn't perfect – both of us had our flaws – but it felt good. When something bothered me, I said so and he said it was the same for him. We parted company because his past is not resolved and we both knew there could be no future until, or unless it is. I am sad that he has gone out of my life but I know the moment will pass and I will keep moving forward because for once I didn't subsume myself in his needs.

Breaking up *is* hard to do. We are not solitary creatures and it's part of the human condition to enjoy having someone with whom to share the minutiae of our days. But you can't sit around waiting for a rescue – you have to make your own life work, on your own terms. If you do, you're much more likely to meet someone who will complement it, if that's what you want. When you are used to being in a relationship, the temptation is to find a new love to superimpose onto the old rhythms and patterns – a recipe for disaster in my book. I passionately believe it's our duty to take time to recover from one failed relationship and to look at and act on the reasons that caused its demise before launching into a new one, but I am all too aware how hard it is to be suddenly alone when the person best able to help you get over it is the one no longer there. Depression seems to be a constant fellow traveller.

For anyone who needs love at such moments, my advice would be to get a 'companion animal'. The unconditional devotion of my Springer spaniel gave me a reason to get out of bed every day and warmed my heart during what seemed like interminable winter. A large tumour in his valiant little lungs killed him a couple of years ago, but I will carry him forever in my heart for being a shining light during a very dark time.

For a couple of years after my relationship ended, I kept a daily journal. I badly needed a survival kit and writing enabled me to slowly process all the noise in my brain. When I reread these journals recently, I figured maybe some of my eclectic observations might be of interest to or even help to other people, if only by re-iterating the message that time really does work its magic and hope will always see off despair – if you let it. Of course, while you're bogged down in a slough of emotional despond any assurances like this will seem incredibly cold comfort.

Six years down the track I am more inclined to see what happened as a lucky escape, although I'd be being disingenuous in the extreme if I gave the impression that the scars had healed – I'm not sure they ever will entirely. Now I recognise the relationship had been subsuming me and getting away from it forced me to take a good look at who I really am, but at the time nothing made sense. One damaged woman-on-the-mend's ramblings may not be of any consequence but I wanted to share them in the hope that they might bring some consolation to others going through a similar experience. My message is a simple one of solidarity: you are not alone, and this too will pass.

Frances Manwaring is an entrepreneur living in New Zealand's capital, Wellington. Director of an electronic greeting cards company, shrewonline.com, she is currently developing an additional business based on virtual technology. Born and educated in Scotland, Frances made London her home for 13 years before emigrating in her mid-thirties.

9.

Diary of a love no-hoper

Louise Chatwyn

The following are extracts from the diary of Louise Goode, a former desperate thirtysomething. She has written this chapter utilising some of her thoughts over ten years on changing, learning and leaving the single life behind to build a loving family.

30 May 1998 – A woman alone on the road to nowhere by Louise Goode

I wake on a Saturday, sun streaming through a gap in the curtains, the sounds of the children next door already playing in the garden. The sky is blue. The day has the promise of clear summer skies, warmth and a balmy, flamingo sunset this evening. Yet I feel a deep sadness, as if someone has died. Perhaps that person is me. A teardrop trickles down my cheek onto the pillow. I am grieving. Grieving for lost opportunities and the children that I might never have. I hide my grief well. When I am presenting at work, when I am participating in a tennis tournament (singles!), when I am standing in church at another bloody wedding, no one has any idea of the emotional pain I feel at not belonging. It was my life plan to marry and have a family; the fabulous career and travelling the world was secondary. I never intended for it to eclipse something to which I feel I have a right.

I am on a fulcrum. I can either redeem my situation – something I have failed to do in 21 years of being ready to find love – or I can tip the balance down and descend into an almost certain bitterness and resentment. And loneliness. Ten years from now, how does a 48-year-old spinster 'seize the day' and be fulfilled? Why should I face a lifetime being excluded from children's birthday parties, making gingerbread men, coping with teenage angst, graduation and grandchildren?

By now you may have put this book down having decided not to read any further about this miserable woman, obviously wallowing in self-pity. Or in a kind of schadenfreude way, you may wish to read on out of curiosity. Somehow this woman is fatally flawed and undeserving of a family of her own. She has manufactured a situation whereby she is unmarriageable, unlovable and not worthy of motherhood. Maybe she has done something terrible and brought the penalty of lifelong singledom upon herself. What on earth could she have done?

I don't know the answer but I am determined to find out. Slipping into despair isn't going to find me a husband so I have decided to dedicate the whole weekend and the next few weeks to deep self-analysis to try and fathom out where I have gone so wrong. Enlisting the help of my sister Sara, I will devise a do-it-yourself home self-analysis kit to rake up my past, sift through comments from former lovers, interview close friends and dissect the reasons for failure in past relationships. I am going to observe couples and how they interact with each other – there must be clues to their success. I need to peel away the layers that keep the truth hidden and try to see myself the way others see me. I'm going to be brutally honest with myself. It's going to hurt, but it needs to be done. The 'formula' that I have now and had in the past doesn't work so I'm going to change it.

27 June 1998 – A woman still alone on the road to nowhere, but now armed with some answers. Looking for the next exit by Louise Goode, 38

I feel liberated and inspired in a kind of spiritual way, almost as if an apparition appeared to me and told me what to do. There is a huge amount of work to be done, but I have shaken off the 'grief shackles' and things are already happening. All this talk about a 'positive mental attitude', it does seem to have 'unstuck' me from my rut.

As we live our lives, we co-exist with people all around us – our parents and siblings, our friends, our friends' friends, colleagues, people at the gym and the tennis club, people we sit next to on the train . . . We have perceptions of each other, but rarely do we reveal what we think. Americans are far more upfront than we British. We just don't have the temerity to 'tell it how it is' and as a nation are more inclined to discuss people's personalities behind their backs than to their faces.

But I wanted to know what I was like, so I asked. Not everyone of course, but with Sara's help, I got my parents, sister, grandmother, cousins, colleagues, friends, friends' husbands, two ex-boyfriends and even members of a professional women's networking group to spell it out for me: the whole truth and nothing but the truth, and no hard feelings.

So, what did I find out about myself? Quite a lot actually! On the downside, I have gleaned the following:

* I expect too much from everything and everyone
* I am not enigmatic enough – too upfront, not mysterious
* I'm predatory – I chase men and think that by cornering them, I can catch them
* Meeting me for the first time, married women don't trust me (I am too obvious about eyeing up all the men in the room)
* I reek of desperation (apparently, according to one male colleague at the office)
* I'm friendly and approachable, but try too much to please
* I am too smartly groomed
* I need to chill out, smile and laugh more
* I put men off because I come across as too clever and successful. I also talk about money and my job too much
* I'm too dismissive of things that don't interest me. (At a friend's house I once walked into a room full of men watching England play an important football match and announced, 'Agghh! I hate football!' Yet I would still expect a partner to accompany me to see an obscure arts film in Italian with subtitles.)
* I am completely obsessed with my biological clock (people can apparently hear it ticking even when I'm not present!)
* I try to map out the future rather than just let it happen
* I can't hide my resentment when people talk about weddings, pregnancy and babies – I blank everything out. People are nervous to talk about these things in my company
* Finally, I confuse sex with love

Wow, quite a lot to take on board there, but what a relief! On the plusside it was unanimously agreed that I am still attractive, most people like me (despite all my flaws) and somewhere beneath the veneer of my failings, I possess a good sense of humour, am generous and show kindness towards others – ah! That's nice.

During my research, I observed and interviewed couples together. One weekend, I went to a café by the common to sit and watch people, particularly couples, and how they interacted. I was struck by how relaxed and natural they seemed in each other's company, how casually dressed they were and how comfortable they seemed to be with themselves. Now I think that's the key to getting started – to be completely at ease with yourself. If you like yourself (not love yourself), people will like you too.

I went to a drinks reception following a christening, hosted by some good friends of mine. Making a concerted effort not to let the baby thing bother me, I spent a while in the garden playing with some of the children running about and actually quite enjoyed it. I knew some of the people at the reception, but not all of them – I thought this would be a good platform from which to commence my factual research. I started with my friends and gradually worked my way through most of the guests (all of them couples), asking how they met and what first attracted them to the other. I jotted down the answers. Most of them met in their early thirties but their answers were surprising and varied. Here are few:

'We met at a university reunion, even though neither of us went to that university – we both went there with someone else. We got married because Edwina fell pregnant but we've been very happy together for 14 years.'

Edwina and Tom, now both 40

'When I first saw Jenny, I just knew she was the one for me. I would have gone to any lengths to get her. I pursued her relentlessly until she agreed to go out with me. Two months later I proposed and we were married within the year.'

James, then 29, now 44

'Ten years ago we were set up at a dinner party and immediately disliked each other. We met again several months later at an outdoor theatre, got talking and found we actually had quite a lot in common. We began a relationship, but Karyn's ex began sniffing about again. It made committing to her all the more important, so we skipped the engagement bit and launched ourselves straight into a secret registry office wedding.'

Karyn and Xavier, 39 and 40

'We sat next to each other on a commuter train travelling through Kent. Because of various rail crashes, rain and safety checks, the journey took three hours. We got talking, exchanged phone numbers and the rest is history. Thank you, Connex South Eastern!'

Paul and Linda, 35 and 37

'We were friends at primary school in Cumbria in the 1970s. I was newly divorced and discovered Chris's name on Friends Reunited. We got in touch and I lured him away from his fiancée. It was easy! We got married a year later.'

Justine, 39

From the people who met in their twenties the initial attraction certainly seemed to be physical: looks were important to them. But the older they were when they met, the emphasis of the attraction changed. People seemed more attracted by qualities such as kindness, mystery, talents or abilities and a connection – a meeting of minds. Now my sample group was very small and wasn't in-depth or scientific research, but it threw up some interesting pointers for me.

1 September 1998 – Opportunities beckon by Louise Goode, 38

It's done now. I have signed up to an exclusive and discreet dating agency, plus I've placed an ad in *The Sunday Times*' lonely hearts column. The only trouble is my manager is sending me to Singapore for a month in a fortnight's time. My colleague who was supposed to be going has appendicitis so I have been taken from the reserve bench. Great timing!

Although it is some way off, I don't think I can handle Christmas with my family again this year. Too many children to remind me of my childlessness and Mum and Dad's enquiries as to whether I have 'met anyone nice yet?' No thanks! Instead, I have booked a massive farmhouse in south Pembrokeshire, which sleeps twelve. The criteria for being a guest at my farmhouse during Christmas week, is that a) you must be single, and b) you must bring someone of the opposite sex who is also single.

10 September 1998

I have had lengthy conversations (taking on board all my 'lessons') with some lovely guys through the dating agency and am sifting through over 200 replies to my lonely hearts ad – 70 per cent dross, 25 per cent possible and 5 per cent almost too good to be true. I think I might invite one or two of them along to my Welsh Yuletide. This could be interesting.

17 September 1998 – Singapore

Unbelievable! My flight on BA was completely overbooked, so they found a seat for me on another airline. I was fortunate enough to be upgraded and sat next to Ed. What a fantastic first date! We had four meals and two bottles of champagne, saw three movies and even fell asleep together. Fifteen hours is quite a long time in which to get to know someone and we are meeting up tomorrow night in Little India for a curry.

Ed works for a pension fund and lives in London. He is 37 and has recently emerged unscathed from a long, unhappy relationship. He is handsome, funny and interesting. He enjoys rugby, opera and skiing. He is well travelled, well read and well heeled. He has Maybelline lashes to die for! Ed comes from a close-knit family of four brothers and originally hails from the north east of England.

Is it serendipity that put me in the seat next to him? Or could it possibly be a malicious plot by some demon spirit guide to raise my hopes and then dash them – a further punishment because I am single? I don't want to hope too much, but I can't help it. Please, please, don't let me screw this up!

2 February 1999 – A woman on the road to somewhere by Louise Goode, 39

A lot has happened in the last five months. I didn't take Ed to Wales for my singles Christmas, I didn't meet any of the men from my lonely hearts ad and I haven't had a single date through the introductions agency. None of these things happened because I am in love! It is a wonderful feeling but I'm not making any plans for the future. I just live each day to the full and am swept up in so many positive, warm emotions as I gaze at Ed's luscious lashes on his sweet sleeping face. There is just one tiny lurking piece of panic in my mind: What if we finish? How would I ever recover? How could I ever meet anyone so superb ever again? Actually, it's not a tiny panic, but a great big one!

7 July 2007 – Two firsts and a second by Mrs Edmund Chatwyn, 47

Today it's Sports Day at the prep school – a bright, windy day and a window of sunshine in this murky summer. Ed came a gallant second in the fathers' race. I look around and see him sipping from a plastic cup of Pimm's (it's only 10.30am!), surrounded by a group of dads, laughter booming and bunting flapping in the breeze. He grins an uxorious salutation in my direction, raises his glass and blows me a kiss.

Across the track, I can just about make out Luca and Oscar sitting with their classmates, coloured ribbons pinned to their shirts. They are cheering excitedly for two 11-year-olds battling out the 300 metres. Gazing about, I drink in the atmosphere and my life as it is now. I think back to how it was nine years ago and feel relief, pride, happiness and gratitude that a twist of fate brought these three fantastic men into my life. And yes, I suppose I am smug.

I could so nearly have missed this, and that's what is so strange because it feels so damn right. Who was that person who took my seat on the plane years ago and forced me onto another one? Why did they check me in next to Ed? How was it that my work colleague who was supposed to go to Singapore got appendicitis and I had to go in her place? How did all these events conspire so that I would finally arrive here? No one could engineer a situation like that, it just happens.

I have learned so much since meeting Ed and having the boys, and I have managed to erase most of the negative traits I previously possessed, or at least I hope so. I have metamorphosed into someone else, someone better and happier. But to me, the most powerful thing is the sheer force of the hand of fate. Very few people meet in a conventional way – good or bad, all our luck is delivered to us by fate. I realise now that one can steer a course along one's predetermined road and set sights on what one desires, but you have to anticipate the unexpected. In a peculiar way behind the scenes are powerful, life-changing forces at play.

With thanks to Louise Chatwyn for providing adapted extracts from her diaries and notebooks. Louise has kept a 'thoughts' diary every day since her tenth birthday.

10.

One woman in three is still single at 35, or is she?

In 2006 the Office for National Statistics (ONS) revealed one woman in three in the UK is unmarried at the age of 35. As we entered the Millennium, this figure was one woman in four while back in 1990, just one in ten was in this position. This demographic shift will have struck fear into the hearts of many mid-to-late-thirtysomethings anxious to buck the trend. Does this mean that with every five years an increasing number of single women will be lonely and unloved? With an already apparent paucity of single men, these statistics imply that in five years' time there will be 23 women competing for the heart of each available man in his thirties and forties. Going on these statistics, nine out of ten of today's female teenagers will find themselves unmarried twenty years hence. But the figures must be true if they're based on ONS data, mustn't they? Well, yes and no.

The ONS slant on the factors leading to this sorry state of affairs is open to interpretation: the downward trend in marriage is attributed to an increase in women following careers, stagnation in the housing market and growing acceptance of couples choosing to live together. Bizarrely, one interpretation in the media attributes the high cost of having a family as being a turn-off when it comes to marriage with people not wishing to struggle with exorbitant childcare and mortgage repayments. (Personally, I haven't heard any women keen to meet 'the one' cite this excuse!)

Analysts believe the introduction of tax credits to the benefit system since

1999 has dissuaded many from marrying, as they favour single mothers. That might be true in certain sections of society, but I don't think it's the case for experienced high flyers with good careers. Figures indicate a couple with children must earn £50,000 a year between them before they are better off together than living apart. From my research, however, economics is not the main limiting factor for the over-35s.

It's the term 'unmarried' in this data that is doubtful. In addition to being genuinely single, this terminology embraces women who are divorced or widowed, or dating someone while living alone, even those who are co-habiting. Married people have a marriage certificate. Those without a marriage certificate are classed 'unmarried' and this is quickly turned to mean single. Research of this kind cannot be valid if all the ONS is doing is counting marriage certificates. These 'freemales' are successful, spirited and single, their growing numbers contributing to the demographic shift in make-up of the traditional British household.

But we shouldn't get things out of proportion. The way we live now is different to ten years ago, and not just for women of a certain age. Quotations from so-called experts are not necessarily helpful either. Robert Whelan of the Civitas civic values think tank was reported as saying: 'This [decline in marriage ceremonies] is an incredible collapse not just because of the extent but because of the speed. If it goes on, we will soon see a majority of women unmarried in their mid-thirties. What we are seeing is a huge and growing gap between what people want in their lives and what they are getting.' Dramatic or what? The institution of marriage is not dead – it's just different. In a fast-changing world, I wish 'experts' would wake up and go with the flow. Hysterical, knee-jerk reactions to statistics magnify perceived problems.

Previously polls have found that about seven out of ten men and women still aspire to marriage but they're just not getting around to it in the same numbers as previously. Scratch beneath the surface and you'll see more happily unmarried couples than ever.

PR director Belinda R, 40 has lived with her partner, a psychotherapist, for 18 years and they have three children. Marriage is the last thing on her mind: 'We're never going to split up, but perhaps it's having that element of impermanence there that binds us together. I liken it to being freelance rather than under contract. We need each other and are bringing up our family in a home we own jointly. It's a partnership in all senses of the word without the official paperwork.'

Stockbroker Gerry K., 48 agrees. He has been happily *un*married to his partner Lucy, 42 for six years and they have two children: 'The institution of marriage signifies to me 'ownership' – giving women the right to henpeck husbands and for husbands to start marshalling the property. Love should be about publicly acknowledging a rapport – it shouldn't be about money or a certificate stuffed away in a drawer.'

It would seem more of us than ever are signing up for *un*marital bliss. According to ONS figures, the proportion of co-habiting women in the UK aged 18 to 49 increased from 3 per cent in 1979 to 16 per cent in 2001, with 40 per cent of children in England and Wales born to unmarried couples.

Having worked in public relations for a number of years, I know all too well how statistical data can be manipulated. Pollsters conduct polls and the results can be presented in a number of different ways. The *Daily Mail* and the The *Guardian* drew completely different conclusions based on exactly the same ONS statistical evidence. It's true that the UK has a different demographic profile now to previous decades, but this doesn't mean that millions of women are being marginalised to the 'spinsterhood'. Of course the media always loves a good story, but this one has been over-sensationalised.

11.

Striving to be happy

Mandy Saligari

*O*ne woman recalls how she pressed her own self-destruct button during her twenties, all but annihilating her relationship prospects. Following introspection and a serendipitous chance meeting in her late thirties, she turned a corner. This set her on the path to recovery and provided unexpected riches in the shape of a loving family and the development of her role as a counsellor.

It's hard to believe the stroke that I had when I was just 27 was to be my making, but it was – despite the fact I had so much going for me. People would tell me I had it all and I believed them. Happiness was my birthright and opportunity fell into my lap. I didn't dream of marriage or children, I just assumed they would be there when I was ready. I had time to play and I took the ride.

What I didn't realise is that there are two things in this life that if you spend them, you may never get them back: one is time, the other health. I spent both as if they were limitless resources with no regard for the consequences. I ignored the sense of impending doom that haunted me and justified away my bad behaviour instead by putting it all down to being carefree but I was actually going into 'care debt'. Years of excess and hidden unhappiness built up to a dramatic watershed and I fell from grace into rehab long before it became 'this season's must-have'. But the drugs and alcohol was just a smokescreen: happy-go-lucky I wasn't – I had issues.

I took a long, hard look at the way I was living my life and the constant sense of insecurity that underpinned all my encounters. Don't get me wrong, I was no wallflower – I stood tall and bright in the crowd. I was a leader, I attracted success . . . but underneath it all, I felt like a fraud and compensated by pretending I didn't care. I had flunked university, taken opportunity for granted, dated unashamedly and fallen obsessively in love with a man who, with the benefit of retrospect, was never going to make me happy.

The age-old argument of 'nature or nurture' raged in my head as I sought who to blame for how I was. On the side of nature was the indisputable fact that I had a self-destructive streak – call it addiction, if you like – but the fact was the way I coped with life hurt me. I anaesthetised myself from feeling vulnerable and supercharged myself to perform; I created a persona who played my part better than me. My self-esteem sank and I was uncomfortable in my skin. I knew this wasn't right but I couldn't help myself, which periodically made me angry, always anxious and never alone.

I sought company to keep me from myself. Like so many of us, I tuned in to the rogue: the one I could change (because I was special) or the one who would love me above all others (because I was special). Part of me was seeking that affirmation, but I was choosing the very person who would perpetuate my low self-esteem because he wouldn't comply. I flipped through relationships like the ball bearing in a pinball machine, bells and lights going off, points being scored. Emotions were currency, sex was power and I played to win.

I know now the wisdom of the clichés such as 'like attracts like' and 'birds of a feather . . .' and so I can understand that all my relationships were doomed to failure. The fact was, no one I was attracted to was emotionally or physically available and despite all the sales patter and window dressing, neither was I. Trouble was, I didn't know it.

Then I met *him*. I didn't like him to start with, but he eventually won me round and persuaded me to go out with him. We ended up in a Norfolk hotel on our first date, returning in the morning to his flat. As we travelled the final mile he warned me that I would meet Suzy at home. I held my breath – aware he held an ace. Suzy turned out to be a motorbike, but I was hooked. He was better at this game than me and it was my turn to fall.

I really believed it was true love – my heart leapt when he rang and days of depression would swallow me up when he didn't. It felt so all-consuming and with the benefit of retrospect therein lies the clue: I would have done anything for him, and thus I lost me. No one could match up to him: he was the one that got away and I held a candle for him for nearly ten years of my life until I was 37.

Looking back, I understand this relationship so much better now and I'm glad I have given it the time to come into focus as it has enabled me to change. I used to think you couldn't help whom you fell in love with, but now I know it's more about how you feel about yourself that drives the attraction. Relationships are jigsaws, the pieces are people and we look for a fit. But it has been hard: over the years I have wanted to get in touch with him, at times craved contact with him more than anything I have experienced, but I didn't act on this. When my body broke, it let in the light: I trusted the journey I was on and that it was about me, not him or anyone else.

So many components of that relationship reflected issues I had with my own background. I began to be able to distance myself from my experience and started to view all my relationships more objectively, seeing them as symptoms of my unhappiness. As many of us could, I looked back on my childhood and pointed the finger, but then I felt guilty. My parents had done the best they could with what they had; they had suffered their own disappointments, so why should they be held accountable for my inability to have a committed relationship too? But home life has an impact on a child and I was no exception. I had been dealt a hand and had to learn how to play it to my best advantage. That meant that I had to know my cards and so once again I looked at my childhood, but this time without the blame that obscured the view and abdicated me from responsibility. Without disclosing too much about them, it was clear that until I resolved my relationship with both my mother and my father, and came to terms with the impact their relationship – and subsequent divorce – had had on me, my chances of forming a healthy relationship with anyone were compromised. Nurture had indeed its part to play.

If the buck was to stop here I had to come to terms with the uncomfortable piece of information that I was the common denominator. Uncomfortable because it implied that I had somehow contributed to my bad luck in love, but I couldn't deny the fact. I looked at my relationships and began to see a pattern of rescuing or being rescued. I followed suggestion and had no relationships for a year. Well, OK, only a short disastrous one but after that I listened.

In that time I concentrated on myself, my feelings and how I behaved as a result; on how control played out in my life and how to be free of resentment. I worked hard because I wanted change. I began to relax and enjoy myself. Life was easier and I felt hopeful. I began to think about the future but the prospect of a relationship was daunting – I felt I couldn't trust my instinct as it always caught the eye of the wrong type. And I knew how easily I could lose myself in a relationship. Life felt so simple when I had only myself to take care of. But I also had to find work as there is a practical world too, and with all formal applications failing, I resolved to take the first job I saw in the local newsagent's window: for a dog walker. I rang the number.

'I'm sorry, but I don't need a dog walker any more.' A woman's voice was gentle, but firm.

'Please,' I said, 'I really need this job.'

I watched a woman in her conservatory two floors down. Her movements coordinated with our conversation.

'Are you wearing pink?' I asked.

She looked up and I waved.

'Why don't you come down for a cup of coffee and we can discuss it?' she relented.

The gods had thrown a double six. Her dog was lovely, and she was kind. I left with a new friend, a job and a dinner invitation. I didn't want to go, but I felt obliged. I watched the guests arrive from the safety of my kitchen and I got changed for the millionth time. Had I known I would meet my future husband that night I would never have found the right thing to wear! Eventually I just left – I couldn't stand the madness of changing again.

I navigated my way through the unfamiliar waters of dinner conversation – sober. Across to my right was a man with sparkling green eyes; to my left a male nurse. By the second course the conversation veered from pleasantries to a more personal nature. The green eyes were interested, the male nurse caring. By coffee I had argued with green eyes, and by the time I went home I had given the nurse my phone number. But all was not as it seemed. One wanted to rescue me, while the other was actually interested in me. Cautious, I took it one day at a time.

Green Eyes became my friend, and after 18 months we went on a date. He rang when he said he would, and I was in love. We were more similar than I had realised and we grew closer every day. But old habits die hard and despite our blossoming relationship and regular conversations about the future, I struggled. We still laugh today about the time when James (he of the green eyes) and I were in Australia, outside a bank in Sydney. He suggested we open a joint bank account as a meaningful gesture to acknowledge our relationship. My response was to run . . . literally. The appeal of a dark alley in downtown King's Cross being greater than the commitment of a joint account with the man I loved – madness! It was the same when he asked me to marry him – I was unusually lost for words. I remember the people at the next table asking if I was going to say yes, as they wanted to buy us champagne and me answering that I didn't drink, more certain of that than my ability to commit.

But I did say yes, and I'm glad that I did. With knowledge comes power, and with faith comes support. We have worked on our relationship, sure, and it hasn't always been easy but the real mileage has come from the work we have done on ourselves: understanding and owning our feelings and behaviour – sharing that has made us close.

It was 20 years ago this year that I faced my Sword of Damocles and I'm reflective as I sit in my sunny office overlooking a tree-shaded garden. There's a thwack of ball on willow from behind the hedge and I hear a shriek of, 'That's a six, Dad!' on the warm summer's air. My daughter smiles up at me as she walks past humming, her hands full of daisies, and my two-year-old is happy with the hose.

I'm one of the lucky ones as I didn't get what I wished for. I thought it was my birthright to be happy, but in the end it took the hardest-working verb to get it. I took the risk to be vulnerable and I live with the consequences . . . some of which have been love.

Mandy Saligari lives with her husband and three children in rural Kent. She lectures at independent schools on addiction and drugs, and on parenting for prevention. She has set up a non-residential treatment centre in London for addictions and relationship counselling: www.charterdaycare.com

12.

Getting your head around being single

Susan Quilliam

I spent a session with relationship psychologist Susan Quilliam. This helped me gain an understanding of the mental anguish experienced by the recent (and reluctantly) single woman who finds herself staring into the nuclear family abyss.

SQ: Whatever the reasons for finding yourself single again 'at a certain age', there will be a raft of emotions bubbling beneath the surface and occasionally bursting out. This is not an easy time for anyone who doesn't want to be single, and because there is a perceived 'tiny window of opportunity' in your life calendar for finding someone, falling in love, settling down and having babies, the very nature of its urgency can instil feelings of panic. While many women in this demographic 'soldier on' bravely, some become burdened by the sheer weight of negative emotions. Help is available, and it could change your life for the better.

AH: What's going on inside the head of a woman alone and emotionally 'at the end of the line'?

SQ: Typically, a woman in this situation will be experiencing a range of feelings akin to bereavement – mourning opportunities lost and potential, the past and present. She may be grieving for the children she hasn't had and might not have, and this can be an overwhelming emotion, manifesting itself with tearful outbursts. Plus there may be fear and despair: 'If I don't move quickly, it will never happen', 'This is my last chance of finding happiness and fulfilment'. Like a rabbit caught in the headlights she is gripped by panic as she wonders how to go about finding someone and what to do first. Inaction is seen as time wasting, although she may well be harbouring negative emotions or regrets from the past. These will undoubtedly hamper her progress.

AH: What other feelings might there be?

SQ: In addition to the feelings above, there may be feelings of anger: 'Why didn't I make my last relationship work?' 'Why did I allow myself to be let down?' 'Why did he eventually choose someone else over me?' At this point blame and self-blame rear their ugly heads. Although a person reading this book is probably past the denial stage, she might be in a state of shock: 'I've wasted the last ten years. Maybe it's all too late', 'I have never made it work in the past – how can I suddenly turn it around now?', 'How did I manage to screw things up so spectacularly?', 'My ex-boyfriend put me in this situation and it could ruin the rest of my life'.

In some cases these feelings may lead to depression and acts of desperation. Real depression is a feeling of helplessness. She will feel upset, angry and powerless to do anything. To give these feelings validity, she will be grieving the loss of relationship. Sometimes, the memory of a former love is the most difficult thing to exorcise from her mind. He will be always there, dormant, ready to emerge when prompted by places, music, key dates and events or moments of loneliness. She will be wondering what he is doing and whether he is missing her. He might be regarded as 'the one who got away' and irreplaceable. There may also be a tiny germ of hope lingering that one day this defunct relationship might be rekindled.

AH: How do these feelings manifest themselves?

SQ: Usually in three ways: attitudes to self, attitudes to the wider world and attitudes to potential partners.

AH: What are her typical attitudes to self?

SQ: She may find herself crying easily, spontaneously and fairly frequently.

She may blame herself, may end up overeating, over-drinking, having one-night stands or taking drugs. All of these self-destructive behaviours are simply ways of trying to get comfort at a time when she feels incredibly vulnerable in her life. Not only will she seek to accelerate an inappropriate liaison into a courtship but she will see sex as a comfort – a needing to be loved: 'It's better to wake up with someone's arms around me, rather than alone.'

But there are positive aspects too. Her state of singleness may instil a feeling of empowerment. If she has enjoyed a successful career and holds down a demanding job, she may take a business-like approach to her situation. She will be proactive and positive in taking steps to change her life around and move things forward. She might decide to join a dating agency or try online dating. She may decide to give the dating game a rest and pursue some new interests. In a way, this is like the end of the bereavement process and acceptance of the situation: 'He left, and he isn't coming back', 'I've got a lot going for me', 'I'm better off without him', 'I'm OK'.

AH: What about her attitudes to the wider world?

SQ: She may find companionship with single friends who are in the same situation. There will be safety and comfort in her peer group, although this might not necessarily be the best way to overcome her manless state. She will start to value herself differently and will shift the way she lives her life to be surrounded by similar people.

Other women may take a different stance. They might cut themselves off from the world by staying in or immersing themselves in their work. Or they might decide to do something radical and different – work abroad, go travelling, do voluntary work or learn a new skill. In the process, they will find a new peer group while learning salsa or German. Whatever she decides to do, although it might be quite manic in its approach, she will work through the solutions to her predicament internally.

AH: How might she come across to potential partners at this critical time in her life?

SQ: Her subconscious will give off signals that she is frustrated at not finding Mr Right. The classic case is that she will move into total desperation mode. She will do anything to get a partner, take anyone, jump into bed, come on strong and fast forward the first date into assessment of a man's potential as a partner and a parent. Her attitude may shoot and destroy a potentially good match in her quest to make it all happen – fast.

I have even heard of some women enrolling in speed-dating sessions and using their allotted three minutes to ask the chaps about timeframes for settling down and having children. It's all too much, too soon, too upfront.

The feelings of bereavement, desperation and anger will not help 'sell' the real woman. It is worth remembering that men who are single and looking for love are emotionally vulnerable too. Advertising for a mate with the aggressive rejoinder 'no time wasters' is unlikely to encourage the perfect man to step forward. I would urge women not to take out their anger or bitterness on men, even if they are deemed unsuitable types. No man wants to be the recipient of someone else's emotional resentment, anger or bitterness.

Sadly, if a woman does manage to find a potentially suitable partner, if she is still holding a torch for her past love (or a voodoo doll), then the man may bear the brunt of her regrets, possibly for some time. This is testing in the extreme for a new relationship.

AH: How much time should a woman leave between one relationship ending and another beginning – given that time is of the essence here?

SQ: The amount of time will depend on her emotional state and the intensity of any feelings she still harbours following the break-up of her last relationship. A classic mistake is for a woman to rush into something too quickly, with an aura of helplessness and fury. A woman may make a bad choice in her haste to fix things.

AH: Why would this be?

SQ: For instance, if a man and woman meet and they have both come out of unhappy, long-term relationships or marriages, they will share mutual emotional and baggage issues but two years down the line, once those particular issues are resolved, they may find they don't actually have too much in common.

She might also latch onto the next available man or (in her mind) the last available man on the planet. Her self-esteem will be low and she would rather be with someone, anyone, than be alone.

I would urge anyone still mourning her last relationship to get over it before even contemplating attempting to find someone else.

AH: How can someone in this state of mind get over her previous relationship? What help can she get?

SQ: The easiest thing is to relax, switch off and look the other way. Open yourself up to be surprised. Change the patterns of your daily life and enrich it by exploring new things. You need to boost your confidence and offload completely your emotional baggage. Clear the path so you can develop relationships with people that you meet along the way.

You may need to change your outlook too. Don't be too precise about your ideal 'type'. It doesn't matter what age you are but you can never conjure up an ideal mate in the exact mould as created in your mind. But don't surrender your standards either – make a list of rules about what you are not going to accept and avoid repeating unsuccessful patterns in the selection of your partners. If it applies to you, be clear that you will not tolerate abusive relationships, addictive behaviour, emotional immaturity or other negative traits you may have tolerated in the past. You cannot change other people but you can change your outlook and your standards. Self-help books or counselling can work wonders too.

AH: What guidelines would you suggest in choosing a counsellor?

SQ: Deciding to go for counselling is a serious and important decision. A counsellor will be an instrument of change in your life, so it is vital that you (as with a prospective partner) choose carefully. You must relate well to your counsellor – you will need to test them and trust your gut feeling before you commit to a programme of therapy. Refer to the British Association for Sex and Relationship Therapy and the British Association for Counselling and Psychotherapy for help. While Relate doesn't provide advice to singles seeking a partner, this national service does offer help on relationship recovery.

AH: If hypnotherapy can work to help people lose weight, overcome phobias and quit smoking, can it be used to help someone panicking about a stage in her life?

SQ: Absolutely! Paul McKenna and Hugh Willbourn wrote a wonderful book with a mind-programming CD entitled *I Can Mend Your Broken Heart*. This is all about overcoming emotional pain at the end of a relationship. Another recommended read is *Cutting the Ties That Bind: Growing up and Moving on* by Phyllis Krystal.

Susan Quilliam is a relationship psychologist and agony aunt based in Cambridge, specialising in intimate relationships, love and sexuality. www.susanquilliam.com

13.

Singledom and the great media myth

Mariella Frostrup

*D*ear Mariella,
 I'm in my thirties and single, and it seems as if everyone has an opinion on this: magazines, television programmes, family and friends. All have explanations and advice as to why I'm still single. I really can't absorb any more information on the subject. Am I old-fashioned in thinking that I just haven't met the right guy, or that I'm just not ready? I want a 'Go, girl' rallying call! Not a depressing and scary monologue about missing the boat, my diminishing fertility (this, I do acknowledge) and that I should just be grateful to meet someone, anyone. All of which seem to be on the lips of everyone around me right now. I'm excited about who I could meet, and my future with that person. However, I feel I'm not allowed to feel this way and should be more remorseful at what I have missed. I suppose I'm writing to you because I want to articulate my excitement – and I'm afraid to among my very intelligent mix of friends. It's ridiculous, isn't it, that we (single ladies in our thirties) are made to feel guilty and fearful about our lives and that we can't celebrate everything that we have achieved and carry that with us when dating?

You certainly don't want to be sitting around boasting about your happy life and proudest achievements if you're looking for a husband, my friend! What on earth is a man supposed to take away from that sort of encounter apart from the notion that you don't actually need him? Perish the thought that your prospective future partner should get the idea that actually you can, and do manage quite well on your own. Or that an ongoing relationship with him would just represent the supplementary icing on your already rich and deeply satisfying cake! The fact that the latter posits what seems a ridiculous and unimaginable scenario merely serves to prove your point.

I don't mind saying it's highly unusual and very refreshing to get an optimistic letter from an unmarried adult for a change. So what exactly is your problem? When it comes to a positive future view you certainly aren't suffering any handicap. As you so rightly point out, you have everything to look forward to and by the sounds of it little to regret. What you may have picked up is a severe case of mediaitis. Over 30, single and childless, you might as well have two heads – and neither of them an attractive one, as far as many publications are concerned. If it's not your selfish, fiscally irresponsible lifestyle that's doing irreparable damage to the fabric of society then it's the danger you represent to future generations by refusing to produce your 2.4 offspring in time to ruin your twenties.

What you've gone and done is read between the lines and discovered that amid the hyperbole there really is no issue at all about being single when you are mature enough to enjoy it. Enjoying independence in your thirties is, if anything, the ideal way to reap the benefits of single life before a virtually inevitable coupling that will leave you nostalgic for those heady days of freedom. A retrospective view is always an enviable one, but I have to admit that my one regret about my long singleton days was I didn't enjoy them more. Instead of fretting about where, when and how I was going to stumble upon a partner I should have been out there celebrating my soon-to-expire state of independence. When I think of all those wasted nights trawling supposed singleton hotspots in the foolish and misplaced hope of meeting my ideal partner I could scream at the utter waste of time. There are so many interesting things to go out and do once you've left behind the hedonistic twilight zone and behaviour-altering insecurity that tend to mar a woman's twenties.

Yet most of us fritter away precious years worrying about a future that will come, no matter what. You can't force yourself to find the right partner, and you're more likely to meet him in a bus queue or on top of a mountain than you are in a bar. You can't help but be aware that your biological clock is ticking. The only thing all those column inches devoted to the 'issue' of thirtysomething singles fail to mention is that it really is just the result of natural evolution. The minute women were given choices, they embraced them in much the same way as men. How much better a partner you'll make coming into a relationship with the confidence and belief in yourself that you display. There's a lucky man out there somewhere, I just hope he comes along in time for you two to have children, but not too soon to spoil your fun. Thanks for making your presence felt – I'm sure there are plenty of women out there who want to know that it's OK to be quite pleased with themselves!

Writing in the Observer *(29 April 2007), agony aunt Mariella Frostrup offered these words of wisdom to a reader's dilemma.*

14.

Pondering the single life

What's it like to escape the dating wilderness and eventually find your life partner? How do you feel if you are still single? This chapter contains the views of some who finally found love, some who haven't and various comedians' take on the whole issue of relationships.

From those who have found love in their late thirties

'After numerous false starts, dashed hopes and being on my own I now feel a quiet sort of relief that I no longer have to search. Seb, my husband is right here.'

Caitlin, 38

'It's not the whirlwind, knockout sort of feeling you have when you are younger, it's more a feeling of stability and companionship.'

Joanne, 39

'Singleness is a state of mind. If we are not happy being single, we view it like a perpetual horizon, stretching away into the distance with no end in sight. Our future becomes distorted and we see demons of our own conjuring, taunting us with feelings of loneliness and isolation. It takes a superhuman effort to eradicate this mindset. If you can do it, then you attract good, positive things. It took me two painful years, then David came along and click, everything became right.'

Andrea, 39

'I met Will through a dating agency. He was my fifteenth "date" and I was beginning to lose heart. I had a predetermined idea of my perfect partner and at first Will didn't come up to scratch. But I did find over time that he had some wonderful qualities that I hadn't expected from a red-blooded male: he liked me doing yoga so he took it up; not exactly a bookworm, he found a renewed interest in literature spawned from my reading group; armed with a Rick Stein cookery book he developed an art for cookery and he got passionately involved with a local charity to protect woodland. He did all these things without changing any other facets of his character or giving up any of his own interests. After just a few months together, I was waking up and wondering whether this was all a dream. Could I really have met my ideal man? Three years down the line, he's a pretty darn good dad too!'

Issy, 41

'My husband is a submariner, so he's away quite a lot. Now that I am married, I have the confidence to do things on my own which I wouldn't have dared do when I was single, like go and see a film, sit at a table for one out for lunch or go solo to the theatre. I can go anywhere on my own without being eaten up wondering if everyone is looking at me and thinking, "Oh look at her, she's on her own! She obviously doesn't have a man. Is she looking for a man? She won't find one here!" All the angst that I had before has evaporated.'

Marie, 37

'We didn't set out on our life plans to get married at 41, have our first child at 42 and our second at 45, it's just the way it happened.'

Greg and Clarissa, 47

'Everyone wants the "best" – the best house, the best job, the best partner, etc. People who won't settle for less than the best are never happy because they're always thinking about the prospect of something better. Compromise can be such a wonderful, releasing thing to do. If you wait for the person of your dreams to come along, you will be waiting forever because they will never show up. Settle for "almost good enough" rather than 'the best' and you will be happy – I am!'

Harry, 40

'My husband says "I love you" to me at least five times a day and calls me Darlingissima. Nobody had ever told me that they loved me before. I can't believe I spent so many years bereft of being really loved and having someone to love back.'

Penny, 38

'I got over myself in my 20s, enjoyed my 30s and am finally slowing down in my early 40s (until my first baby is born in six weeks' time). I think I am the happiest I have ever been. I feel like I have arrived at something which had previously been out of my reach.'

Angeli, 39

'As I got older I forgot how to flirt or at least it didn't really seem appropriate at my great age. Since I was getting panicky about still being single, I decided to take a new approach. I'd just turned 38 and was invited to a glitzy evening function through work, and decided this would be the perfect launch pad for the new, flirty me. I tried a different dress style and made a concerted effort to chat up men, flatter, tease and show just how impressed I was (without being insincere). Married men really don't expect anyone to flirt with them, so they were good "training material" and I was encouraged by their response. It wasn't long before one of them introduced me to a single guy – Jonathan. We are now married. It's true, flattery really does get you everywhere. Flirting is easy and can quickly be relearned – a bit like riding a bike.'

Becky, 38

'At the age of 45 I attended my first school nativity play as a parent. Looking around me, I realised what a very near miss I had had. If I hadn't met Carl on the train, then none of my now-epic life would be playing out before me each day.'

Rosemary, 43

'By their late thirties, the female of the species has matured to become more womanly and worldly. Like a good wine, women definitely improve with age.'

Max, 38

'I wasted years of my life dating the wrong kind of men, with each ephemeral relationship crashing and burning. I found it impossible to achieve permanency in a relationship so in my mid-thirties I made a conscious decision to be single. When I wasn't looking for love, at the age of 37 it found me. Sean was the exact opposite of all the guys I'd dated

before. Over time I have discovered so many things I didn't know I wanted
or needed from another person.'

Roberta, 41

'My girlfriend of six years gave me a marriage ultimatum – just as well, really
because I was never going to marry her. So we split. Within six weeks I had
met someone younger, happier and more gorgeous, and within six months
we were married. Sometimes you need a kick up the arse to really know
what you're looking for!'

James, 38

And for those who have not yet found love

'Never allow someone to be your priority while allowing yourself to be their
option.'

Mark Twain

'Single women are frightening. If you get to 41 as a single man, you're quite
battle-scarred.'

Hugh Grant

'My baby clock's not ticking and I don't have the marriage gene.'

Lucy, 35

'*Quirkyalone* stands in opposition to saccharine, archaic notions of romantic
love. It stands for self-respect, independent spirit, creativity, true love and
confidence. People are hungry for different ways to look at being single. We
don't want the old ideas rammed down our throat, that if you don't have
someone you are socially stigmatised. We don't want dating turned into a
job, feeling the pressure from the online dating industry and speed-dating
services that have revved up in the last decade, and the reality dating TV
shows where people are desperate to find someone. We don't want to think
we should change in order to be in a relationship and be validated by family
or society. So much of our economy is based on encouraging us to buy
lipstick and bikini wax so we won't feel inadequate if we are not in some air-
brushed relationship.'

Sasha, 34

'OK, so I'm single and childless. I don't need to be pitied (poor woman,
she's probably infertile) or judged (there's more to life than luxury holidays

and Jimmy Choos) or sneered at (too career-minded to settle down). I'm actually quite content with my lot – sorry to disappoint.'

Sharon, 38

'I stood at the altar clutching my small bouquet and cringed. Whatever possessed my best friend to want to humiliate me on her wedding day by making me wear a Little Bo Peep frock and be her bridesmaid? It's bad enough being single, but weddings, lovely as they are, do have a way of rubbing salt into the wounds. Having to wear that hideous dress only served to enhance my age and discomfort at being past my sell-by date. Was Natalie thinking that by including me in her big day this would somehow make me feel better, like it was the next best thing to actually getting married?'

Heather, 38

'Each year it's the same. The only difference is everyone seems younger, except for us. As perpetual singletons, we endure the festive jollity of Christmas and New Year, and grind our way through various social gatherings. Our parents' generation shrug, "Oh dear! Still not met anyone nice yet?" Newly engaged couples flaunt sparkling rings, fecund women aglow with pregnancy smooth their bellies and sip elderflower water, while the chaps marshal surly Boden-clad toddlers away from the presents under the tree. Will the next Christmas holiday be the same, or will the emphasis have shifted onto one or both of us a bit? We live in hope!'

Jenny and Catriona (sisters), 37 and 38

'There has been a long tradition of "walkers" for single ladies of a certain age. A walker is gossipy and good-looking. He flatters, protects and possesses impeccable manners. He is a true gentleman and represents the perfect foil for female insecurity. I have walkers who step beside me when I need to display "my other half" at corporate events and dinners. In this accepting society in which we exist, no one bats an eyelid if you are accompanied by your gay lover or a toy boy or someone else's husband, but God forbid that you should attend an event as a single person! In my particular industry that would not do at all, so Stuart (who happens to be discreetly gay) is displayed as my partner, and I reciprocate for him. Harry is my reserve for when Stuart isn't available. We look good together. There are no obligations, complications or sex. And in the whispers and rumours circulating by the office water cooler my single status is completely overlooked.'

Simone, 42

'You know when you walk through the Nothing to Declare section at the airport, you feel guilty, even though you're innocent? In the same way when you reach 40 and you are still single, you just look and feel desperate, even if you're not.'

Carol, 40

'When I was 25 I met Louisa, who was perfect to me in every way. I should have married her, but I considered myself too young. I let her go and heard that she married someone else. Although I have matured and am still the same person inside, I have never met another Louisa. Maybe I should stop making comparisons and carrying a torch for someone from my past, but no woman I meet ever comes close.'

Spencer, 39

'Think what you will about me, but don't you *ever* feel sorry for me.'

Laura, 40

'Being alone. You visit your museums and cultivate your interests. You make out To Do lists – reorganise linen cupboard, learn two sonnets. You dole out little treats to yourself – slices of ice-cream cake, concerts at Wigmore Hall. And then, every once in a while, you wake up and gaze out of the window at another bloody daybreak, and think, *I cannot do this any more. I cannot pull myself together again and spend the next fifteen hours of wakefulness fending off the fact of my own misery.*'

Barbara Covett, late 50s, fictional character from Zoë Heller's
Notes on a Scandal, Penguin, 2004

'After my first date with Samantha, I texted her saying that I'd enjoyed the evening and would she like to meet up again. She texted back, "I liked meeting U2, but b4 we arrange anything else, can U let me no where U stand with regards to C?" I texted back, "What is C?" Instantly she responded one word – COMMITMENT. And these women wonder why men run a mile!'

Andy, 36

'Single is a state of mind with which I am happy. Although I don't live with anyone, I have such a busy life that I can't actually dwell on the fact that I am single. If I met someone tomorrow, I really don't know how I would integrate him into my life. I just couldn't fit him in, so to speak.'

Miriam, 40

Textual advance made by Victoria (38) to Larry (43), who lives with Roberta, his girlfriend of ten years (Victoria got Larry's mobile number from his website): 'Hi Sweetie! Remember me? I'm that gorgeous QT U flirted with at the Finches. Couldn't believe my luck – the only hunky single guy in Kent! Perhaps we cld get 2gether & get 2 no each other a bit better? U free Friday? Call me. Yrs hopefully, Victoria xxxx' Larry had a vague recollection of being introduced to this woman, but was only at the event for 20 minutes and was with Roberta all that time. He later found out that another friend at the same event had received the same text!

'After thriving for years in my role as a prolific seducer of women, I finally received a wake-up call and a summoning to the next chapter in my life. It all happened when I experienced a pang of envy seeing my friends dancing with their kids at a wedding. In that thunderbolt moment, as I shot my champagne on the sidelines, I wanted more than anything to be married. I wanted a family of my own, I wanted to belong, to protect and to be loved.'

Andrew, 40

'It's rude to snoop, I know, but I casually flipped open a notebook on the coffee table. What I saw made me gasp and sweat prickle on my forehead. I had only been out with Jo for three dates and she was getting ready in the next room. In curly, girly writing she had written *her* first name and *my* surname on every line to the end of the page. To me, this just about summed up the emotional insecurity of today's single woman. Jo wasn't some love-struck teenager, she was a 36-year-old chartered surveyor.'

Gary, 37

'I don't need a permanent woman in my life. If I want sex or to have something cleaned, cooked, organised, designed, written or repaired, I pay someone else to do it for me. My life is cool, uncomplicated and angst-free.'

Mark, 43

'I'm single, bitter and resentful and there's nothing I can do about it. The older I get, the worse it becomes.'

Jen, 35

'Love is a compromise and I'm just not prepared to accept second best. I'd rather be single than stuck with someone second rate.'

Rachel, 38

'In the rarefied upper reaches of high-altitude careers where the air is thin, men have a much easier time finding oxygen. They find this in the form of younger, less driven women who will coddle their egos. The hard fact is that most successful men are not interested in acquiring an ambitious peer as a partner.'

Dr Sylvia Ann Hewlett

'As women glide from their twenties to thirties . . . the balance of power subtly shifts. Even the most outrageous minxes lose their nerve, wrestling with the first twinges of existential angst: fear of dying alone and being found three weeks later half-eaten by an Alsatian.'

From *Bridget Jones's Diary* by Helen Fielding, Picador, 2001

'Women in their late thirties seem to have a desperation about them. You know on the first date that you are being assessed for your marriage potential.'

Simon, 38

'Friends set me up with "an ideal date". This contrived meeting put a lot of pressure on our first (and only) evening out together. Throughout dinner she looked tense, worried and preoccupied – as if she was putting all her concentration into turning me into her soul mate. At times she even looked traumatised. Pity really, because she was lovely. I just think she was pressuring herself into seeking instant compatibility and true love from the outset.'

Bill, 38

'You have to ask yourself what are the reasons for a man of 42 to be still single? Is he going to suddenly get his act together and sweep some gorgeous 38-year-old woman up the aisle? Somehow I don't think so.'

Charmaine, 38

Now, let's not get too morose . . .

'Everything was going great until I said, "I love you," then he got this look on his face like he'd taken a wrong turn in a really bad neighbourhood.'

Roz Doyle, *Frasier,* Paramount Television

'I fall in love real quick, which can scare guys away. I'm like, "I love you, I want to move in with you, I want to marry you." And they're like, "Ma'am, just give me the ten bucks for the pizza and I'll be out of here."'

Penny Wiggins

'I've learned that you can't make someone love you. All you can do is stalk them and hope they'll panic and give in.'

Emo Phillips,

'I've never been married, but I tell people I'm divorced so they won't think there's something wrong with me.'

Elayne Boosler

'OK, I want to know the man for a year before I get engaged, another six months before I get married. Then, after a year, we have our first baby, then two years later we have another one . . . so, by then I'll be . . . Good God, I need to meet my husband tonight!'

Monica, *Friends*, Warner Bros

'Somehow a bachelor never quite gets over the idea that he is a thing of beauty and a boy forever.'

Helen Rowland

'Homosexuals and single women in their thirties have natural bonding: both being accustomed to disappointing their parents and being treated as freaks by society.'

From *Bridget Jones's Diary* by Helen Fielding, Picador 2001

Boyfriend: Do you want a lift/lunch/to go out tonight?
Thirty-seven-year-old girlfriend: 'NO! I WANT A FUCKING BABY!'

From Channel 4's *Spoons*

'Odds on meeting a single man: 1 in 23; a cute, single man: 1 in 529; a cute, single, smart man, 1 in 3,245,873; when you look your best, 1 in a billion.'

Lorna Adler

'Why is it so difficult to find men who are sensitive, caring and good-looking? They all already have boyfriends!'

Jane Caron

'If he hasn't called you in about three weeks and you have no idea where he is, the chances are he's not in an emergency room moaning your name.'

Diane Conway

'I waited for the phone to ring, and when at last it didn't, I knew it was you.'

Karen Muir

'If you love someone, set them free. If they come back, great! If they don't, they're probably having dinner with someone more attractive than you.'

Bill Greiser

Cautionary tales

In your quest to find love and happiness, learn from the collective errors and informed judgement of others.

'As the evening progressed, I began to notice her tattoo, faintly at first, and later very clearly. Across her forehead in big letters "I just want to get married and have babies!"' Rory

15.

Are you a tail-ender?

Jacqueline J.

I was once a tail-ender, but not any more. There are lots of tail-enders out there, most of them blissfully unaware they have this moniker attached to them. Some have been tail-enders more than once. One thing's for sure: whatever happens in the future, not one of them will be a tail-ender forever. You see, to be a tail-ender you do not have to be the ultimate girlfriend of a lovely man. No, you have to be the *pen*ultimate girlfriend of a lovely man. You are the long-term girlfriend, loyal and loving partner, committed (but with no strings attached) lover, who invests heavily in this, the best relationship you've ever had. And one day, the lovely man will show his appreciation of you and all you've done for him by proposing marriage . . . to somebody else.

You see, at some point the serial monogamist (or stringer) has to reach the end of his dating life. If the spinning bottle in this particular game of lovers' roulette stops with you, then you are the loser. The winner is the next woman, almost certainly younger than you, whom he'll meet before your tears have dried. She will have a whirlwind romance with this lovely man, be rushed up the aisle and go on to live in a beautiful home, own a cuddly dog, give up her career and have lots of babies, seemingly all within six months. You, on the other hand, will have already grown older, gone to endless weddings of friends, been stuck in the same job and dedicated years of your life to the physical, emotional (and quite possibly, financial) welfare of this lovely man. Now, like in a game of snakes and ladders, you have just slid right back to the beginning.

There are laws to prosecute individuals who falsely dupe the innocent into parting with their investments. You can go to prison for wasting police time, for causing actual bodily harm or taking things that don't belong to you. But the lovely man who strings along a series of women over the years, deluded as they might be, and steps off the bus when he has had enough of a particular journey is completely unaware, unaccountable or indeed apologetic for any damage he may have caused. I'm not being overdramatic when I say that the damage he casually inflicts with impunity could ruin the rest of a woman's life.

So, to all those tail-enders out there, or friends of tail-enders, you must learn to identify this most criminal variety of man to stop him from perpetuating his cruel and well-hidden intentions. You must spot a serial monogamist, however gorgeous he may appear, and deal with him appropriately and promptly or you could wait until the next one trugs along and surrender the next few years of your life to him. It's up to you.

Nine years ago, I was a tail-ender but I had the good fortune to meet my husband, Doug, two years after I was tail-ended. When we met, I was still recovering from the emotional destitution of being passed over for a young wife. I was determined not to get involved in another relationship, so Doug had to work hard to pursue me. He says this made me more attractive so I am happy that I was able to turn around such a negative experience into a positive one.

So, how do you know if you're a tail-ender and how do you spot a serial monogamist as he attempts to capture your heart and play for time until Ms Right shows up? Perhaps I should recount my own story first. I was 32 and had my own media buying company in London. I had a Fulham house, a Mercedes SL, a big bunch of friends and felt fulfilled with my lot. However, there was a gap in this near perfect life, and quite a big one too: a husband and children of my own – a family. So I couldn't believe my luck when I was invited away to a house party on the coast one New Year and found myself receiving the attentions of James and Mike, two dashing, eligible men over the course of three days.

Back in London, James wooed me relentlessly, so I declined further dates with Mike and it wasn't long before James and I became an item. We made a great team and although we didn't co-habit, we saw a lot of each other and enjoyed a good social life. But I had to be careful to give James 'some space' and allow him to indulge in cricket and golf in the summer, squash midweek and let him support Wasps rugby team at every home match during the winter. He had a côterie of mates and a close friend from university called Ian; he needed time to meet for five or six pints with these buddies after work and the occasional weekend to visit his family in Chester to see 'the most wonderful woman in the world' – his mum.

But I was always there for him when he did come back to my house, with a delicious supper, a bottle of wine open, a recording of something he'd like on video, laundered shirts and a big comfortable bed. We always stayed at my house and I didn't spend a single night at his place. His rather tired maisonette was filled with oddball lodgers who more than paid the mortgage and bills while he got to stay in a stylish home with all facilities provided free of charge – just like a five-star hotel, without a bill at the end. Quite a good deal, I'd say, and with a compliant girlfriend who made few demands to boot.

However, I did have to give up my Saturday morning art classes and three weekends away a year to attend a creative writing course because otherwise we would have seen so little of each other. I knew (or rather hoped) we were going to be together forever so there would be plenty of time to pursue my interests in the future. I didn't want to upset James or he might finish the relationship and I would be left alone. I just couldn't risk that through my own selfishness.

Eighteen months after we met a close friend Camilla married Ben, her boyfriend of two years. Camilla didn't throw her bouquet – she marched through the crowd and plonked it firmly in my hands. 'You're next!' They moved to Devon and began renovating a barn complex. That year James and I went to eight weddings, and I became godmother twice. Gradually, my core of friends began to dissipate out of London but for me, it was business as usual with James.

One long weekend, four years after we met, James, his two brothers, his friend Ian and their girlfriends all went to New York for a long weekend. He didn't want me to come as I had spent a year there in the past and he 'didn't want me to spoil the novelty of it for him.' I was inconsolable, but to keep him, I accepted his reasons. To get over this rejection, I went down to Devon to see Camilla and Ben. Quite out of character, I felt a surge of jealousy when I saw their spectacular barn conversion. When I was introduced to their beautiful baby son, a pang of longing was triggered deep inside.

That weekend, I became an emotional, snivelling wreck, knocking back the wine and bemoaning the fact that every aspect of my life seemed to have become stuck. I hadn't moved on with a new house, I'd gone as far as I could with my work and all my friends had settled down. My relationship with James just seemed to be jogging along as it had always done. It wasn't leading anywhere, I wasn't going anywhere and the only things that were changing were that I was getting older and more pissed-off.

I drove back to London, resolving to do something about my situation. During the journey along the M4, I became aware of a lingering odour in the back of my car. I stopped to investigate at a service area and found James's sweat-sodden squash kit in a sports bag, festering behind my seat. I vaguely remembered him requesting 'clean kit' for his forthcoming match with Ian the following week when he got back from New York. So, my friends got a barn conversion and a baby, plus each other while I got to wash my absentee boyfriend's putrid sportswear. Meanwhile he was going large in the Big Apple with his mates. Great!

So what did I do? How did I address this problem? I'll tell you, my friend, I did what most tail-enders do. Absolutely nothing. Life carried on exactly as before. My epiphany came, unexpectedly, when a group of us had been out for dinner and went back to another couple's house. Well, it wasn't their house, it was *her* house, but her boyfriend lived there most of the time – Cindy and Chris had the same situation as James and me.

While we had all been out, Cindy's washing machine had gone wrong and the kitchen was flooded. Chris didn't give a damn and was cheerfully pouring us drinks and turning up the music. He told Cindy it was her machine, her problem, so she should clear up the mess, call a plumber (at 11pm on a Saturday night) and stop bugging him about domestic issues. Now, I would have just got on with the job in hand, always ready for an easy life, but Cindy was having none of it.

She ordered all of us out, then ran upstairs and packed a bag for Chris and chucked him out too. Both yelled abuse at the other in the street and Cindy slammed the door on him, making it clear that he shouldn't bother coming back. Ever. A week later, Cindy and Chris got engaged and we went to their stunning wedding at the end of the summer.

Some months later I discussed with Cindy her outburst and subsequent nuptials, and told her how much I admired the fact that she wouldn't take any nonsense from anyone. Her advice was to be your own person and don't behave any differently because you're scared of losing him. If he really values you as a person, he will take the rough with the smooth, and he will respect you more if you stand up for yourself and your beliefs. If he legged it for good just because of a row over spilt water, he wouldn't have been worth having in the first place.

So I decided to take action and delivered a six-month ultimatum to James. 'Marry me, or let me go.' He thought that was reasonable and so we trundled along just as before. But a marriage ultimatum isn't the same as paying an invoice on the final day. I didn't really expect him to wait until 14 March at midday, exactly six months hence, and deliver his verdict – 'Yes, I do want to marry you' or 'No, I don't want to marry you.' You can't decide things of this magnitude just like that – you may as well roll a dice and if you get one to three dots it's no, and four to six dots means yes, but James thought it was perfectly reasonable to wait until 'Decision Day'.

Two months later there were no hints or signals as to which way he was thinking, so I made the decision for him. We would split up. So that's what we did, and he was able to pack all his possessions at my house into two carrier bags and leave. He rang me regularly to say that he missed me terribly, but that was only because he had no one to go to the cinema with him or to cook him meals in the evening, and he didn't like hanging out with his odd-ball lodgers.

For me, the emotional fallout was far worse. I do not regret that I had a 'revenge shag' with his best friend Ian three days after our split. It was good to be desired, it was wicked, it was fun and it was right. And no one else knew or ever found out. But it took me at least two years to cut the emotional ties from James. I carried him around in my thoughts perpetually – I was reminded of him by pieces of music, from hearing the rugby results on TV, places we had been . . . every tiny thing seemed to have some significance.

We saw each other once when he took me out for lunch on my birthday (we split the bill, of course) and he told me he had met Katie and that they were engaged. It had all happened so quickly. Ian was going to be best man. How thrilled I was for them both! I may have had revenge sex but he had got me back with a full-scale wedding. Oh the anguish!

You probably don't want to hear about one woman's pain. If you are reading this, then you may already know about the emotional devastation something like this can do, but perhaps, dear reader, you may wish to identify the various facets by which you yourself might be branded a 'tail-ender' so that hopefully you can avoid or deal with a serial monogamist when he presents himself.

The seemingly committed boyfriend who *isn't* going to marry you will exhibit some, or possibly all of the following traits:

* A lack of emotion when it comes to you. He will never say 'I love you' and will give the impression of being detached – an empty vessel. He is likely to be emotionally immature or emotionally lazy.

* You will *not* be the most important person in his life. You will be very low in the pecking order: after friends, siblings, his mother, his job and

recreational things or sport. Do spot-checks regularly and jot down where you stand. If you don't move up the order, you are a tail-ender.

* Does he do things without you, while expecting you to give up things for him? Don't stand for selfish behaviour. If he doesn't want to share the good (or bad) times with you, he won't want to share a marriage with you. It's tough, but this is *your* life he's messing about with.

* As a sure sign of his commitment to you, he will have his own bolt hole although he will spend a lot of time with you at your place. He will be reluctant to share things or undertake anything that could be seen as permanent, such as moving in together or opening a joint bank account.

* Just how long is a courtship supposed to be? A courtship is effectively a trial period. How many years does a man need to make up his mind? Approximately two years is the typical time people take to move from meeting to commitment, and this timeframe is shorter for someone in her mid- to late thirties. This is also the biological time for the first flush of romance to die and the calmer, more commitment-oriented hormones to kick in. Therefore if this dilatory individual hasn't committed to you within two years, he's probably not going to, either because his feelings for you aren't strong enough or because he hasn't made the shift to commitment state. Let's face it, who wants to end up with a man who vacillates and prevaricates over important decisions anyway?

* Is he a commitment phobic? If he never talks about the future or alludes to your life together, view this with suspicion. Couples who are going to marry have a steady and continuing rise in the commitment signals they show – spending more time together, swapping door keys, moving in together . . . This shouldn't be curtailed (it would be equally worrying if this all happened in the first six months, though) but if there isn't a moderately steady progression then it's reasonable to assume there will be no progression at all. Men tend to live for the moment while women anticipate the future, and a lot of men find it hard to express their feelings. They also like to keep their options open so a lack of commitment is more commonplace, but bundle this with other aspects of the serial monogamist and it just adds to your case against him.

* Perfectionism plays a large part in the serial monogamist's thinking. He has an ideal woman in his mind and whatever other good qualities you might have, you will never measure up to the goddess in his head. Also, tough as it is to take on board, you just might not be 'the one' for him or he might not be emotionally ready to settle down right now.

* Childhood influences also a play a large part. Bad role models from parents, such as constant arguing and the fallout from divorce, give serial monogamists an inherent fear of commitment. They are unable to cope with the pressure of the family unit for long periods of time and eventually seek their independence once again. If the partnership begins to show problems similar to those witnessed in childhood, then it will no longer mirror the ideal the serial monogamist has in his head.

* Have you been left off the guest list at (his) family events? Have you ever had to make alternate Christmas arrangements because your boyfriend had other plans that didn't include you? A serial monogamist usually doesn't involve his uncommitted girlfriend with domestic, personal or family affairs. To his mind, there's no point – you are not family and you aren't going to be in the future. Read the signs and take the hints.

* Many tail-enders believe they are the one to change the serial monogamist's way of thinking. Invariably, this is a futile effort. The pattern of serial monogamy is often so established that the serial monogamist can predict the month or year that the break-up will occur. No one seeks to end a relationship willingly if there are no problems. For some serial monogamists, the fear of commitment is beyond their control.

* Some people hold that serial monogamy is a psychological problem. They believe the only way to deal with the serial monogamist's state of mind is through psychological help. But can you really see your boyfriend, who is perfectly happy, seeking out such services because you suggested it? Not really. Others think that the term 'serial monogamist' is a cop-out. It can be used as a way for people to give weight to their incapability of sustaining a relationship. Psychological or not, serial monogamy is usually not a state of mind in which most people are happy to live forever. One day he will break the pattern, quickly settle down and live happily ever after – only not with you. So, ladies, if it isn't happening for you, sweep away hope and look at the reality. Act on it and move on while you still have time!

With thanks to Jackie and the many tail-enders (there are a lot of you out there) who emailed me their thoughts. Thanks too for the opinions and suggestions of two of the UK's best agony aunts in helping with the 'serial monogamists' profile'.

16.

The serial monogamist answers back

Imanaged to track down James T., who has been happily married to Katie for nearly ten years. They have three children and still live in London. He was not prepared to contribute an article but was willing to be interviewed about his previous embodiment as a serial monogamist. He read Jacqueline's article with a wry smile. This is his response.

What was your initial reaction to Jackie's article?
JT: Incredulity. I had no idea that Jackie was, and continues to be, so bitter. I didn't force her to go out with me! Guys in their thirties are not obliged to marry their girlfriends just because they [the girlfriends] want a house and a dog and a family. Women in their thirties have much to offer but they spoil it all by getting so hung up on commitment.

Do you think you behaved in a selfish way when you went out with Jackie, pursuing all your sporting interests while denying her, her own recreation?
JT: Absolutely not! I had (and still have) a very demanding job. Sport is an important part of my life. We have all grown up a lot over the last ten years or so, and I no longer do the pub thing after work but if any woman had tried to curtail my interests, then I would have ended the relationship in an instant. Jackie was absolutely free to pursue her own interests – it was she

who decided not to do things because they would interfere with our time together. That was one of the things I found annoying about our relationship: I didn't really know what made her tick because she didn't have any interests.

How did you feel when Jackie gave you an ultimatum?

JT: Fine. I agree that at the time there was no obvious end in sight to the relationship, nor any big plans for the future so a focal point seemed like a good idea. I was never in a million years going to marry Jackie, so I thought I would pan it out for another six months or so. I actually didn't have a room in my house because of all the lodgers and I didn't function well on my own. Lots of guys need to have a woman around – not just for the sex, but they don't have to marry someone just because they have been out with them for a while.

Why did you go out with Jackie when you had no intention of marrying her?

JT: For an easy life, and I was the sort of guy who needed to have a girlfriend – I was hopeless at being single. I know it sounds stupid, but people make all sorts of judgements on men of a certain age who are always single. It wasn't that I was 'making do' with Jackie – she was a great girl and we were good together. She had a lot of good qualities but it's hard to put my finger on it. She wasn't quite what I wanted. As I said, I didn't want to be on my own – I never did enjoy dating loads of women, I always preferred one long-term relationship at a time.

Do you feel guilty that you wasted Jackie's time during her mid- to late thirties?

JT: No, I didn't waste her time. I didn't lead her on and dump her at the altar. I didn't break a deal – there was no deal to break, there was no contract. If I recall, *she* finished with me. She was the one who clung on – she could have left at any time. I wasn't ready for marriage or even co-habitation on an official basis – not to Jackie, not to anyone. There are loads of men who are railroaded by determined women into all kinds of binding situations, often with bad results. A lot of damage can be done. Look at the divorce rate and all the legal stuff you have to go through. Men think about the ramifications of this sort of thing far more than women do. Women just seem to be governed by the imperative of their fertility and it clouds their judgement.

Do you think that you were a serial monogamist, as described at the end of Jackie's article?

JT: No! (Laughs) All that is a load of bollocks – it's the women who need their heads examining! You could categorise all types of men – what about womanisers, bigamists, deviants, mummy's boys, men who can't cope with rejection? You could take any guy and dissect his personality and behaviour, and come up with something dysfunctional about him. I wasn't a bad person – I wasn't violent, I didn't behave badly, I was faithful. I was actually quite generous and we had a good time together. We went on big holidays to Australia, Thailand, skiing in Canada – she didn't mention any of that in her article. My brother was getting married and the New York weekend was a kind of family thing. Jackie wasn't family, so I didn't want her to come. I was just a normal guy, leading a normal life, who didn't want to marry someone he didn't love. Where is the weirdness in that?

What do you think of her act of lust with your best friend?

JT: Well, we had finished and Ian was in a bad relationship himself so it didn't really surprise me. A short while later [after we had split up] I met Katie. Ian never did tell me and I find that a bit unusual – we discussed all sorts of things. I don't know how he'll feel when he sees it published in a book!

When and how did you meet Katie?

JT: When Jackie and I split, I went on holiday with one of my brothers to Portugal to play golf for a couple of weeks, staying in my parents' villa. Katie is a good golfer and we met on the veranda of the clubhouse. We ended up playing as a mixed four and she beat me. I was impressed and attracted by everything about her.

How did you know that Katie was 'the one'?

JT: I just did. She was actually seeing someone else at the time but I was determined to win her over, so for the first time in my life I had to really work hard at courting her. Because I couldn't have her, it just made me even more determined. I also knew that I couldn't just keep on in the same pattern as I had done for nearly 16 years. She was 31, very pretty, sexy and not afraid to speak her mind. I liked her independence, feistiness and the fact that her life was full and exciting. She didn't really need a boyfriend in the background, so I created a new role for myself as the leading man. It sounds a bit cheesy, but that's how it was.

Don't you think it was a bit thoughtless to tell Jackie about your engagement on her birthday?

JT: Well, we had just got engaged and I didn't want her to hear it from someone else. Her birthday just happened to occur that week. I knew it would be hurtful, but what could I do?

What advice would you give to women in relationships with 'serial monogamists' – as you were then? What should they do to get these men to commit?

JT: Read the signals. If he hasn't shown any sign of commitment after a few years, then chances are he is holding out. I would suggest dumping him with great determination. If he does want you, he will come running back, beg to get you back and probably make you an offer. If he doesn't, then better to know now rather than a few years down the line. A lot of men need a wake-up call for many reasons. By the way, can you lose that title 'serial monogamist'? It's straight out of *Four Weddings and a Funeral* – very nineties and completely meaningless.

17.

Looking For Mrs Goodbar

Toby Young

When it comes to sex, America is supposed to be the land of opportunity. As a young man growing up, I was regaled with stories from well-travelled friends about how sexually voracious American women are. They usually quoted that famous statistic: in New York, single women outnumber single men by such a large amount that an unmarried woman in her thirties is more likely to get struck by lightning than find a husband. By all accounts, the island of Manhattan was a single man's paradise.

So it was with considerable enthusiasm that I set off across the Atlantic in 1995 as an eager 31-year-old. My initial plan was to go for just four weeks. Graydon Carter, the editor-in-chief of *Vanity Fair*, invited me to spend a month at the magazine's New York headquarters. I had already written for *Vanity Fair* at this point and the idea was that I'd get to know some of the staff and then go back to London, where I'd continue to contribute on a regular basis. But I became so bewitched by Manhattan, I decided to stay put. It was just so much more glamorous than London. I felt as if I had been plucked from a rubber dingy bobbing about in the middle of the Atlantic and given a first-class berth on the *QE2*.

I should have known better. I got an inkling of what life in New York held in store on my first day at work. I was in the elevator, about to go up to *Vanity Fair*'s offices on the fourth floor, when a beautiful model stepped in beside me. She spotted a friend in the lobby and stuck out her hand to prevent the doors from closing. Instead, they snapped shut, almost trapping her hand.

'They're fashion sensitive,' I joked. 'If you're not wearing Gucci or Prada, they'll take your arm off.'

'But I am wearing Prada,' she said, deadpan.

I later discovered that trying to strike up a conversation with a woman in the elevator – particularly a beautiful woman – came under the heading of 'inappropriate behaviour'. About a week after I arrived, I found a memo on my desk entitled 'Policy on Sexual Harassment'. Behaviour that was strictly verboten included 'sexual remarks, advances, propositions', 'repeated requests for dates or other social engagements' and 'comments about an individual's body'. Trying to laugh a colleague into bed was out, too: 'A joke considered amusing by one may be offensive to another,' it said.

It's just as well *Romeo and Juliet* isn't set in contemporary Manhattan as Romeo would probably end up in jail.

The sexual harassment policy at *Vanity Fair* was quite liberal compared to other New York offices. Another ex-pat told me that at his advertising agency men were not allowed to enter a elevator if the only other person in it was a woman in case being alone with a man made her feel 'uncomfortable'.

Needless to say, the women who required these elaborate rules and regulations to protect them weren't exactly shrinking violets. On the contrary, it was men who needed protecting from them. New York women, particularly smart, attractive ones in their 30s and 40s, are extremely predatory – only, they're not looking for a good time. They're looking for husbands.

On the few occasions I managed to persuade New York women to go out with me, I was amazed at how unselfconscious they were about sizing me up as a potential partner. They invariably had a checklist of questions that they shamelessly ran through over the course of the evening. What did I do for a living? What part of town was my apartment in? What kind of car did I drive? It was less like a romantic encounter than an extremely tough job interview. By the time the bill arrived I was surprised they hadn't asked for a urine sample.

In London, I'd never had any problem getting women, relying on the gift of the gab. But in New York I simply couldn't get any of them to laugh at my jokes.

For instance, I was at a party once on the Upper East Side, talking to a beautiful woman, when she pointed out a plastic surgeon on the other side of the room.

'Tell me, Mercedes,' I said. 'If you could have one cosmetic procedure, what would it be?'

'Oh, gee, I don't know,' she replied. 'I guess I'd have my breasts reduced.'

As you can imagine, it took a superhuman effort of will not to glance at her chest – but I managed it.

'How 'bout you?' she asked.

'Oh, that's easy. I'd have my penis reduced.'

I was expecting a smile at the very least, but instead she looked deadly serious.

'Oh really? Why? D'you have a problem?'

I was tempted to string her along – 'Yes, actually, I've got a HUGE problem' – but I knew it would only lead to disappointment at the end of evening so I told her I was only joking.

'Oh,' she said. Thirty seconds later she was gone.

I think one of the reasons I had a problem – apart from my uncanny physical resemblance to Phil Mitchell – is that the women could sense I was just out for a good time. From a courtship point of view, contemporary Manhattan is very like the world depicted by Jane Austen. Most of the women I met, if they weren't already in a relationship, felt under an intense pressure to find a man. And the reason so many of them were still single is because not just any man would do. He had to be a prize worth having – the kind of man it would enhance their status to be seen with. It was less about finding a well-resourced mate to provide a secure environment in which to raise a family than it was about impressing their peers. I remember a conversation with *Sex and the City* author Candace Bushnell late one evening when we were both in our cups in which she confessed that she was 'a real snob' about who'd she'd go out with.

'I wanna go out with someone who's really successful,' she explained. 'I feel like I'm successful, I'm gonna be more successful . . . I wanna be with somebody who's like maybe *famous*, you know? I wanna be with somebody who's like me. I sort of feel like I've earned that.'

The willingness of New York women to enter what is essentially a 19th-century marriage market is surprising. After all, the cause of women's emancipation is more advanced in Manhattan than in any other city in the world. They might not describe themselves as 'feminists', but if these women experience any form of discrimination they're straight on the phone to their attorneys. They're more ambitious, better educated and less oppressed than any previous generation and yet they're prepared to go to almost any lengths, however demeaning, to secure a suitable husband. Without a successful man in their lives, they feel incomplete. In that respect, New York is a much more sexist city than London. Yet as far as I could tell it's a form of sexism perpetrated entirely by women. The reason they feel they have to make good marriages is because they don't want to look like failures in the eyes of other women.

Eventually, I met a nice English girl and returned to London to be with her. I wouldn't call the five years I spent trying – and failing – to take Manhattan a waste of time since I got a best-selling book out of it. But for me, America wasn't the land of opportunity. It was the land of the unreturned phone call.

Toby Young is the author of How to Lose Friends & Alienate People *and* The Sound of No Hands Clapping. *He lives in West London with his wife and four children.*

18.

Mr Right or Mr Write-off?

Amanda Platell

When Jennifer Aniston and Vince Vaughn's relationship finally collapses in the 2006 movie *The Break-Up*, there is always a stunned silence from its (mostly) female viewers – a sigh of collective sadness, of universal recognition. This is not because the film reminds women of the utter heartbreak of a doomed love affair, but because in real life the adorable Jennifer Aniston reminds us of a newer, more devastating social trend: the emergence not of Mr Right but his wicked twin Mr Write-off, as in he's a total write-off. He may not be a womaniser, but he is a serial swine.

He woos a woman in her twenties, stays with her for eight to ten years – long enough to give her every expectation that they will marry, have a family and spend the rest of their lives together. Then – and here's the rub – he dumps her for a younger woman with whom he usually promptly has the child his ex so longed for.

The most devastating aspect of Mr Write-off, who has a highly developed ability to move on without a backward glance, is that he dumps a woman literally in no-man's land. Bitter and desperate, in her late thirties, she must start all over again to try to find another partner and, more urgently, a father for the children she may soon be too late to have.

So when women cry watching *The Break-Up*, they are actually identifying with Aniston's real-life dilemma. She met Brad Pitt in 1998, but after nearly seven years together – but no children – they separated. Just months later he was in Angelina Jolie's bed – producing a brood of children. Brad Pitt is the ultimate Mr Write-off. He was 41 when they split. Jolie was in her late twenties and Aniston in her mid-thirties. Within a year of their separation, he and Jolie had a child.

And whereas it is easy to dismiss this as a tale of Hollywood heartbreak, we see the same social trend all around us in Britain. Most women dumped by Mr Write-off are left with literally nothing but the memories. These women, in the twilight of their fertility, who believed they had their lives sorted, are cast off with no partner and, crucially, no babies.

Most interesting is that this is not a problem predominantly on our council estates, but a middle-class phenomenon. It is happening to well-educated, highly successful, post-feminist women who thought they could have it all when they wanted it; who postponed their families to enjoy the 'me' decade in their late twenties and early thirties. Families and commitment could wait.

But they didn't. Or at least he didn't. Of course, men are mostly culpable for this trend, but women must shoulder some of the blame, too. As a society, we have loosened the obligations on both men and women to commit to one another permanently.

It is an inevitable and long-predicted by-product of a co-habitee society. With our ultimate desire for a father for our children, and a fertility window that slams shut sooner than any of us ever expect women were always going to lose out when we replaced marriage with co-habitation. Marriage protects a woman in a way that living together does not. We have made it so easy to move in together, to have the appearance of a stable relationship – but one of the reasons marriages work is they are harder to get out of. And who can blame men for taking advantage of a system women created? The feminist movement wanted to break women free from the chains of marriage, and it succeeded. The government finished the job.

Of course, women can have children throughout their forties, even up to their sixties now with donor eggs and IVF. But the chances of having a child naturally decrease drastically every year over 35. One in four 40-year-old women do not have any children – and most of these are not by choice. Mostly they are left without the families they long for because they've made the wrong choices about men.

Part of the problem, surely, is that feminism taught a generation of women that they did not need men and they did not need marriage. We enabled men to become commitment-phobes. What man wouldn't at least consider trading in his thirtysomething partner for a nubile twenty-something, given the opportunity? What man would not hang onto his youth until the very last minute?

It is part of the modern alpha male psyche to hunt and gather – but now he hunts women and gathers partners. And with so many women putting motherhood off, they can make themselves vulnerable to the alpha male who simply cuts and runs. The simple fact is that it is more difficult for a decent man to leave a relationship if there are children. That's why Mr Write-off avoids them at all costs. And what are we left with? An increasing number of men who think nothing of robbing a woman of the best child-rearing years of her life, and a new set of women left not holding the baby. It's a social tragedy in the making.

Amanda Platell is a journalist and political commentator. She has a regular column in the Daily Mail *and has made numerous TV and radio appearances.*

19.

Always the mistress, never the wife

It would seem that there are a lot of married men out there, enjoying a bit on the side. The people running the big dating agencies in the UK should know. They meet scores of women who have tired of the hollow assurances and empty promises that their lovers will leave their wives and families, but never do. Being a mistress may suit some women, but for the woman in her late thirties who is holding out for the man in question and wants to have children with him, her wishes probably won't be fulfilled. Whatever benefits or advantages there may be, it would appear that a mistress is neither for Christmas, nor for life.

The mistresses

Natalie, 38

I have been mistress to William for ten years. He is 64, lives mainly in Hertfordshire and is on this third marriage. He has six children, the oldest of whom is older than me and the youngest is four. William is very wealthy. I am not a gold-digger, as I am financially independent and see him only once or twice a week in London, when we go out to dinner and stay at his City apartment. We occasionally go away for a long weekend. This suits me fine. As a person, I avoid love and don't seek emotional involvement. I also don't want to have to work at a marriage. At any one time I only need to be sexy and glamorous for a few hours then when he's gone, I can slob out.

His wife does not know about us, but I believe she has her suspicions. William tells me that she 'bought in' to the marriage, understanding what he was like and accepting that he would not change. She leads a charmed life, and I have no doubt that he loves her. A few of his friends are aware of our relationship, but everything is kept discreet and low-key.

Our relationship is a physical and intellectual one. We find each other intriguing, interesting and attractive. I myself enjoy the freedom from commitment and have no wish to settle down or have children. I work hard to keep myself physically in good shape. I don't love William and probably won't know the extent of my feelings for him until our relationship ends. Apart from looking good and the sex, his only requirements of me are discretion and silence. Technically, I don't exist.

I have always had an affinity to married men. They can be kept at arms' length, emotionally and physically. I cannot imagine being tied to one person for the rest of my life. I would never wish to hurt anyone, and always block out the image of 'the wife', their marriage and family life.

Katie, 36

Phil is unhappy in his marriage. He sleeps in a separate room to his wife (on a different floor even). He is trapped because he can't afford to be divorced. He has a big house, a big mortgage and three children to support. He works incredibly hard and is loathed by his wife. They married on impulse in their early twenties and were happy, initially. They had their first child ten years later, but his birth triggered stresses which turned their once-happy marriage into a loveless one.

For the last two years we have been seeing each other. I know that we will never be together in the real sense, but I am able to offer some respite. Phil is a wonderful man: he is fun to be with, generous and loving. He comes over to my house twice a week. Sometimes we go to the theatre, the cinema and out to eat. Sometimes we just stay in. He keeps me in the background as he doesn't want to alert his colleagues or friends to my existence but I am cool about it. We usually manage to take a week's holiday together once a year and go to out-of-the-way places where we are unlikely to see anyone we know. I enjoy all the subterfuge. We once went to a private view at a gallery together, which was packed with mutual acquaintances and his wife was there too. Phil and I had to ignore each other throughout the event and at a dinner afterwards. It was so exciting! Although I am financially self-sufficient, Phil buys me luxury items – I have a real weakness for handbags and shoes. He spoils me.

In recent months I have been feeling quite broody. I would love to have a baby. Phil's keen on the idea, but does not want to be the biological father. He feels this would complicate further his already complex and financially encumbered life. We have discussed sperm donation and it will be good to have his support so that I won't become a mother alone.

I know that I am a mistress. My parents and friends disapprove massively, but I see Phil because I love him, and I don't need anyone's approval.

Lynne, 36

I have been Dickie's mistress for eight years. He has been married for nearly quarter of a century to Mandy and the second of his two boys is starting at university next year. Ever since we first met, Dickie has promised to leave Mandy when the boys leave home. That time is coming.

I want a family of my own with Dickie and I am aware that my fertility has a time limit on it. I try not to plan, but I'm desperate for us to be together permanently. When we first started our affair, I felt very guilty – Mandy was suffering from osteoarthritis and had two hip replacements, but now I have no guilt. She has recovered and I want what I feel I have a right to. I want Dickie to myself. I have been waiting, but next year it will happen. We won't have a big wedding – we will probably go abroad and we'll live in my house to start with until he reaches a financial settlement with Mandy. I love being with him, but I have tired of all the clandestine arrangements, the hiding, communicating in code (I am listed as Peter Lambert on his mobile), sudden cancellations and waiting in the car in the next street. I want to come out of the mistress closet and be a married woman and mother in my own right.

Hayley, 38

Robin and I had a crazy time. Sexually, we pushed all the boundaries, although we never really connected mentally. I was therefore surprised when Robin called round unexpectedly late one evening and sobbed his heart out to me. Apparently his wife of 13 years had been having an affair for a year with a young university lecturer. He was incredulous, very hurt and emotionally devastated. I poured him a brandy and cradled his blubbering head. He cried like a baby, and kept saying over and over, 'I can't believe it! How could she, how could she?' The phrase 'Pot calling the kettle black' ran through my mind. After two years of rampant extra-marital sex, Robin climbed into his Meno-Porsche and drove out of my life forever.

Sarah J. Symonds, 39

Having been a well-documented mistress for most of my dating life, at 39, people could say I have left it late to look for my own husband and settle down. Ever the optimist, I disagree: I believe there isn't a right age or time to get married. Whether you are 18 or 80, the situation purely depends on if you have met the special person you deem good enough to call your life partner. If you never do, then I strongly suggest a woman never settles for a man in order to fit into society. It's far better to feel lonely – even miserable – while being single, than to feel lonely and miserable in a relationship or marriage.

Through my life experiences of being 'the other woman', and while researching my first book, *Having an Affair? A Handbook for the Other Woman* I have heard *all* of the lies and excuses used by married men. A cheating husband feels that words alone give him the right to cheat on the woman he took wedding vows with – the mother of his children. And, I can tell you categorically I would rather marry late – or even not at all – than have been the wife of one of those cheating duplicitous men. More often than not, these were men who married young, and who had grown bored with their situation; hence my argument for marrying later being better.

When you marry later, you are generally more developed as a person. You have learnt what you want (and more importantly what you *don't want*) in a partner and in life. Also, you have lived and seen more of life so you aren't typically searching for those things you used to be. All this points towards a stronger propensity to be faithful and a greater commitment to making a marriage work.

I think that getting married later in life is the way to go, and provides more chance of happiness and longevity, although I always find it rather funny that if a man leaves it late to marry, he is often described as a 'playboy' etc, but if a woman decides to leave it late to get married she is often described as 'desperate and on the shelf'. (Life is so unfair, sisters!)

Now – with my New Year's resolution to become a 'reformed other woman' – I am in the pursuit of happiness myself, and I finally feel ready to settle down and actually look for Mr Right rather than continually wasting time with Mr Wrongs!

But can the mistress ever go on to become a Mrs? Yes, and no. Yes, if she makes a fresh start and finds a single, unmarried man. But no if she ever believes she will marry the very man she is a mistress to. Even if she did marry him – since they say 'a leopard doesn't change his spots' – he may *always* be looking outside the marriage for sexual fulfilment. Which will be equal misery for her. Ultimately, my point is that being a mistress isn't necessarily a fast track and sure-fire way to end up with your perfect man!

To be even handed though, we do know people whose great second marriages have been born out of affairs. Sting and Trudie Styler immediately spring to mind. I truly (not Trudy) believe that a mistress can make for a brilliant wife as she has picked up so many of the dos and don'ts along the way. A sort of starter wife, if you will . . .

Through my work as a relationship expert and infidelity analyst, I coach multitudes of women on how to end their affairs with married men, and look for available love. In the heartfelt letters and emails I receive daily from the secret society of mistresses who write to me for advice, the common grievances shared are 'annoyance at wasting so much time with the wrong man and believing his lies and empty promises, thus leaving it too late to find the right one'. I always tell them it's never too late to love yourself and create the right relationship. I hope, in reading this book, disenchanted mistresses will be empowered to wait for the right man rather than settle for the wrong guy!

The blog 'Pillow Talk' is a forum for mistresses and can be found at www.havinganaffairthebook.com

The wives

Cleo, 46

It's different in France, where mistresses are viewed as potential saviours of marriages on shaky ground. But in the UK, it's encouraging that people – friends, family, colleagues, the media and (in the celebrity world) the public, tend to rally round and support the wronged wife. Take Annabel Goldsmith, Victoria Beckham, Mary Archer and Jilly Cooper. They all emerged from 'sensational' revelations of their husbands' infidelity fragrantly, with dignity and overwhelming support.

An anonymous woman, claiming to be a former mistress, called me at my office one day and informed me that my chief executive husband was having it away with a new lady friend, every time he stayed overnight in London (at least once a week). If I cared to call The Lanesborough Hotel, I could be put straight through to their room and interrupt the proceedings.

Rattled by this bombshell, I didn't feel capable or indeed willing to confront my husband, if indeed he was *in flagrante* with some tart. After all, the phone call could be a cruel hoax. But I did call The Lanesborough and the receptionist confirmed that my husband had a current room reservation.

When he came home the following day brandishing a guilt bouquet of roses, I asked him which hotel he had stayed in. As soon as he replied The

Hilton, I knew. I hate being lied to, and my anger empowered me to extract the truth from him.

What I hadn't bargained for was that he said he was going to continue to see her. He knew I wouldn't seek or be brave enough to instigate divorce proceedings or separate, and he thought I would take this all lying down – so to speak. So the lustre in my life has been dimmed. I continue on in the knowledge that I am a cuckold, feeling a cutting wound when I see couples being happy together.

Jayne, 42

Sex, lies and phone calls. The forensic evidence I have is as follows:

* Long blonde hairs on a comb that aren't his (or mine) in his overnight bag after a conference
* The washing machine full of sheets (he forgot to empty it as he *never* does the laundry) after the children and me had been away for the weekend
* Shredded credit card and mobile phone bills – these are normally filed
* A speeding ticket in Shropshire when he was supposed to be playing golf in Surrey
* A new smart-casual sartorial look even though he 'never shops for clothes'
* His frequent working-late-at-the-office sessions, even going in on Saturdays to cope with an increased workload – such loyalty to his employer!
* A sudden decrease in his highly charged libido leading to zero conjugal activity in our bedroom
* Making mobile calls from the bottom of the garden in the rain
* Taking a shower after going for a drink at the pub with 'friends'
* Completely stonewalling an attractive woman in her late thirties we were introduced to at a charity ball. Meanwhile, she kept sneaking looks at me. Was she a lesbian with the hots, or was she shagging my husband and mildly curious to see what wifey looked like?

I could go on, as there's plenty more evidence. Does he think I'm completely stupid? At first, I felt a frisson of uncertainty about our established, happy marriage of ten years. Then I felt paranoia, followed by anger and a need to avenge myself. These emotions are against a backdrop of fear. If I confront him and we get divorced, will I lose the house? What about the children? When I got married, I felt so safe, so secure and so loved. Everything emotional, financial and practical was taken care of.

Now, I have fallen head over heels out of love. I am determined to find out about this 'other woman'. As I walk the dogs on the common each morning, I concoct outlandish plans to catch them *in flagrante delicto* and humiliate them both – plans that obviously I'll never see through. And I ask myself again and again, 'How could I have married someone so false?'

Joelle, 42

I had a nervous breakdown when my husband of 15 years told me he was leaving me. He had been having an affair with a woman a little younger than me for three years. I had absolutely no idea, and truly believed our marriage was rock solid. He moved out and my life fell apart. I went into hospital and our two boys went to live with my sister, changing schools.

Then three months later he came back. His mistress said she felt so guilty about what he'd done to us, so she ended their relationship.

I'm not glad to have him back. It's not the same. There has been so much treachery and deceit. My heart has been broken and the boys are traumatised by what has happened. My seven-year-old has started wetting the bed. I have chronic insomnia and have had to resign from my job. If I ever meet this other woman, I swear, I will kill her. She has destroyed our family.

Karen, 41

It's not that I *mind* my husband *having* a mistress. I knew when I married him that he had a roving eye and an insatiable lust. What I do mind is that he spends money on her and that she is more attractive and considerably younger than I am. (I have seen her Facebook entry.) The wealth in our family is all on my side and the courts would come down on Harry like a tonne of bricks if we ever got divorced. I don't want to be alone. I don't want him to divorce or leave me, so I have accepted what is happening. I just want to lead my life, enjoy my friends, travel, have fun and raise my family without coming back to an empty bed. I think he's pathetic needing to take a young lover to satisfy his urges, but I am amused by his lies, complex stories and cunning plans because he thinks that I don't know. Hopefully, in a few years he will grow out of it – and grow up.

He has just packed for a last-minute weekend 'conference' that apparently he must attend. I have sneaked a look in his bag. At least he's using condoms at this conference, but will he really need 50? So I have wiped a fresh slice of chilli over the crotch area inside his underpants – just to spice things up at his 'conference'. That'll teach him to have hot weekends away!

Marrying the mistress – does it work?

Apparently not very often: men who cheat on their wives usually do so more than once. So the mistress, who shunts the first wife out of the way and changes her status to Mrs, should know what she is dealing with. As Sir James Goldsmith famously put it when he divorced Ginette Lery and married Lady Annabel Goldsmith, 'When you marry your mistress, you create a vacancy.'

'I spent ten years holding out for Henry,' says Anne, 45 who is sensible, church-going and thoroughly unmistresslike. 'Finally, when his children had grown up and left home, he divorced his wife and married me. I entered into this arrangement with such naivety, thinking that marriage would be an instant cure for all my frustrations – no more waiting to see him, no more weekends cancelled at the last minute, no more subterfuge. We could have breakfast together every day, go on holiday and even spend Christmas in each other's company.'

In the event the marriage was short-lived. 'I traded in the flowers, cashmere and dining out for life in a tiny flat waiting on him hand and foot. When I wasn't working, I was queuing up at Tesco, clearing up all his mess and being assaulted by the TV, which was permanently tuned to sport. I had transgressed from lavished love bunny into a domestic servant.'

After just 14 months, Anne left her lover of ten years. 'By waiting years for Henry, I surrendered my chances to have children. I wanted him so much that I thought this was a sacrifice worth making. But almost as soon as we moved in together I realised I didn't know him at all. I'd only ever seen his good side – the clean, attentive side outside the home.

'After just a month of being with him full time I began to empathise with his ex-wife. I had never noticed it before, but he was lazy and slovenly. Nothing ever got done. I also found myself uncomfortable with the seething resentment emanating in my direction from his grown children and our financial constraints – his wife had scooped the jackpot when she divorced Henry and now I was financing our relationship.

'Initially, I had felt guilty about breaking up the marriage, but now I am certain his wife was glad to have him off her hands. However, they remained on suspiciously good terms and he seemed to get on better with her after they split than when they were married. I realised that our part-time, covert relationship worked simply because it was part-time and covert. The 24/7 relationship held no mystique or magic for either of us, the tables had turned – Henry's ex-wife suddenly had the allure of being "the other woman".'

Dr Janet Reibstein, visiting professor at Exeter University, whose research into infidelity reveals that marriages following affairs are particularly brittle, often breaking up faster or not really becoming established in the first place, says: 'The more you integrate yourself into someone's life, the more likely you are to experience conflict and disillusionment.

'People do not realise how dependent an affair is on the marriage. In other words, an affair needs the marriage to keep its lustre in order to look good in comparison. People believe that they are revealing their true selves in an affair. All those deep conversations, candlelit dinners and long nights give lovers a chance to share their innermost thoughts in a way that a married couple – with children, work, in-laws and domestic humdrum – never have time for.'

And of course, this only applies to the small percentage of mistresses who actually marry their lover. The vast majority never do.

20.

Settle for less in love

Elizabeth Williams

Adrian's proposal was utterly romantic. We had walked out onto the restaurant balcony in Corfu, and against the sunset, with a dolphin's silhouette leaping in the harbour, he asked me to be his wife. We were both 32, captains in the Army and had only been seeing each other for six months. He caught me off-guard and, hesitatingly, I accepted.

But in my heart, this wasn't what I wanted. I liked Adrian, but I didn't love him. He was a good man but he wasn't good enough – for me. Our holiday continued, and we rang friends and family to tell them the news. My acted smiles and happiness were a mask: in my mind I struggled with ways to exit this quandary without hurting anyone.

We returned to the UK and I continued with our engagement charade, stalling wedding dates and plans. I asked my CO if I could have an alternative posting. When that time came, like the true coward that I was, I wrote Adrian a classic 'Dear John' letter – it's not you, it's me type of thing, enclosing the ring, and bailed out of my base and my relationship.

So what was wrong with Adrian? Little things, I guess. He wasn't particularly tall and he had come up through the ranks. Unlike my family, he came from working-class roots in Derby, and I found that difficult to deal with. One of his brothers was a welder and the other had been unemployed for two years. I was a snob, as well as a coward. Adrian possessed a great sense of humour and was popular with the officers and men. He had integrity and good leadership skills. Affectionate and caring, he was plainly besotted with me. I was unable to reciprocate his love, though pretty good at faking my affection for him. But his attention to detail and the fact that he did everything by the book irritated me. On principle he wouldn't cook something from a recipe unless he had all the ingredients. He was crazy about Derby County FC to the point of obsession, which I found tedious. Outside his job, Adrian wasn't a risk taker and to my mind, lacked imagination and spontaneity – I needed someone more exciting, with more class, who didn't follow me around like a lovesick puppy all the time.

That all happened nine years ago now. I've long been out of the Army and have retrained as an accountant. I'm still single and childless. In the intervening time, I haven't met someone caring, popular, with integrity, humour and affection, who is besotted with me . . . I let Adrian go – I pushed him away in the hope of landing a better catch, and I failed.

I saw Adrian last year at a reunion. Now a major, he is exactly the same and greeted me warmly – always the gentleman. Recently back from Afghanistan, he introduced me to his pretty wife and their three children – a perfect family unit. Later that night, alone, I went back to my little flat in Tooting and wept.

Some months later, on a scorching July day, I had a reunion of a different kind with two friends from my school days – Belinda and Sian. Belinda is married to Howard and gave birth to Alexandra on her 40th birthday. Sian is unmarried, but has a two-year-old daughter, LuLu. She won't discuss the father, who has no role in their lives. With the two babies on a rug, we sat in the shade of a sweet chestnut tree in Kew Gardens and contemplated our respective lives, and whether or not we were happy.

Belinda: Yes, I am happy. It hasn't always been easy and Howard is a tricky individual. I think I am the only woman who has ever been attracted by his rather odd features (big nose, wild grey hair, 19 stone on the scales) and have overlooked his, at times, pompous and conceited attitudes – things that have made other people see red. I have learned to deal with his laziness around the house – he does work very hard and earns good money. He argues only about stupid little things, never majorly important issues, and as a lawyer, regularly puts me in the witness box for interrogation over minor domestic misdemeanours.

His social life dominates – he goes to the rugby at Twickenham, he plays golf and watches the cricket in the summer. He often drinks late with his colleagues, eats dreadful junk food on his way home to dinner I have prepared and obsesses about military tactics in World War I. I spend a lot of early evenings in on my own and have sole responsibility for all matters domestic and child-related. I am also carrying six points on my driving licence, which he has lovingly earned and transferred to me. The good things are: we're well off, we love each other and I get a great buzz from being with him. He's proud as punch to be a dad and is eager to have another.

Was he the best I could have had? I'm not sure. Did I compromise myself when we married? Yes, at first, but I don't feel like that now. If we'd met when I was in my twenties, I wouldn't have given him a second glance but at 38 I was running out of options. Yes, I think I did settle for less, but my life has changed dramatically for the better. Being loved is the most important thing. And how does being on your own equate to being with someone you have grown to love? It just doesn't.

Never having been married before, I didn't know what to expect. But I had a maturity and composure that I didn't possess when I was a frenetic account director in advertising. With marriage, you are a team player. It isn't the same as being in a relationship: a relationship is a choice. A marriage is less about passion and more about partnership, companionship, doing things and making decisions together. It's knowing you have someone alongside to face the next chapter in your lives and grow old with.

Sian: For some reason, and I'm not sure why, I missed out on the marriage/partnership thing. It just didn't happen. I've had lots of relationships and I don't think I was attracted to the wrong kind of men. I just always hoped that I would find someone better – someone better looking, more success-ful, funnier . . . I think in our media-obsessed society there is an imperative among women to strive for perfection. I have actually been proposed to twice, but either I wasn't ready or he wasn't the right guy. Why are women so fussy? It's not as if they have to make do with some grossly inadequate monster – everyone is flawed. None of us is perfect, yet we seek some kind of unattainable perfection in others. So what do we do? Give way to panic when our fertility system gets ready to shut down and marry the next guy who asks? Maybe, if he's asking, but no one was. I always wanted a child and I couldn't wait forever, so I had LuLu.

My baby is the most precious thing in the world but she has wiped out any prospects of meeting a single, eligible man (if such a thing exists). Picture this: somehow – don't ask – I meet a wonderful guy and we go out for dinner a few times. He's single, never been married and he seems to be looking for some permanence in his life. And he likes me. What are the odds on that happening at 40?

He invites me back to his house, but like Cinderella, I have to dash back and pay off the babysitter. He asks me out again, but this time LuLu is ill, so no can do. A week later we go out once more and this time he comes back to my place. The babysitter ogles at him a bit too much as I pay her at the door. And then I gasp with horror as I try to clear the fuzzy felt off the carpet and move LuLu's pink play kitchen out of sight. The whole of the downstairs of my house resembles a crèche. We are woken at 5am with LuLu yelling, 'MUMMY!' I lift her out of her cot and she screams in terror when she catches sight of my new lover. Try nurturing a relationship along with that as the backdrop!

So, what can we conclude from this? As we get older, we change. We mellow away from the thrill-seeking, fun-loving, hedonistic lifestyles we might have enjoyed in our twenties. Then we were too flighty, nomadic and optimistic to settle down with someone who was OK, but not perfect. But getting older is a double-edged sword. With maturity come higher expectations, inflexibility and greater discernment. For the older woman, second best just won't do.

So who would make the ideal partner? Obviously we're all different, but it would seem that friendship in a team mate is a general requirement, someone who understands your quirks and foibles, someone who can share the mundane with the exciting, who can support you, second-guess you, put up with your moods and share the responsibility of family and decision-making. So what if he's short, fat and bald? If he loves you, values you, respects you intellectually and makes you laugh, grab him while the offer's hot!

To me it seems that all the best men have been snapped up. The dating pool has dwindled. Maybe it was plundered by all the women who rather than hold out for the zenith of perfection opted for Mr You'll Do Nicely instead. Meanwhile, the fellas don't get wound up about Ms Right, taking second best, settling for less, etc. They meet a woman, and if she's right and the time's right for him – bingo! Wedding bells. But for women with a deadline for marriage, who wouldn't previously lower their partnership aspirations, they now have to compromise or remain solo. They must be prepared to make greater concessions than they would have done fifteen years ago. The only men left seem to be older, divorced guys, shell-shocked and financially disembowelled by a previous marriage. But by accepting Mr You'll Do, do you really want to take on board complex family issues and resentful step children?

So, ladies, get off your high horses and get real! As someone on the outside, I believe that settling for less *is* the best option. Otherwise, you face

21.

Is settling for less really best?

I managed to find three women, who considered when they finally walked down the aisle in their late thirties that they had compromised on their choice of husband. In the interests of confidentiality, all names have been changed.

Steph

I knew it wasn't full-on love when I met Tony. It was more of a convenience – better to have someone around than to go solo all the time. He was a good companion and I thought that I could change the little things that I found irritating: his penchant for sun-beds and cravats and his less-than-sexy spectacles. Other than that, we had quite a lot in common and he seemed fairly uncomplicated. But it wasn't love. I knew from the reactions of friends and family that they were taken aback and surprised when we announced our engagement. At 38, I was a year older than Tony. I was no spring chicken and I felt that I was unlikely to meet Mr Perfect at this stage in my life, so we got married.

Our daughter, Amelia, was born less than a year later and proved to be a distraction for me from the feeling of sliding disappointment. I came to find fault in everything Tony did or said – the way he coughed, his fastidious attitude to everything, the smell of his aftershave. After two years we divorced. We'd bought our property jointly, so we split our assets down the line, even though I took custody of Amelia. So I went from living in a large country house to existing as a single parent in a tiny cottage. I was relieved that I was free, but we still had to see each other every week to drop off and pick up from nursery and allow him 'daddy time'.

It was only after we separated that people started to say what they really thought. 'A tosser doesn't change his spots!' from my brother, and 'What on earth possessed you to *marry* him?' from my best friend.

I am blessed to have a wonderful daughter, but I am an awkward individual at the best of times so I must share some of the blame. Tony has since told me that he felt he was taking a massive risk when he married me. As far as he was concerned, it wasn't love either and he didn't think I was 'marriage material'. However, he hoped that I might mellow with time and that perhaps he would grow to love me.

Looking at myself, I am most definitely guilty of 'making do' in the marriage stakes, and I paid the price in the end. Tony and I are both still single. I can't get back into the dating game with a small child in tow and I have had my fingers badly burnt by this experience. I feel second rate, and I don't believe there is anyone out there who could really love me for being who I am, and who I could love back.

Paula

I met Guy on a windsurfing holiday in Tenerife. I'd gone with a mixed group of people and first set eyes on him in the bar, where he treated me with aloe vera for a bad dose of sunburn. I was immediately attracted to him: he was handsome and funny, with a good job in advertising, and astoundingly bright. We embarked on a passionate, long-distance relationship on our return to the UK. It was a whirlwind romance, and after a few months, he told me about his ex-wife. That is, ex-wife number one – they had married ten years previously and divorced after two years. Then he told me about wife number two: they had married four years ago and divorced two years later. The reasons, he cited, were irreconcilable differences, but the reality, he said, was that on both occasions they just left. There was no infidelity on either side; they just grew apart. Privately, I was incredulous that two women could walk out on such a fabulous man. He was top dollar.

We went out for about a year, and then he told me about his mental illness. He had a history of paranoid schizophrenia, but it was completely under control and he was on medication for life. I had never seen any sign of depression or manic behaviour, and his confession made me feel protective towards him. He assured me that his illness had nothing to do with the break-up of his marriages.

Then he was fired from his job, and it transpired this was not for the first time. By now, I was beginning to notice the reckless abandon with which he spent money – money that I assumed he had. The façade was beginning to crumble, but I was still buying the dream man I had first met.

Maybe he sensed some hesitancy in me because one weekend, after we had climbed to the top of a hill, he proposed. Confused but exhilarated, I wanted with all my heart to be married and so I accepted. However, I had nagging doubts about my survival chances in this marriage and shut out any suggestions in my own mind, or from my friends that I might be making a mistake.

A month later we had a registry office wedding and went off to Mallorca (courtesy of *my* bank balance) for a honeymoon. By now it was too late to change anything, although I had a terrible feeling of dread in the pit of my stomach. Something wasn't right – there were too many things over which I had no control that could affect me.

'On the honeymoon, Guy forgot his medication and plunged into a deep depression. He lay in darkness in our hotel suite for nearly ten days. When we returned to my flat, I didn't recognise the man I had married. Two days later he hit me.

I picked up on the bad signals before we married and could have stalled or even stopped things. It's a big regret and has cost me dear, emotionally and financially. The writing was on the wall – I chose to ignore it. Now at 39, I am resolutely single and childless.

Yvonne

From an early age I had an improbably glamorous image of the man I would eventually marry: someone tall, dark and handsome; someone wonderfully funny and gregarious, with lots of money. He would sweep me off my feet when I was in my mid-twenties and we would make love on his yacht in the Mediterranean and organise extravagant parties for other bright young things. We would lead a hedonistic, indulgent lifestyle and travel to the most exclusive and expensive destinations.

The reality was somewhat different. I am now married to Adam: he is shorter than me, quite bald, and getting a little rotund around the middle. He doesn't have loads of money, although we are comfortable. We have three children: George, Henry and Francesca – and we love each other to bits!

I was pushing 39 when Adam proposed after a short courtship. I shudder when I think that as I planned my wedding, I went into my old bedroom at my parents' home and wept. I cried because I felt I was accepting less than my dream; I was accepting second best and I had run out of time to find a perfect life partner.

It is only now that I feel so fortunate. Adam has attributes I would never have included in my 'wish list': he has a dry, witty sense of humour and a generous smile, he's creative (he's a professional photographer), plays the violin and is practical. He cooks all the meals – *yes*, even breakfast for us all, and is a doting dad. Through his eclectic tastes he has introduced me to many new and exciting things, including Russian literature, bird watching, jazz and modern art. Through his work for *National Geographic*, we have travelled to remote parts of the world (on occasions with the children) and when he's around, there's always a buzz of positivity, music and creativity.

It was on our honeymoon that I really fell in love with Adam. To me he epitomises everything that can be good about a person and I feel privileged and honoured to be married to him.

I realise that my early aspirations were out of touch with reality. Now I can look back to the shallow and selfish individual I was when I conjured up these stupid ideas. Although I feel shame (and I have never discussed my true feelings prior to our marriage), I now understand that this was a level from which the only way to progress was up. Through Adam, I have grown as a person too. I have changed my values and how I regard other people and feel a sense of completeness, having such a beautiful family.

22.

Running shy of the bunny boilers

Tom is in his mid-forties. Handsome and sporty, he cuts an impressive figure, flysurfing in the winter waves off the beach near his cliff-top home on the Sussex coast. Tom sold his medical supply business when he was 39: he was able to retire on the proceeds and pursue his sporting interests, travel and manage an extensive property portfolio. He was married, briefly, in his early thirties and doesn't have children.

'I've been called a lot of things in recent years: bastard, stringer, serial monogamist, time-waster and little boy lost – those are the printable descriptions! I have also been described as being emotionally immature, selfish, self-obsessed, narcissistic, a closet gay, also vain.

'I suppose there's no smoke without fire, but all these and other less than complimentary descriptions of my being have come exclusively from women I have been out with. This bewilders me as I can honestly say, hand on heart, that nobody else – friends, acquaintances, family, neighbours and former colleagues – would ever describe me in these terms. I'm quite a nice guy, actually. These epithets all have to do with the fact that I openly enjoy being single and have no wish now, or as far as I can see in the future, to live with or marry a woman (or a man, for that matter).

'There was nothing wrong with Julie (my farmer wife), but I just found the institution of marriage stifling. I'm very controlling and found I couldn't be accountable to another person. I agree that I lacked the emotional maturity and any sense of responsibility for somebody else: I was great at managing my business but pants at marriage! It felt like I couldn't breathe and suddenly there was this pressure to become a father – my life became governed by fertility dates, thermometers and a calendar dictating when we must have sex.

'As for children and babies, I have never wanted them. Julie didn't ask, she just assumed that is what we would do – have kids. I grew up with two brothers and my father spent all his time philandering about with other women. He wasn't really there with us to do boyish things like football and build tree houses. My memories of my parents' marriage were of fights, shouting and tears, followed by a relentless and inevitable round of suitcases, taxis, slammed doors and separations. To me, marriage just didn't look like a great prospect. I am too selfish to be a husband or father – I enjoy my freedom and an uncomplicated existence too much.'

Although Tom has long been released from 'the confines', as he describes them, of marriage, he continues to find himself 'fair game' at the hands of an expanding group of women. According to him, ladies of a certain age, 'can't believe their luck' when they stumble across this most eligible of men.

'I don't go looking for relationships, but they have a way of finding me. I may sound big-headed, but all the women I meet seem to think I am some kind of prize and I've been waiting all these years for her to show up. If I begin a relationship with someone, after a short while her eyes glaze over and she begins to think, as if she has some divine powers, 'I can change him. No one else has been able to convert him into a husband and father, but *I* can!' They look around my modern, minimalist house, fretting about the dangers of the cliff at the end of the garden and the open plan stairs, worrying about the safety of our – as yet – unborn children. Some have even secretly looked at property details so that we can move to a more family-orientated house.

'I'm always straight with them. My feelings towards them are purely amatory – I don't want anyone to move in, I don't want to get engaged, married or have children, either in or out of wedlock. But this seems to make them more determined than ever. I'm also not interested in anyone who already has children. Why would I want to give up my surfing or golf so that I could take somebody else's kid to a party or a swimming lesson? I don't want children of my own and I certainly don't want to be responsible for anyone else's.

'I'm not looking for someone to share my life with, but my ideal woman would be financially independent, independent in nature and independent in spirit and without an urge to procreate. It's not very romantic, I know, but I do feel victimised by every woman I meet. Perhaps my ideal woman would already be married to someone else, who has no intention of leaving and just wants a bit of fun.

'I had a great time in my teens, twenties and early thirties, and always went out with women of roughly the same age. I may be emotionally immature, as I've said, but I really don't want to hang out with women decades younger than me. I might be mistaken for being their dad! While I might still have concupiscent yearnings for nubile young women, I'd prefer to give clubbing and camping at rock festivals a miss. I do find the company of women in their thirties and forties most stimulating – they are more worldly. I just don't want to settle down with them.

'I haven't gone so far as having a vasectomy, but I am extremely careful when it comes to sex. I don't take any chances and am genuinely fearful that I will be tricked into making someone pregnant. A girlfriend sees that I'm wealthy and even if she decides to go-it-alone on the parent front, she knows there is some financial security waiting for her. If a relationship progresses (in my case beyond six weeks), the woman begins to feel I don't trust her (which I don't), and that creates tension. We split and then, often as not, she reveals her true colours by turning into a crazy bunny boiler.

'I am extremely wary of starting any kind of relationship. Women seem to interpret this fear as playing hard-to-get, and my "shyness", as one 38-year-old put it, "is my most attractive quality". One-night stands fulfil a physical need, but I'm not in my twenties any more, and there is something a bit grubby about just being in it for the sex.

'This relationship thing does blight my life. I feel hunted. The more freedom I have, the more intense the hunt. I'm not like other guys, and I hate the feeling that I have to do so much rejecting and create so much disappointment after just a few months.'

Asked what would be his advice to women who are hoping to get married when they come across an eligible bachelor, who is proactively single, like himself, Tom replied: 'Believe him if he is adamant he doesn't want commitment. He will be very clear about this. True, there may be stringers out there who lead a merry dance but a large proportion of the blame must be attributed to women who have left it too late. These women are hell-bent on getting a wedding and a baby, and like some bonkers evangelist set about trying to "convert" male "candidates" into husband material.

'Single women in their late thirties and early forties who don't want to be single are rapacious and scary. They come across as predatory and calculating, and try to get what they want through stealth. If a woman *does* find someone and the prospects for her look good, I would say, don't force it. Don't imagine a glorious summer wedding under silk-lined canvas when you've only just met. Guys may not be as intuitive as women, but they will read your mind on this one, you can be sure. Don't sacrifice everything you have achieved so you can rush headlong into a relationship. What about being a bit aloof – make him curious about you? If you're the right person and he thinks he might lose you, he'll commit. If he lets you go, then it was never going to work anyway.'

I asked Tom if he thought the time would ever come when he would decide that he might like to settle down and have a family. Would he still be happy and fulfilled in twenty years' time if he was on his own? 'Who knows? I know I don't!' was his reply.

Two of Tom's old flames from the 1980s (both now married with children), give their responses to this interview:

Rosie: Oh Tom, what a wanker you have obviously become! You were such a dashing, gorgeous hunk and I really thought you loved women! You were always so bold and innovative in everything you did; you pursued the things you were passionate about. Now, you just sound like a narcissistic nutcase! I think you just want to hang onto all your money and keep away those gold-diggers and would-be yummy mummies itching to lay their hands on your cash and bear your children. Chill out, Tommy!

Jessy: Tom, you are so wrong! Wrong about women in general, and wrong about kids. You obviously crave a lifestyle where you are served by other people in restaurants, as tenants, in your business – other people's children in fact, yet you are blinkered to the joy that having your own children could bring. Ask any guy who's a parent whether he would have preferred to be single, without a woman in his life and without his kids – I think you know the answer. Poor old Tom! You appear to be consumed by selfishness, so on second thoughts perhaps you would be a lousy dad and husband after all. Pity, in 1986 you were quite a catch!'

Louise, who has never met Tom before, but read this interview, says: 'I feel rather sorry for Tom. He has obviously been deeply traumatised by something in his life. As with women who become fixated on getting a man, Tom should relax a little and try not to be alarmed by every encounter he has.

23.

Where have all the men gone?

Professor Robin Dunbar

For every 100 females, 108 males are born in the UK, but owing to the higher mortality rates of young males, by the mid-teens the numbers have evened out. This remains the case until old age when a surplus of women arises again.

In some big cities, including London, there are more women than men. There is debate about the reasons for this but it is nothing new. The thirty-something single status *is* new, however – mainly because women now leave it later to marry. In their mid-thirties they find themselves in a predicament, whether they outnumber men of their age or not.

A study I carried out on lonely hearts ads indicated that, while single females typically advertise for men three to five years older than them, men advertise for women of a certain age, irrespective of their own. Their preferred age is 24 to 25, so the men that the women want are looking for women, but younger ones.

So, should a woman in her mid-thirties be looking for a man in his forties instead? Perhaps, but only in his *late* forties. I was involved in research that looked at how the sexes perceive their market value – i.e. what they think their 'package' is worth to the opposite sex. The results suggested that males in their early- and mid forties overestimated their standing the most. They are getting richer by this age and become self-deluded about what they can get in return; they also want to attract a twentysomething but are less likely to succeed than younger men. Only in their mid- to late forties, when their risk of death increases (they may be rich, but they may also die), do they become more realistic.

In short, women seem to hang onto the ideal and many get lucky, but when they start wanting to settle down, they opt for what biologists call the Hobson's Choice Strategy. In layman's terms, they opt for something over nothing.

Professor Robin Dunbar is professor of Evolutionary Anthropology at the University of Oxford.

24.

Try this instead

Andrew Clover

Most single men want love, but they are also terrified of failure, poverty and being trapped. They are scared of turning into their dads or, if divorced, repeating their old mistakes. They are scared that their women will make them throw out their comics, their motorbikes and their dreams of writing novels. It doesn't really matter which type of man you go for – younger, older, divorced. What matters is that you go for him.

Personally, I think the divorced man is more realistic. He's not like a young man who can't commit because he yearns for a fairytale goddess whose heart he may one day capture. The older man just wants someone who won't shout at him. If it takes her two minutes to get into the car, she's ideal. If she's giving, and laughs at his jokes, he'll love her forever. Give those bruised men a try. Stop expecting to find 'the one'. Find someone, and give him love recklessly.

Or you can snare one of the single man-boys, but you must be cunning. You must wait for him to call but when he does you must be devoted and give him glorious sex in flattering lighting.

There is only one time when a man knows, for certain, that he loves his woman and will stay with her forever: when she has just chucked him. The rest of the time he's not sure. I remember the first time my wife said: 'Let's have children!' I knew this was an historic moment – I must respond like a man. So I ignored her. Men's heads are filled with confusion, fear and football statistics. And whenever they are made an offer, they always feel the negatives first – and if they can't express them, they clam up like oysters.

In which case, trapping them may involve trickery. After five months – preferably during a three-day trip to Paris, so he can't get away – you must say, lightly and just before sex: 'I love every part of your life. I want to see you richly succeed, but you must marry me.' Then you must change tack and become very soft. You have touched on his deepest fears. Listen. Tell him to write that novel. Tell him that you love ELO. After a two-day sulk, which will be immensely wounding for you, he will begin to express his horrid, selfish fears, and thus you will be stumbling towards your perfectly imperfect life.

Try not to worry about what happens. Remember, there are also loads of men like me: the ones who hatched, and still went bad. We wish you luck, we wish you love. We'll see you by the swings in five years.

Andrew Clover is author of Dad Rules *and is a columnist for the* Sunday Times.

25.

Are you an Urban Cougar?

I couldn't compile a book about trying to meet a man and settle down without mentioning Urban Cougars. Now I'm not making a judgement here, merely a passing reference. An Urban Cougar reading this book would probably toss it to one side and laugh. The chances are if you're single, in your late thirties or early forties and more than anything want to settle down and have a family, then you are *not* an Urban Cougar.

Since Urban Cougars fall into the same age bracket as women reading this book, then I believe a short definition is required. The term Urban Cougar, as defined by the urban dictionary, was spawned in America (where else?). It's used to describe 'a sophisticated species of female who seeks the pleasure of younger males. An Urban Cougar avoids the entanglements of a "relationship" in favour of the freedom of the hunt.'

In other words, she dates younger men just for the fun of it. While Mrs Robinson from *The Graduate* immediately springs to mind, it is worth remembering that Anne Bancroft who played the predatory neighbour was actually in her late thirties when she took up this role. Urban Cougars are considered 'older' women, because they seek to romp with delicious male totty, many years younger. Either they have done the marriage and family thing to emerge confident and sexy the other side, or they have eschewed the whole family model.

In dating these frisky stud muffins rarely is the Urban Cougar looking for husband material. In most instances, the men themselves are 'dating up'. This isn't just in age, but the women in question are dominant. That is, they have plenty of money and are confident and successful individuals. They are not looking to settle down and start a family – these ladies just want to have fun.

Sonya is a sleek-looking 42-year-old from Los Angeles. She is a high-flying corporate lawyer, who, when time permits, indulges in the close attention of her latest fling, Lars. Lars is a 23-year-old blond surf dude from Manhattan Beach with a slim build, a dark tan and a rippling six pack. His sun-bleached hair is long and tied back. He drives an old, rainbow-sprayed VW Beetle convertible. On Saturday evenings, after a day's reef breaking and tubing, his car can be seen parked on Sonya's sandy driveway of her beach house, his surf board sticking out of the back.

'I can't believe how much fun I am having! He never gets tired – all the surfing invigorates him. And he is just so cute! I call him My Little Pony.'

Of course, the older a woman becomes, the harder she has to work on her physical appearance. The Urban Cougar will enforce upon herself a relentless programme of high maintenance – toning, waxing, tinting, buffing and looking sexy in and out of great clothes. Above all else, she will need to feel and look good in order to attract sexually athletic younger males. Is this something you could or would want to pull off, so to speak?

Baby, I want you

'When a childless woman turns 40 it's as though she has a huge neon sign above her head which flashes 'LAST DAYS FOR BABIES! LAST DAYS FOR BABIES!' in giant lettering. The rest of the world is full of unhelpful advice: there's so much more to life, have one on your own, you've still got lots of time, doctors can do wonderful things these days . . .'

Dillie Keane

26.

Motherhood: to be, or not to be?

That is the question for older women desperate to have children. This chapter extracts various professional viewpoints relating to the age-related decline in fertility and the risks associated with pregnancies in later life.

January 1961: in a small market town in Cheshire, England, a woman on the cusp of 41 emerges from the local hairdressers, her greying hair tightly curled and set. She pushes her shopping trolley to the corner shop, where she purchases frozen fish fingers, peas and some loose potatoes to make fries. Ravenous for their supper, her teenage sons and 11-year-old daughter will already be on the bus after a busy day at school. Before she begins cooking she must first call in at the surgery to see the family doctor. After a short wait, she is summoned and closes the door quietly behind her. With just a hint of disdain, the doctor sombrely announces, while holding up some notes: 'Mrs Tennant, you are quite right in your diagnosis – you are indeed pregnant.'

As winter turns to spring and the trees start to blossom, Patricia Tennant's belly starts to swell. The community is abuzz with the news. Huddles of women in the post office tut about the pregnancy. Not that she will be an older mother, more the fact that she has 'been intimate' at her great age. Surrendering to her husband's conjugal rights in her forties, whatever next!

On 30 August 1961, at the Royal Liverpool University Hospital, Patricia

Tennant undergoes a caesarian and her baby daughter Caralyn is lifted into the world, screaming with indignation. Back in his office, Michael Tennant takes a phone call from the company's managing director. Congratulations! He has become a father again and it's a girl.

Thirty-nine years later Caralyn, holding the hand of her boyfriend Rudi, pushes their firstborn, Sol, into the world. He has been conceived using IVF. Over the next three years Sol will be joined by his sister Esme and brother Jack, both created from frozen embryos. From a variety of beginnings, life goes on in the Tennant family.

But no one tut tuts any more when a woman becomes pregnant in her early forties. Today's fortysomethings look very different to their mothers' generation. They dress younger, they act younger and they feel younger. Physically and mentally, they challenge the ageing process. Clichéd maybe, but 40 really *is* the new 30. Perhaps a few crows' feet or a twinkling of grey roots slightly gives the game away, but often it can be difficult to determine a woman's age. She could be anything from 32 to 46. And like the sisterhood in their twenties and thirties, a woman in her early forties can now comfortably embrace motherhood without prejudice. That is, until her fertility falls off a cliff.

So, what can the woman nearing the end of her natural fertility realistically expect if she yearns to give birth to a child? Research suggests the trend towards later maternity is strongest among women with better educational qualifications, with many postponing child rearing to pursue a career. In addition, some women who have already brought up a family wish to have another child with a new partner, while some simply haven't met the right partner until later in life. Advances in fertility treatment and greater aspirations have contributed to a record rise in older mothers. These factors have prompted a demographic shift, with more women than ever starting families when they themselves are older.

Figures from the Office for National Statistics revealed that over ten years (1996–2006), the average age for giving birth in the UK increased greatly. By 2006 there was an almost 50 per cent increase in the number of women over 40 who had babies. And in 2006, the number of women giving birth aged over 45 had doubled on the 1996 figures. The statistics include those giving birth for the first time.

Women in their late thirties and early forties yet to become mothers are in good company. They can take reassurance and encouragement from the host of celebrity and figurehead role models who become mothers in later life: J.K. Rowling, Elizabeth Hurley, Sarah Lancashire, Celia Imrie, Jennifer Lopez (twins), Sarah Jessica Parker, Julie Walters, Melanie

Griffith, Julia Roberts, Courteney Cox Arquette and Jodie Foster. And the following all had their first (or subsequent) babies in their forties: Madonna, Elle McPherson, Bette Midler, Iman, Brooke Shields, Caroline Quentin, Emma Thompson, Jo Brand, Mariella Frostrup, Helen Hunt, Jerry Hall, Annette Bening, Julianne Moore, Lowri Turner, Halle Berry, Anna Ford, Esther Rantzen, Meera Syal, Sophie, Countess of Wessex, Nicole Kidman and Ulrika Jonsson. At 44, swimmer, Sharron Davies had a baby while *Desperate Housewife,* Marcia Cross, produced twins.

Cherie Blair, Mimi Rogers, and Jane Seymour (who had twins) raised the stakes by having babies at 45. Susan Sarandon and Geena Davis (both mothers of twins) and Christie Brinkley upped the figure to 46, while Holly Hunter was 47 when she gave birth to twins. Bridget Jones's creator Helen Fielding produced babies at 46 and 48. Topping them all is Beverly D'Angelo, actress and Al Pacino's ex, who delivered twins at the ripe old age of 49, making 40-year-old mothers look positively juvenile.

So, are these women exceptional? How easy is it to become pregnant in your forties? And how many women are forced to resort to IVF with donor eggs? Some doctors warn that women who delay motherhood are 'defying nature' and increasing the risks for themselves and their babies, provoking a backlash in some quarters from women who sense a conspiracy against older mothers.

Daisy Waugh, TV presenter and a first-time mother at 39, attacked the double standard whereby ageing rockers such as Paul McCartney and Rod Stewart (who both fathered babies in their 60s) were congratulated with a slap on the back and a nod and a wink, while 'old girls' like her were gently encouraged to worry. Media coverage about older mothers is plentiful, but rather than celebrating it, the tone is cautionary and, in my opinion, slightly negative. While a clan of celebrity mothers is seen to endorse the late motherhood trend, women who want children cannot afford to be complacent about the right age for childbearing.

Anyone on the receiving end of a rant from a successful woman lamenting her failure to bear a child will witness the grief, regret and bitterness. This was meant to be the easy bit, right? Not like getting into Cambridge or being appointed to the board. A baby should be a gift from Mother Nature – a female rite of passage. Anyone can do it. And with modern medical science devoted to resetting the biological clock, why can't a Mistress of the Universe have a baby late in life?

Experts warn that older mothers face significant health risks in delaying childbirth and many women who leave this until their forties will suffer the heartbreak of infertility. The age limit for women who seek fertility treatment on the NHS is 39, which means older couples (or singles) have to pay privately if they want to become parents. Each batch of treatment currently costs around £3,000.

Gynaecologists warn that fertility levels in fortysomething women tend to plummet. The older the woman, the greater the risk of miscarriage, birth defects and high blood pressure, as well as complications in childbirth.

Obstetricians also say they are under increasing pressure because of the 'precious baby' syndrome, where pregnant women who have delayed motherhood are so anxious about complications they insist on giving birth by caesarean section. Dr Gillian Lockwood is medical director of Midland Fertility Services, near Wolverhampton. She believes increased life expectancy and improved medical care mean there is no reason for women not to give birth later in life, but she also warns that many who leave it until their late thirties and forties face the heartache of infertility having been lulled into a false sense of security because they still feel young. They wrongly assume their reproductive systems too are as young as they feel.

'Given life expectancy, I see no particular problem with women extending the time in which they have babies but I think it's vital that women recognise – even though, in their late thirties and forties, they look and feel so young – their ovaries may be past their sell-by date,' she says. Lockwood also warns that although some older women will be able to conceive one child, they may be disappointed when they are unable to have a second: 'They think, "That was easy" and two years later they want a sibling and discover it's not happening. Then they press the panic button.'

Dr Peter Bowen-Simpkins from the Royal College of Obstetricians and Gynaecologists and co-medical director of the London Women's Clinic has said the health risks are substantially increased for older mothers, but he points out that the trend is no different from the Victorian era, when it was common for women to give birth in their forties, although most would already be mothers: 'Medically speaking, the best time to have your baby is between the ages of 21 and 25. The chances of complications are increased if you leave it until late in life, but having said that, I don't think older mothers place a particular burden on society. Forty-year-olds plus today are much fitter and are more likely to be able to afford the cost of parenting.'

Fairly typically, when someone in the medical profession says one thing it is immediately countered by another specialist. According to one obstetrician in Scotland, late motherhood, however achieved, can have an adverse effect on health. Older mothers suffer more problems during pregnancy (higher rates of stillbirth, ectopic pregnancy, haemorrhaging and pre-eclampsia) and are thus more likely to require caesarean sections. Worse still, their age means a higher probability in battling with arthritis, depression, cancer and heart attacks as they bring up their kids.

Birth abnormalities

Age of mother at delivery	Chance of live-born baby with Down's Syndrome	Chance of live-born baby with chromosomal abnormality
25	One in 1,350	One in 476
30	One in 909	One in 385
35	One in 384	One in 179
40	One in 112	One in 64
45	One in 28	One in 19

On the face of this evidence, the prognosis looks grim. That is because the medical profession looks at risks and presents them in a particular way. There is about a 1 in 20 chance for a woman aged 45 to give birth to a baby with chromosomal abnormalities. This looks like quite a high risk, especially compared with the figure for 25-year-olds (1 in 1,350). 'But 1 in 20 is actually only five per cent, so you still have a 95 per cent chance of having a baby with healthy chromosomes,' counters Mona Saleh, genetic counsellor at the Centre for Genetics Education in Sydney, Australia.

Screening for abnormalities is now very sophisticated and accurate. Sensitive counselling is also available for those forced to make critical decisions based on their screening results. Often women who leave it late to embrace motherhood are criticised for gambling with their fertility and risking their own, and their baby's, health. But, a leading American academic argues that it's better for many women to delay getting pregnant.

Until now older women have been worried that they risk their own health and the welfare of their babies by choosing to start a family later on, but that view is challenged in Professor Elizabeth Gregory's book, *Ready: Why Women are Embracing the New Later Motherhood*.

Director of the Women's Studies Program at the University of Houston, Professor Gregory says 'the new late mothers' are more likely to be financially secure and happy to put their careers on hold while they bring up their child. Also, they are more likely to be in stable relationships than younger, first-time mothers. And they live longer.

Professor Gregory's book is one of a number of recent works in praise of older mothers. One study of 4,300 older mothers, published in the *Journal of Epidemiology and Community Health*, found that women who delay starting a family are more likely to have brighter, well-behaved children. The explanation, according to the authors, could be both biological (older mothers make sure they have better nutrition during pregnancy) and social (they may have a more established home life that is highly conducive to learning).

But there could be hidden costs to later motherhood. For example, there is likely to be an increase in the number of children who will lose their parents at a younger age, while their children will not experience having grandparents.

John Mirowsky is the author of the study and is a member of the Maryland-based National Institutes of Health's scientific review panel on human development and ageing. He believes the prime age for childbearing, in terms of maternal health and longevity, lies between 34 and 40: 'Mothers in that age band are healthier than childless women of their same age because while younger women are more fertile and biologically fit, older mothers tend to be more mature and less likely to engage in risky behaviour, and they are more settled educationally, financially and emotionally.

'Women who wait to give birth enjoy better health, live longer and have healthier babies. There could be a number of reasons for this. Getting an education and establishing themselves in a good financial situation raise the chances that people will have good healthcare and make informed decisions about their health.'

His study is backed by others, including the ongoing New England Centenarian Study led by Thomas Perls, which found that women who give birth after the age of 40 are four times more likely to live to be 100 or more than women in the general population. Nevertheless, Gregory believes the best argument for later motherhood is an emotional one: 'For the women I spoke with, and for their families, the new later motherhood experience has had overwhelmingly positive effects. These women live in a very different world from the one the media portrays. They enjoy motherhood immensely and most combine it with satisfying work. These women feel they've come to motherhood prepared and that their children, their marriages, their careers and their sanity are the better for it.'

That's one view, but every argument has its detractors and there is a counter view to Professor Gregory's theories. What really irritates Daisy Waugh and her supporters are pronouncements from gynaecologists such as Dr Susan Bewley, a consultant at St Thomas Hospital, London, who declared women who put off childbearing until their late thirties or beyond were risking disaster. Writing in the *British Medical Journal* in 2005, Dr Bewley and colleagues stated: 'If you want a family – and most people want a couple of children – and you are going to complete your childbearing by 35 and leave time for recovery in between, you would be wise to start before 30 . . . People are aware that ageing is a bad thing but the bio-panic women had on their 30th birthday has moved up to the 40th birthday. Surveys of older mothers show that half say that they delayed because they had not met a suitable partner. Maybe instead of waiting for Mr Right, they ought to wait for Mr Good-Enough, if they want children.'

Naturally the article caused a storm when it was first published in 2005, and reverberations continued for some time. Dr Bewley was later forced to apologise on the website Mothers35plus.com after she compared the problem of the post-40 mother to the pre-20, teenage one. 'The last thing I want to do is insult anyone,' she wrote. 'However, my colleagues and I have been concerned about the increasing distress and complications we are seeing in our professional lives. There are rising amounts of infertility, miscarriage and complications of pregnancy as the average age of child-bearing goes up.'

In the same journal a comparison to teenage pregnancy was intended to point out there were problems at each end of the reproductive spectrum, one more social, the other more medical. While in the UK the number of teenage pregnancies was falling those in women over 35 were much higher and rising dramatically. Dr Bewley added, 'What I am concerned about is why, over the last 30 years or so, women are having babies later and later, with more risks, when we are generally much more risk-averse nowadays.'

She is not alone. Many obstetricians who witness daily the heartbreak caused by infertility warn of the risks to women who 'want to have it all, when biology hasn't changed'. Sam Abdalla, clinical director of London's Lister Fertility Clinic, believes society imposes a 'massive strain' on women by forcing them to choose between family and career: 'It puts more of a burden on the women because it reduces their chances of conceiving and puts more strain on IVF treatment. In women over 40, treatment is less successful, with fewer pregnancies, a high miscarriage rate and a lower live birth rate.'

Older mothers face other problems too. All the complications of pregnancy, from birth defects to premature delivery and caesarean birth, increase with age.

Ultimately, this all comes down to statistics generated by fertility experts. Fertility peaks in the mid-twenties. At the age of 30, three-quarters of women will fall pregnant within a year, but this drops to two-thirds at 35. Although most pregnancies over the age of 35 go well, a minority run into problems, some very serious. At the age of 40, less than half (44 per cent) of women become pregnant and give birth within a year. By this age, a woman who doesn't conceive quickly – assuming she has regular intercourse – will be anxious about time running out, and thinking urgently about IVF, *if* she and/or her partner can afford it. Even conception is no guarantee of a live birth – half of all over-40 pregnancies end in miscarriage.

Many childless older women reassure themselves there is always IVF to fall back on, but this, too, often turns out to be a mirage. Fortysomething women are the fastest-growing group seeking IVF (up from less than 1,000 women in 1991 to more than 6,000 in 2006 in the UK). But for the vast majority, treatment ends in failure as doctors run up against the barrier of the biological clock. Over the age of 43, more than 95 per cent of those undergoing IVF are unsuccessful. Among those who fall pregnant, half use donated eggs so they are not the genetic mother.

Several celebrities who have had babies in their forties are thought to have had IVF using donated eggs, but few admit to it, fostering the impression that it is still perfectly easy to become a mother of your own genetic child into your fifth decade. Whenever an older celebrity has twins, speculation turns to an alleged egg donation.

Figures from the UK's Office for National Statistics show that among younger women, medical advances and improvements in technique have seen success rates for IVF treatment improve dramatically. Overall live birth rates have risen from 14 per cent per cycle in 1991 to 21 per cent in 2006. Past the age of 35, success rates fall rapidly, declining to 12 per cent per cycle at 40.

Disappointingly, the over forties have not seen the improvement in live birth rates experienced by younger women. While modern IVF techniques can rejuvenate an older womb and prepare it for pregnancy, they have not yet succeeded in pulling off the same trick with older eggs. This is the untold story of late motherhood. Among young women, IVF has matched, and in some clinics bettered birth rates achieved by natural conception, but in older women it has only done so by using younger women's eggs, of which there is a shortage, with growing demand and lengthening waiting lists. Some women have frozen their eggs for later use (usually while undergoing cancer treatment), but the technique is still in its infancy and only a few hundred babies have been born worldwide from frozen eggs. With a few notable exceptions, IVF has significantly failed to *extend* the reproductive lives of most women.

As American economist, Dr Sylvia Ann Hewlett, states 'In just 30 years, women have gone from fearing their fertility to squandering it – and very unwittingly. The decision of whether to have a child will always be one of the most important any woman makes; the challenge is not allowing time and biology to make it for her.'

Thankfully, I had none of this information to hand when Steve and I decided to have children at the end of our thirties. Anyone who has ever browsed through a medical encyclopaedia will have been alarmed by some of the mild symptoms attributed to life-threatening illnesses, 'Yes, I get a pain there! Maybe I've got X!' Too much information for an older woman trying to conceive will, in my opinion, put undue pressure on her – not a good thing. With a solitary NCT book on pregnancy and childbirth, and mindful of the tick-tock biological clock urgency, we ignored the pessimists and concentrated on making babies. I was fortunate to fall pregnant on both occasions after just a couple of months' trying (although I did have an earlier miscarriage). Both pregnancies and deliveries at 40 and 41 were normal, and out of six women in the labour ward when I had my first baby, four were older than me.

I found pregnancy and childbirth exhausting, fascinating and very positive experiences. Having babies brings you into immediate contact with a range of new friends – other new mothers of all ages. The trials and tribulations of conception, pregnancy and birth appear, from my limited perspective, to be random. With ages ranging from 23 to 42, some women (in my unscientific study) had difficulty conceiving, others didn't. Some were dangerously ill during pregnancy while others bloomed. Some women popped their babies out like a slippery bar of soap, and others laboured for agonising hours with an army of consultants in attendance. Age seemed irrelevant to our individual experiences.

Ultimately, women (and their partners) have to choose. Do they ignore the doom-mongers and just get on with it, or accept that biology discriminates and brace themselves for failure, or possibly having a disabled child? This is not an easy choice and there are no easy answers, but if you really want a baby, there may be no time like the present.

With grateful thanks to the health professionals, academics and Jeremy Laurance, health editor of the Independent *in assimilating the research for this chapter.*

27.

Pregnant and single — am I brave or selfish?

Mariella Frostrup

The dilemma

Dear Mariella,

I recently had a short fling with a man I am very fond of. He ended it, which upset me more than I thought it would, and then I discovered I was pregnant. My close friends have been incredibly supportive, but I sense their disapproval. I am a professional woman in my mid-thirties and have been feeling the increased pull to have a family for a year, but I imagined doing that with a good man. My ex has made it clear he does not want me to go through with the pregnancy but I am overjoyed to be pregnant, and am ready to be a mother on my own, though I'm not kidding myself that this would be easy or in the best interest of the child. On the other hand, I am realistic that the chances of me meeting Mr Right and having a family before I'm too old are getting smaller by the year. Am I being courageous or incredibly selfish?

If I go ahead, I know it will cause my ex a lot of anxiety but this is not revenge for his ending the relationship or an attempt to get back together with him. By way of some background, he has just come through an acrimonious divorce, in which access to his young children was restricted.

Courageous or incredibly selfish, you ask. I'd say neither. It's funny, isn't it, that the background you choose to give me is about your ex? Having established quite firmly in your letter that this desire to become a mother is unrelated to him, you then decide to fill me in on his family circumstances. What about your own? Your ex has made his situation clear: he's reluctant to go ahead with having a baby because he did not want to continue the relationship with you. Are you guilty of trying to add Freudian dimensions to his understandable decision? The only need for you to add that final detail was to make even clearer why the poor man has reservations about becoming a dad again.

I say 'poor man', but the truth is I don't feel that sorry for him. Whether it's a one-night stand or a six-year relationship, it's disingenuous for anyone having sex to be surprised if their partner becomes pregnant unless they've been actively deceived. I'm seriously hoping that is not the case here. However, this does offer you some leeway. I'm not taking sides, but for every man who professes horror that his girlfriend is with child, there's a man who never considered prevention his business. If responsibility for his own actions wasn't a priority for him before, then this is, at best, a wake-up call.

Not that this exonerates you. I've no idea how culpable you are, but we are all perfectly capable of telling lies to ourselves. Are you quite sure this isn't something you helped along in an effort to secure an affair you didn't want to see end? A child born out of deception and a misguided determination to underpin a relationship is not to be recommended.

My instinct is to give you the benefit of the doubt. And while kids do emerge from much less functional unions than yours and live to tell the tale, there are medical arguments that back up your sense of urgency, and we ignore them at our peril. Both my kids were born after I'd hit 40, but it's not a route I'd recommend. No one need remind me how close I came to missing the boat. So while your fears aren't entirely rational as you hit your mid-thirties, and your panic is at present premature, your concern is justified. It's all too easy for five years to slip by and a dramatic decrease in your fertility to become terminal.

I realise none of this directly answers your question about what to do, but it's not a decision anyone can make for you. If you feel lonely and confused now, be aware that by embracing single motherhood those are emotional states that will become more familiar. There will also be rewards, but those you don't need me to outline. At present it's more important that you consider the disadvantages. Having a child isn't easy or idyllic, and however hard you imagine it will be it's ten times more challenging. You'll most likely encounter discrimination at work, and it will restrict your career options at some stage.

Do you have family or friends around you who will help shoulder the enormous responsibility and time-consuming drudgery of having a child? If not, the challenge you are setting yourself is huge and daunting.

I love my own children more than anything I imagined myself capable of feeling, but given the choice between not having them or having them alone, I'm not sure what my decision would, or should have been. There are plenty of men and women out there who have chosen or been forced into single parenthood and are rising daily to the challenges. In this instance they're probably the best people to ask.

Writing in the Observer *(22 July 2007), agony aunt Mariella Frostrup offered these words of wisdom to a reader's dilemma.*

28.

Going solo — having a baby without a partner

significant proportion of single women in their mid-thirties and beyond develop a burning desire to have a child before it's biologically too late. The yearning for a child is a very powerful emotion. For a quarter of a century our monthly cycle reminds us of our potential to procreate. While there will be some women who have no desire to have a child, and those who may find it difficult or impossible to biologically produce a much-desired baby, options are open to single women today to help them on their way to motherhood before their fertility ends.

This chapter briefly examines the biological and practical options, together with the legal implications for those seeking motherhood as a single person. And it looks at the emotional fallout, too. I am grateful to all the people facing childlessness or who have had a child alone, who have spoken from the heart.

Some thoughts from childless women

'I'm OK, but everywhere I go, I see babies, mothers, toddlers, families. Society and urban environments remind us all – quite rightly – of the importance of children and so much is geared to them. I desperately want to have a baby. I have to say that all this emphasis often makes me feel like some kind of failure.'

Nicky, 37

'More than anything else, I want a baby. I cry often for my unborn children. In my mind I am reaching out to them, but I can't quite touch them. When New Year comes around, I hope upon hope that this will be the year when I have a child, or at least get started on one. I visited a wonderful psychic and she said she could see two little souls, waiting to be born to me. Those words have given me tremendous hope.'

Lin, 37

'There is obviously something about me which doesn't attract men. Maybe I give out the wrong energy. I have never been in a long relationship and I doubt if I am going to settle down with Mr Right now. I do think I would make a good mother, though, and I am going to try AI through a donor programme. I need someone to love and someone to love me back.'

Monica, 40

'The pain is intense. I don't want to hear if someone is pregnant, I don't want to admire or hold a baby; I don't want to see a complete stranger pushing a buggy. Babies and children remind me that I am not a mother. I don't want any of these things unless they are happening to me – which they aren't. It is like a smack in the face every time I hear news of people and their babies or children. I know my friends tread on eggshells when they are around me, but I am a cauldron of emotions. I regret the decisions in my life that landed me in this predicament and I feel a great sense of personal loss. Hopefully, over time things will ease a bit but I don't want to be lonely when I grow old.'

Jane, 40

And from those who did have children . . .

'I deliberately became pregnant when I was 38. I was in a half-hearted relationship with Phillip, a man I didn't love or even want to be with. I know this was not fair on him, but I wanted a baby so much. My gorgeous, clever, handsome son, Daniel, is now going off to university. In the early years, Phillip contributed financially to Daniel's upbringing until he married, but he has never had much involvement with his son, which suited me. I was fortunate to have my sister and her family nearby, because raising a child alone is hard.'

Paula, 57

'I have a daughter who I never see. I had a brief liaison with Megan, who, I didn't realise at the time, was a hormonally charged sperm bandit. Her sole objective was to get impregnated by a man, *any* man before her time was up. She told me she was pregnant a month after we split up, but that she didn't want anything from me. She gave birth to Zoe five years ago, moved from Edinburgh to London and hasn't accepted a penny from me, Zoe's father. I have had to go through the courts to gain access to my daughter and I have no say in any aspect of her life – her schooling, her upbringing or activities that she might do. It's really tough. I am biologically a father, but I am not able to be a father to my little girl.'

Paul, 43

'Having Emily was the best thing I ever did. Bringing her up alone was the hardest thing I ever did. By all means be a parent, but take seriously your obligations and responsibilities to your child. And think of the complications – the father and his role, and his parents; you are tied to another family forever. Christmases, holidays and birthdays are particularly complex and this becomes even more complicated when you meet someone to settle down with and he has two children from his first marriage. My world is full of stepchildren, exes, loads of grandparents and various uncles, aunts and cousins for my daughter. Diaries are juggled, and we spend large proportions of every weekend driving up and down motorways.'

Laura, 49

In 2001, Jonathan E., a high-flying young businessman, met Corinne T., 34 at a club in Leamington Spa, shortly after he had split up with his wife. He spent the night with her and they went on to have several torrid encounters at her house in a sexually driven relationship. He was careful and always used a condom. A few months later, Corinne dropped a bombshell . . . she was pregnant. Jonathan, who had no wish to become a father, was shocked and devastated by her announcement, but reluctantly acknowledged that he was one of the unlucky statistics: condoms are only 90 per cent safe.

Just as he was coming to terms with the idea of fatherhood, Corinne revealed the truth: she had taken sperm from Jonathan's used condom and inseminated herself while he was in the shower. She went on to have a baby daughter and since then Jonathan has been forced through the courts to pay thousands of pounds in maintenance for a daughter he rarely sees.

Another case of desperate sperm banditry occurred when Fiona W., 37 began a half-hearted relationship with Mike W., 35. They weren't particularly happy together and for both of them, it was a just a case of making do for the time being. Fiona was on the Pill and kept her contraceptives on the shelf above the washbasin, where one pill disappeared on each day of the week: Monday, Tuesday, Wednesday . . . The only trouble was, Fiona wasn't taking them – she was flushing them down the toilet instead.

After three months together Mike told Fiona that he wasn't getting anything out of the relationship and was going to walk away. Fiona said he could do that, but she had just found out that she was pregnant – 'Obviously the Pill hadn't worked.'

Fiona and Mike now live together with their baby son. Shortly after his birth, she told Mike how she'd conceived. He responded by demanding a DNA paternity test as he couldn't trust her. As Mike put it, 'The door is always open – I can, and will, leave at any time. I will always take my responsibilities to my boy seriously, but I cannot grow to love a woman who has been so duplicitous.'

'I desperately wanted a baby, but it just wasn't going to happen. So, as a single woman, in 2005 I adopted Maria from Perm in Russia. The process was rigorous, lengthy and expensive, but I have my baby daughter and I am hoping to adopt again soon so that she can have a brother or sister. It was very hard at first. Although only a year old, nobody had ever loved her, she was malnourished and emotionally damaged. But I adore my new role as a mother and want to give her the best life I possibly can.'

Sandra, 46

For further information contact The British Association for Adoption and Fostering: www.baaf.org.uk

Gabriella's story

Gabriella was 39 when her married sister encouraged her to find a way to have a baby before it was biologically too late. She knew that by this stage in her life her fertility was waning and she had been single for six years. However, she remembered a male friend's promise that if they were both single at the end of their thirties, they should have a baby together.

As a mother of two already, my sister Theresa was far more aware of the complexities and problems of having children and urged me to make an informed choice about whether I could have a baby. My medical history wasn't great (I'd received treatment for endometriosis) and my age was a factor too, so my clinic advised that IVF using donated sperm would give me the best chances for becoming pregnant.

On the Internet, I tracked down my old friend Yannis, who was a lecturer at a university in Athens. He had two sons, but was now divorced and single. Even after ten years, he still remembered our pact and was thrilled to accept his role as surrogate father.

At the clinic, I opted for treatment with a 'known donor' because I wanted my child to know the identity of his or her father. (This was before the lifting of donor anonymity.) We had to endure a frustrating six-month wait before treatment could begin while Yannis's sperm was screened. It was odd because although we'd been very close friends at university and afterwards, we had never actually been lovers. The whole process – begetting a child – was incredibly intimate, personal and biological (not to mention financial).

Only two eggs were collected, but they were of the best quality. We were excited when both were fertilised and placed back in but joy quickly turned to devastation when this cycle was unsuccessful. It was terribly disappointing, but it made us more determined than ever. Yannis and I decided we would have three attempts before abandoning our quest to become parents together. On the next occasion, the two fertilised embryos were replaced on my 40th birthday.

I was hopeful, scared and smug at the same time. My friends couldn't understand why I passed on the champagne at my party, but I knew! A week later, I shook with excitement as I examined the results of a pregnancy test. It was positive! At the six-week scan, I could see a flicker of a heartbeat on the peanut-sized embryo, and the life growing inside me. I bloomed during the pregnancy and towards the end, staggered about like a galleon in full sail.

I was fortunate that friends and family supported me throughout. I was encouraged by everyone around me and was quickly ensconced with a new group of compatriots at antenatal classes. And in the wider world, nobody batted an eyelid because of the way my baby had been conceived, because I was going to be a single mother or because of my age.

I don't think using a known donor will be a suitable option for everyone. Yannis and I know each other pretty well and as he lives abroad, we knew from the outset that he'd always be a long-distance, hands-off parent. We also discussed the impact on our arrangement, were I to find a permanent partner. We agreed that as Androu's birth father, we would do all in our respective powers to reinforce Yannis's role in his life. We plan to be honest with Androu about our own personal lives. And he will know that his mummy and daddy were friends, who wanted him very much and both love him.

Becoming a single mother is a lonely and at times frightening process but do summon support. You will find that friends feel honoured to be asked for help. Procedures such as egg collection are truly awful and you will need someone to hold your hand, blot your tears and drive you home.

And don't underestimate how difficult it is to bring up a child on your own. It is the hardest thing I've ever done – it completely consumes your life. Anticipate this and never compare the freedom you had before with your hectic life now. I still have fears – for my son's future and how I can ensure he does boy-things without a father – but I guess that mothers everywhere worry for their children.

What you will soon learn is that having a child delivers immense rewards. Bringing a new person into the world is the most wonderful thing and however successful you are professionally, having a child will be your greatest achievement, never to be topped.

Amber's story

Amber, 41, lives in Sydney with her son Ollie, now two, whom she conceived using an anonymous donor while living in the UK.

I always wanted children, but I didn't want to settle down with someone unsuitable just because my dwindling fertility dictated it. Then I was made redundant at 37, which enabled me to take some time out. It was a real wake-up call – I realised that while I'd never really wanted to be a career girl, I'd thrown myself into work in the absence of family and emotional commitments.

I looked in the mirror one morning and I suddenly thought, 'Having a child – it's now or never.' I chose an anonymous donor because I didn't want my child to feel that his or her father had elected not to be part of their life, and it would also leave the door open for a future husband. After much research I opted for a donor from a bank in Denmark, which was accredited by the HFEA. I was able to access in-depth profiles, including information about interests, hobbies, talents, favourite things – I wanted my child to have some sense of how they came to be. Reading through the profiles was weird – like a dating agency, but much more surreal. Do I choose the blond, blue-eyed, 6ft 5in athlete who likes poetry and surfing over the good-looking neurosurgeon with a penchant for opera and collecting decanters?

The sperm was imported through Midland Fertility Services, and as my fertility wasn't in question, they suggested IUI (intra-uterine insemination) rather than IVF. It took six attempts before I conceived. Unfortunately, tests revealed severe chromosomal abnormalities, and at 16 weeks I made the decision to terminate. I would advise all women thinking about being single mums to consider that there might be complications – you need to think through how you'd cope.

I didn't realise this before, but one in four pregnancies ends in miscarriage. Getting pregnant is hard enough, but once pregnant, nothing is definite. Pregnancy is a precarious state. Friends and family were magnificently supportive, but in the end the decision was down to me. I really missed having someone else to share the decision, the process and all the stages of pregnancy with on an intimate level.

After all the setbacks, I decided to continue with treatment as I wanted a child more than ever. Maybe it was all the hormones, but the desire was at times overwhelming. After the sixth IUI attempt, I couldn't bear to look at the reading on my pregnancy tester. I left it in a mug under my bed for two hours while I cried and panicked downstairs. But the little blue line declared that treatment had been successful and I was indeed pregnant. This time, everything felt just right from the beginning and despite the awful morning sickness, I loved being an expectant mother.

I had great support – my close friend Sarah was with me during the birth and my parents came over from Australia to wait outside the delivery suite. They stayed with me for a month to help out. Their involvement was invaluable. I had no idea how tumultuous the arrival of a baby could be on a settled, organised routine. I realised then that I could never have done this completely alone. Everyone needs help.

I loved those early weeks and months. Of course, neither Ollie nor I knew what was going on as we were trying to work each other out, but it was great. We formed a very strong, bond and motherhood felt like the most natural thing in the world. It was as if I had discovered my whole raison d'être.

There are lots of positives to being a single mum: you get to set all the rules, and no one lets you down – there's no one to get fed up with for not pulling their weight. I do find it difficult to fit in 'me time' but I think that's the case for all mums. Not being able to put myself first has actually been good for me and has made me less selfish. I have also found new levels of patience I never knew existed.

I feel very proud of what I've achieved and I can't believe how lucky I am that I realised what I really wanted just in time – another year or two and I think I'd have left it too late. It's the single best thing I've ever done.

Information on fertility treatment, egg donation, clinics and legislation is available through The Human Fertilisation & Embryology Authority: www.hfea.gov.uk

Midland Fertility Services: www.midlandfertility.com

National Gamete Donation Trust: www.ngdt.co.uk

Tara's story

I had an incredibly normal first part of my life – normal family, normal education, normal friends . . . I was unremarkable in almost every sense of the word. I went out with various men during my twenties and early thirties. Again, there was nothing earth shattering about my relationships and none of them went beyond mere dating; I didn't move in with anyone and no one proposed. My job was fairly neutral too. I was a secretary before 'my big change' (which I'll come on to) and working for a bank in a London suburb. I tapped into a big network of girlfriends, so there were always plenty of people to go on holiday, or out with on a Saturday night.

But by the time I was 35, I began to question all aspects of my life. Why was work so utterly dull? Why were all my friends moving out of London or settling down? What about me? Would I ever meet a guy who I would love and who would love me? And the biggest question of them all, would I ever have children?

Something happened to me one weekend (I won't go into details, but it made me completely re-evaluate how I wished to spend my life, and I decided to instigate big changes immediately). So I applied for, and got a job as a producer's assistant at a West End theatre and started living a whole new life.

I quickly established a clique of friends, most of whom were gay men working in the Arts. I wouldn't class myself as a fag hag, but I thoroughly enjoyed their quirky humour, creativity and vibrant lifestyles. I became very close to Austin, who lived with his partner Andrew. Over time, I fell in love with him, but I wasn't so blind that I knew we could never be together physically. He adored me, but he loved Andrew. I found myself in a happy, dysfunctional, unconventional love triangle.

One drunken evening in their mews house we came to an agreement whereby I could have a child and Austin would be the father. Having first screened Austin for HIV, I began to monitor my ovulation cycle and using a good old turkey-baster, did the deed in their spare room by myself a few days before Christmas.

Two weeks later my period came. After five attempts I found myself pregnant at 39 and wafted about the theatre with a smug grin and a matronly glow. I gave birth the following winter to a beautiful baby girl, whom we called Sky. Austin and Andrew were with me at the birth, which was the first time they had ever seen a woman's you-know-what! The birth was so exhausting I couldn't even turn my head on the pillow and it left them both traumatised. We were all elated.

We are all still very close, and Austin takes an active role in the upbringing of our daughter, who lives with me. The staff at the nursery she attends are curious about this slight, effeminate and quite obviously gay doting father, who minces in twice a week with his daughter. My parents and brother were exasperated when I announced my pregnancy, but they have come round to their new role as grandparents and uncle, and have welcomed Austin and Andrew to family occasions.

Austin and Andrew recently got married at a rose-bedecked civil ceremony in the gardens of an exquisite mansion and I was maid of honour. We have a happy ménage-à-trois with our daughter at the centre. Unconventional it might be, but I feel honoured and privileged to have such a close-knit, loving family and to be mother to such a beautiful little girl.

A short comment from a married mother

'I was sitting waiting for an appointment at the antenatal clinic in Canterbury. I was hot, uncomfortable and irritable because my baby was late, and I was jealous that my husband was enjoying the day on the beach with our two-year-old daughter, Tilly. Then I looked up and saw something that immediately made me thankful for everything in my life: a woman I had met at antenatal classes when I had had Tilly was struggling to get in through the doors of the clinic. I remembered that she was a single mother, the same age as me. Here she was now, still a single mother, heavily pregnant, on crutches with a broken leg, and a toddler in the process of throwing a terrible twos, carpet-biting tantrum.'

Alison, 39

29.

Who needs dads, anyway?

Steve Hampson

I'll tell you who needs dads, children do! Our increasingly feminised society has undermined the status of men for a number of years. Medical advances, political correctness and legislation have conspired to make men's roles as fathers obsolete. Sure, plenty of women raise children as single mothers, and many children are caught in the crossfire of divorce, but this doesn't make it the best option for the kids involved – *they* are the casualties. Numerous studies show an association between fatherlessness and a wide range of social pathologies, including drug abuse, promiscuity and delinquency. Who wants to add to these statistics? Raising children in a nuclear family is difficult enough with two parents as we try, bloody hard, to do a good job. Bringing up kids with just one parent must be nigh-on impossible.

So, for whatever reason, a 38-year-old woman has left it too late to find a partner to make a baby with – it must hurt being childless and seeing families all about. But wait! There's a quick-fix solution to this problem: donor insemination. This solo operator, this one half of the genetic code, doesn't need to form a relationship with anyone (she's already failed thus far), and she doesn't even have to have sex in order to procreate. She won't need to cook any meals for someone coming in late, or turn outside-in dirty socks, or put the toilet seat down, or tolerate Sky Sports on TV. No, like the latest consumer must-have she can have a baby without a dad in sight!

Just you wait: parenthood is not something you train for – in its magnitude it's the biggest responsibility of your life. Until you become a parent, unless you have qualified as a nanny or nursery teacher you will have no understanding of what it's like to bring a baby home and raise that little person into a child, a teenager and an adult. At work we are sent on courses; if we do sports, we train. If we play a musical instrument, we practise . . . We rehearse and there are people there to support us. If we stop liking these things, we can jack it all in and do something else instead. Not so with parenting! Your real work is cut out for you the day your first child is born, and we busk this parenting lark from the outset.

And still the feminists say a father doesn't matter. Tell that to the pregnant soldier's widow, tell it to those adults whose fathers died when they were just children, tell it to the little boy who dreams of one day being a great dad; tell it to the girl whose single mother has just been diagnosed with terminal cancer. And tell it to the millions of hardworking fathers out there who are striving to protect and provide for their families.

I have two sons and a daughter. From the moment their lungs first screamed their resentment at arriving in this crazy world, I have been as involved in their lives as much as is humanly possible, given that I have a full-time job. When they were little I changed, bathed and burped them and read them stories. I did rocket launches with the babies, pushed the buggy and took them swimming; I clowned about at birthday parties, built a wooden fort in the garden and soothed them when they had fevers. Now they are older, I help out on the school run, oversee homework and stand on the touchlines at football, yelling encouragement at my boys. I idle away an hour a week at the riding stables when my daughter has her lesson and I ferry them all back and forth to sleepovers, parties and play days.

I am a parent and a team member: the team comprises me and Claire, my wife. Team Hampson works flat out! I honestly don't know how single parents manage 24/7, year after year. How does a single mother manage to do all the domestic drudgery – laundry, cleaning, shopping while simultaneously working and managing the complicated and demanding role of parenting? How does she do any of this if she or her child is sick? How does she simultaneously take one child to a swimming lesson and the other to a friend's house to play ten miles away, fit in the MOT on the car, do a big shop at Sainsbury's and wait for the gas man to come and fix the boiler?

How often does she rugby tackle or wrestle with her sons, or kick a football about or take them to the tank museum? How does a single person alone make important decisions about education, particularly if one of her kids is falling behind? How does she deal single-handedly with issues like bullying or shyness or genius? How does she manage to give her time, the very best opportunities and unconditional love if she is doing ten million other things at the same time? And when does she take a break or integrate a love interest into her life?

We haven't got there yet, as our children are all under ten, but when they hit their teens, there will be a whole raft of new issues to contend with. Surely even the most hard-nosed, devoutly single mother would agree that fatherly influence during this critical, emotional, hormonal and peer-pressured time would be just a teensy bit useful?

Yes, single parenthood can strike at any time – through separation, divorce or widowhood. It's a tough world out there and even the most rock-solid partnership or marriage feels the strain at times. Often, there's no choice for the single parent other than to soldier on bravely, calling on the goodwill of friends and family for support while buying in childcare, but to deliberately conceive a child through artificial means for one's own personal gratification seems to me to be an act of wanton selfishness.

Children don't need dads? My arse!

Steve Hampson is a 44-year-old insurance broker, living in Surrey.

30.

'Creeping nonchoice' – American study into executive childlessness

Dr Sylvia Ann Hewlett

At the beginning of the millennium a disturbing study about American women by economist Dr Sylvia Ann Hewlett revealed that, 30 years into the women's movement, female executives still don't have what they want – and probably never will. Although this study is now almost ten years old, the findings are relevant to many women in the UK today.

There is a secret out there – a painful, well-kept secret: at midlife, between a third and a half of all successful career women in the United States do not have children. In fact, 33 per cent of such women (business executives, doctors, lawyers, academics and the like) in the 41 to 55-year age bracket are childless – and that figure rises to 42 per cent in corporate America. These women have not chosen to remain childless. The vast majority, in fact, yearn for children. Indeed, some have gone to extraordinary lengths to bring a baby into their lives. They subject themselves to complex medical procedures, shell out tens of thousands of dollars, and derail their careers – mostly to no avail, because these efforts come too late. In the words of one senior manager, the typical high-achieving woman childless at midlife has not made a choice but a 'creeping nonchoice.'

Why has the age-old business of having babies become so difficult for today's high-achieving women? I was shocked by what I found in the survey. Forty-two per cent of high-achieving women in corporate America (defined as companies with 5,000 or more employees) were still childless after 40. That figure rose to 49 per cent for women earning over $100,000. Many other women were able to have only one child because they started their families too late.

The findings are startling – and troubling: they make it clear that, for many women, the brutal demands of ambitious careers, the asymmetries of male-female working relationships, and the difficulties of bearing children late in life conspire to crowd out the possibility of having children.

During my research I was prepared to believe that the exhilaration and challenge of a megawatt career made it easy to opt out of motherhood. Nothing could be further from the truth. When I surveyed these women about children, their sense of loss was palpable. Consider Lisa Polsky, who joined Morgan Stanley in 1995 as MD after successful stints at Citibank and Bankers' Trust – she managed to make it on Wall Street, the ultimate bastion of male market power. But when we met in 1999, our conversation focused on what she had missed. Polsky was 44 then, and her childbearing days were over. She said: 'What gnaws at me is that I always assumed I would have children. Somehow I imagined that having a child was something I would get to in a year or so, after the next promotion, when I was more established.'

Kate, 52, a member of the medical faculty at the University of Washington, felt the same way. 'Looking back, I can't think why I allowed my career to obliterate my thirties,' she told me. 'I just didn't pay attention. I'm only just absorbing the consequences.'

And there is Stella Parsons, 45, who had just been offered a chairmanship at Ohio State University the day I interviewed her. But she waved my congratulations away. 'I wish some of this career success had spilled over to my private life. I just didn't get it together in time.' Then she whispered, 'I'm almost ashamed to admit it, but I still ache for a child.'

'For most of the women that I interviewed childlessness was more like what I refer to as 'creeping nonchoice.' Time passes, work is relentless, and because of the travel and the long hours relationships are hard to sustain. By the time a woman is married and settled enough in her career to think of starting a family, it is all too often too late,' says Hewlett.

From 'Executive Women and the Myth of Having It All' *by Sylvia Ann Hewlett,* Harvard Business Review, *April 2002*

31.

Grief and salvation

Donna Grieg

I have a pain deep inside me: a deep gnawing, raw pain that never goes away. Most of the time it's dormant and someone meeting me for the first time would be completely unaware of my agony. But it's always lurking.

I am not ill, not in the conventional way, but I suppose what I have is some form of malady for which there is only one cure. So what's wrong with me? I just want to be a mother. I gave up on the idea of capturing the heart of a man long ago. I was married briefly in my early twenties; we were too young and although we loved each other, we were both single at heart. In a funny sort of way, I am still single at heart now, even after all these years. All I want is a child – to have and to hold, for richer for poorer, in sickness and in health, 'til death us do part.

It's as if my life is somehow incomplete. There is a big chunk of it missing, a gaping hole. And this is what causes the pain. It is like being bereaved or constantly grieving for the child I have never had. It's a very powerful emotion, which creeps up on me unsuspectingly. I have welled up in tears at board meetings, in shops or while driving. I put on a stoic face when I have to attend events where there will be children, but babies move me to cry. I want one so much, but can't bear to hear about, see or hold one. If someone walks past, who is pregnant or with a new baby in a papoose or buggy, I have to move away. And then the pain begins all over again.

Everything today is so child and family-orientated. 'Baby on board' on the car window in front; a Mini Boden catalogue shoved through my letterbox when I never asked; mums in a gossipy huddle by the school gates; women with an assortment of buggies enjoying social motherhood outside the café . . . These are constant reminders to me about my state of childlessness.

I was crossing the staff car park the other day, behind our office. In the visitors' parking bay, I noticed my client's red Audi and recoiled when I saw through the glass two children's car seats in the back and a toy dinosaur on the passenger seat. After a positive morning's business, the pain returned to my solar plexus in a knuckle-punch. Someone else had children and I didn't.

Maybe I'm psychotic and need professional help, but these symbols and images are there to taunt me: 'We've got children, why haven't you?' But every month when my period arrives, it screams out a taunting reminder, 'Ha, ha! No chance!'

I long for simple things – to hold a child in a towel, fresh from the bath; to tumble about on the floor pretending to be a monster; to dig in the sand together on the beach; to kiss a soft skinned forehead goodnight.

I am fearful for what I am now and how lamenting and empty I will be when it really is too late. I worry about the loneliness and the lack of purpose in my life. How can any experience or dream fulfilled be worthwhile and enjoyable, when it will always be a long, long way second best?

My friends and colleagues tread cautiously about me. They pick their words carefully. I am included in non-threatening childfree events and excluded from child-orientated or family ones. They don't dare to match-make me: she's the crazy woman who hasn't got time for a man because she is too busy wallowing in her perpetual state of childless misery.

I look in the mirror and see a sad woman: still attractive with a good bone structure and a (rare) beautiful smile. My eyes used to be laughing, but they have a hollow melancholy about them now. I may be sad, but I am not bad. I have always been generous and kind, and believe it or not, a happy individual. I have never hurt anyone or been bitchy; I have never taken anything that didn't belong to me; I have been hardworking, gregarious and am well liked. So where did it all go wrong?

I think it's all about age. Thirty-nine. Now there's a number. Even if I got pregnant today (highly unlikely), I would be 40 by the time I had a baby. So as every sunset draws to a close, I notch up an incremental deterioration of my eggs and a decrease in my prospects for motherhood.

Then there is work. I need to work in order to survive. I earn a good salary, but have an enormous mortgage. I can't afford not to work, although

I could stretch to paying for childcare. So what hope is there for someone like me?

A *few weeks later* . . .

Desperate measures where no one gets hurt, that's what! I have found on the Internet a sperm donor programme. It is logged in my favourites and I look at it every day. It is drawing me in – a salvation for my bereavement. Somewhere out there, frozen in a dark cylinder might be half the genetic code to my future child. What started out as a wistful longing has blistered into a raging desire: I want a baby so much. This is the uncomplicated, achievable way to quash my grief and experience love and realise my whole purpose.

I have already written a long letter to my, as yet, unconceived child. While the act of obtaining a child by whatever means may appear selfish, I have solemnly declared to be a good and loving mother and to always do my best for my little one. I have so much love to give and my life truly depends on making this happen. Without a child, I am nothing.

Donna Grieg is a part-time PA working for a film production company. At the time of publication, Donna had just given birth to a daughter, Charlotte, conceived using a donor programme.

32.

Meet my family

Hi,

My name is Nick. I'm a university student, 20 years of age and I live in San Diego, California. I'd like to introduce you to my family.

First, there's my mom, Cecilia, who works as an administrator in a bank. Then there's my stepfather, Scott, who's a vice president of a software company. He formally adopted me when he was still married to my mother. They split eight years ago, and although he no longer lived with my mom, I still saw quite a lot of him and went on vacations with him and his new partner Lisa and 'the boys'. 'The boys' are Scott's two sons, Randy and Robert, from his first marriage and they were my stepbrothers. They are now my ex-stepbrothers but we're still close. Randy and I both share the same birth date and were in the same grade at high school – a bit like twins, but different. Lisa also has two boys from an earlier marriage: another called Randy and one called Nicholas, just to keep confusing everyone!

Then there is Georgia, my half-sister, whose parents are my mother Cecilia and my adoptive stepfather Scott. She lives with my mom. It's a complicated family portrait and my grandparents on my mother's side find family events such as Thanksgiving totally baffling. They keep asking, 'Who's that boy over there? Which one is his mother?' Well, the picture gets even more confusing . . .

My biological father is someone called Günter F. He is German and lives in a city in the north of Germany. He was a medical student in LA during the late 1980s. My mom paid for fertility treatment using his sperm through artificial insemination at a donor clinic, resulting in my arrival in this world. At the time, Günter was an anonymous donor and received $35 for jerking off over a porn mag! Romantic, eh? That was the total of his commitment and legal obligation to me.

A couple of months ago, while travelling in Europe, I tracked down Günter F. and met him in the cafeteria of the university teaching hospital at which he's now a consultant urologist. I look very much like my father – same eyes and eyebrows, same height, same ears and our hands are quite similar too. Like me, he has a double crown and a thick head of hair. He is married to Sonia and they have two sons, Peter and Henri, and a daughter, Ingrid. So these are also my three German half-siblings. (It's ironic, but Sonia actually had to have IVF in order to conceive.) But there's more. Quite a few more sperms-in-law, in fact, all shot from the same barrel. I have 27 known half-brothers and sisters, who are the result of Günter's exertions for cash. Some are in the US and some are in Germany. My father has met six of them and been contacted by others; there could even be more who are yet to surface.

It's weird spending the first ten years of my life as an only child and now ending up with over 30 blood relations, most being roughly the same age group. Now, I have no real concept of who I am, and Günter is struggling to come to terms with the impact that I and all the others have had on his quiet life. Sonia has taken the news of all her husband's additional offspring badly and feels cheated. She wonders where all this will end. For me, this is more than I want to know and I feel as if my identity has been diluted. I wonder about my half-siblings. Do they look like me? Are they similar to me in any way? Do we share a predisposition to any genetic irregularities? I will probably never know.

I have checked out the websites of a number of fertility clinics. While these appear to be predominately there to help infertile couples have babies, there is a lucrative sideline in providing single women with the necessary ingredients to create children in the absence of the biological father. The words 'discreet' and 'confidential' crop up continuously. It's real cosy and nice – for whose benefit, exactly? But the word that lured my father all those years ago was 'anonymity' and that now seems to be missing. The donor is informed when his 'donation' has made someone pregnant and then 18 years later a posse of curious teens pitch up wanting to clarify in their own minds their sense of identity. On an emotional scale, this is easily as big as an adopted child finding his or her birth parents.

I am grateful for having been given the opportunity of life, but it does come at a price – that of confusion and identity. In the future, how am I going to explain my family tree to my own children? How can it be allowed that two healthy people who have never even met can beget a child in a financial transaction when there are so many unwanted children in this world? To me it all seems completely crazy, irresponsible and selfish.

33.

Child-free — I'm not ill or nasty, I just don't want to be a mum

Kate Battersby

It's because I'm ill, you know – and selfish. My illness makes me selfish, or my selfishness makes me ill, I'm not quite sure. But I'm definitely ill and selfish, anyway. I'm also strange, and probably nasty.

My illness is not catching, but increasing numbers of women have it. It's called 'nulliparity'. *Chambers Concise Dictionary* defines a nullipara as 'a woman who has never given birth to a child, especially a woman who is not a virgin'. Twenty per cent of British women fall into this group. Moreover, 20 per cent of British women in their thirties have specifically opted to be childless. The very word 'childless' suggests loss or absence, and I can't imagine how painful it must be to yearn for children while being unable to have them. But I don't yearn for children, or find them fascinating and adorable. I never wanted them, and am grateful to be able to exercise my choice.

The many who are evangelical about breeding are dismayed, bewildered or offended by my decision. Inevitably, I'm required to explain. 'Why not?

Do you hate children?' 'Don't you have any maternal instinct?' 'Is it a physical problem?' 'Isn't that terribly selfish?' After that comes: 'You'll regret it', or 'You'll change your mind'. The diagnosis never changes. This is just a phase and I'll get over it, either in time to rectify matters or not, in which case I will get the lacerating unhappiness I deserve.

The idea that I've made a positive choice is apparently very strange indeed. But like grave-digging or shelf-stacking, motherhood is not a job I ever wanted. So I was glad to contribute to a book by Nicki Defago, a former senior producer of BBC's *Newsnight* and deputy editor on Radio 2's *Jeremy Vine Show*. Nicki is not a lobbyist or campaigner for the child-free but as a married woman who has chosen not to have children she wrote *Childfree And Loving It!* at the age of 39 when she realised not a single relevant book existed on the subject.

'Amazon offers more than 1,000 titles on the single subject of what children eat,' she explained. 'But if you are resolutely childfree, or even undecided about starting a family, you'll go hungry.'

For years the Americans have tuned in to the electively childfree trend. Over there, 42 per cent of women without children read truckloads of books on the subject, all featuring contentedly upbeat titles separating motherhood from female identity: *Sweet Grapes*, *Pride And Joy*, *Cheerfully Childless*, *No Kidding* and my own favourite, *Families Of Two*. I have a family quite separate from the one I was born into – I mean, the family comprising myself and my partner, the kind of family ignored by politicians.

'The thing that really makes me rabid is the British government's £250 gift to every new baby,' foams a friend. 'I strongly believe there's a communal interest in the tax system. I have no problem with universal health and education systems, or with targeting support where there is need. I do have a problem with giving money to kids' savings.

'There aren't any breaks for people without children. At work, flexible contracts are offered to those with children, or to carers. These are entirely legitimate. But their work doesn't go away. Cover has to be found for it, and those who give it are not recognised. Meanwhile, when I broke my leg in six places, my partner was refused carer's leave and made to feel very uncomfortable.'

We nulliparae sound cross, don't we? Well, we *are* cross! It's just one more negative characteristic to add to the list. Personally, I bristle when being informed I will soon see the light and change my mind. It seems quite reasonable to reply: 'Really? Is that what happened to you after you had children?' Then the evangelicals look offended, because my reply is indeed intended to offend, in the hope that they will spot how offensive their question is to me. But they never do. Hence I am not only ill and strange, but also nasty.

And then of course, I have a dog. Guess what? The mummy mafia smile knowingly and diagnose a child-substitute. Sigh. Pay attention at the back! How can a dog be a 'substitute' for something I don't want? I love my dog in his own right: I want him specifically.

'Ah, but a dog won't change your life. Children will,' lecture the mummy mafia. Sawing off my legs would change my life, too. I just don't feel any urge to try it!

Kate Battersby is a journalist who writes for the Daily Telegraph *and other national newspapers, predominantly on sport and motoring.*

34.

Birth mothers, not

Here, four single women share their own experiences of childlessness.

Camilla, 46

For as long as I can remember, all I ever wanted was a husband and children of my own. I witnessed my sisters' and friends' weddings and a rapid succession of nephews and nieces. As my sisters and most of my friends settled down into routines of domesticity and child rearing, I climbed the corporate ladder at a pharmaceutical company and dated a string of eligible, but wholly unsuitable men.

I endured my share of heartbreak and disappointment on the dating front and stoically attended a batch of weddings every summer that passed. I admit that I cried a lot and felt sorry for myself. I wallowed in self-pity, resented the happiness of others and longed for my prince to rescue me, the damsel in distress, the hopeful lady-in-waiting . . . My only consolation was music – I play the piano – and it became an outpouring for my bitterness. But there came a point when I glanced up from resentment and saw that my nieces and nephews were growing into wonderful little kids.

I had always been close to my sisters, particularly my twin, but backed off when they got married. In a typically English way, I thought that nobody would want a spinster sister sticking her oar into family life. But I was wrong.

On the morning of my 42nd birthday, I had what some might call an epiphany. Since it was now extremely unlikely that I would have a family of my own, the only way I could combat my isolation was to get involved with the families closest to me. So I got over myself and my perpetual state of singledom – and became a yummy auntie instead.

I relished Christmas with my families, lent a helping hand at children's parties and became hoarse with shouting at school sports days. I got involved with one of my nephew's schools and played the piano in the school play when the music teacher was ill. Suddenly, my network of friends expanded and I found a renewed passion within my humdrum life.

I am always there for my sisters and their families, and wherever possible, for my godchildren and friends' children. I can offer my support, and when my hectic work life permits, take great pleasure arranging outings for the kids or having them to stay the weekend. We camp in the garden, go to the cinema or the ballet, have barbecues, hunt for fossils in the cliffs and take long, muddy bike rides in the countryside. I occasionally baby-sit, but limit this to a few times a year – I don't want my good-natured availability to be taken for granted.

Since music is my passion, I have taken ownership of piano lessons for Chloe and Emily, two of my nieces. I bought them a Bechstein piano and have funded their lessons right up to Grade 8, swelling with pride and wiping tears away when they have played in concerts.

I have carved a role as friend and confidante to these children, as musical sugar-auntie to two of them, and as an unencumbered extra pair of hands at family events. It's wonderful to love and be loved, and to admire their youth and vitality. And do you know what? It's not such an odd role in this family – this is the way of life for large Italian families.

And just as soon as having my own children was off my radar, something in me changed and I met Andrew – a handsome divorcé with four grown-up daughters. We live about 100 miles apart and both of us are unwilling to compromise our current lifestyles, but I suppose you could say, I do have a love interest there. He doesn't want commitment, and neither do I – that would mean giving up on my children and my extended family.

So, I didn't get what I envisaged in life, but I took the next best thing and it has fulfilled me. I had the option to be bitter and twisted with my lot, but I chose not to take it. And right now, I wouldn't have my life any other way.

Fiona, 42

There is a time and place for everything and being single, the wrong side of 40 and living in the countryside is quite a tough package. Throughout my younger life, I had always envisaged being married and having lots of children to make up for my fairly solitary upbringing. My only brother lives in Canada with family and both my parents are dead. But instead, I found myself leading an insular life in rural Lincolnshire.

The problems, as I saw them four years ago, for a single woman of a certain age living in the countryside are as follows:

1. Everyone is married with children.
2. Everyone is involved in farming.
3. There are no single men.
4. On the off-chance a single man *is* in circulation, he is automatically invited to everything and is always paired up with a woman whose husband is working through the night sowing crops or ploughing – he is never matched with a real single woman.
5. Women think you are somehow going to make a move on their husbands (and some of the husbands hope you will).
6. Everything is geared around family life.
7. Any other singles are about twenty years younger.

Most of my friends were old enough to be my parents, so I lived in my little house, with its empty field, surrounded by flat landscapes, lambs and crops of peas and maize. I commuted into Peterborough to work in financial services – out early, back late and bored. Life was pretty dull and unfulfilling. I was an angry and selfish person to boot, resentful of my predicament and desperate to change my life, but unsure how to do so. Should I move into a town? Would that somehow be better? I wasn't sure. Like Bridget Jones I would stare despondently at an empty chardonnay bottle, trying to blot out my miserable life. I started dating online, but that too proved expensive and disappointing. I was altogether in the wrong mindset for a relationship.

Then one day, Eric – my elderly next-door neighbour – asked me if I would mind keeping a horse in my field. Eric had been asked by the vet if he knew anyone who might take on Rowley, a five-year-old Irish Draught, whose five-year life had obviously been tough – he was badly schooled, malnourished and due to be put down. At first, I resisted the idea. My experience with horses was limited – I could ride, but I had never looked after one before.

After sleeping on it, I decided to give Rowley a go, and so he moved in. I cleared out the cobwebby stable and tracked down Sophie Ostler, a brilliant Horse Whisperer. Together we worked to rehabilitate Rowley.

Professionally, I worked increasingly from home and began to build a menagerie of small animals: two kittens called Ying and Yang, a rescue mongrel called Kafka, an owl named Towitt and a donkey – Sabba. I now had a role to play and creatures that depended on me. I started riding again, joined the hunt and am learning falconry. I'm on the organising committees of a local air show and a charity ball. I stopped thinking about myself all the time and amazingly, people's attitudes to me – and my attitudes to them – started to change.

I began meeting people and far from being regarded as a dotty woman with lots of oddball animals, I found myself more acceptable in social circles. I think I came across as less threatening without a 'poor me' or 'desperate for a man' aura about me. I've even met a nice farmer, Richard, three years my junior.

Yes, I would have liked to have married and had a family but I've created a new family now and have plans to expand it with more horses and injured birds of prey. I have a full and varied life, which brings me into contact with a rich and diverse cross-section of people. And living in the country is not so bad, not so bad at all.

Rowena, 45

When I was 33, I made an assumption that the man I had dated for three years, the man who proposed to me, who married me and carried me over the threshold wanted to have children. But I was wrong. Our viewpoints were completely polarised, and in just two years, our happy marriage was feeling the strain. To make matters worse, I became ill and needed a hysterectomy. My wretchedness at being denied parenthood by my husband was compounded by the surgeon's knife. Six months later, our short marriage finally broke down for good and we divorced.

I experienced pain, regret, resentment, bitterness, overwhelming sadness and a kind of black void. It took a long time to shake off and I have to confess to recoiling at the sight of a new baby, or feeling like I had been punched whenever a pregnancy was announced by a friend or colleague.

I had a good counsellor, and between us we worked through this and other issues I had. A few years later I met Rod, who was divorced with three children: Paddy, Hamish and Annabel. Shortly after his divorce, cancer claimed the children's mother and he took custody of his brood.

The children, who were all under 14 at the time, regarded me with suspicion and resentment. They felt I was muscling in on their father and trying to assume the role of their mother. I understood this, but it was still very hard. If they weren't ignoring me, they were rude or sullen. I could do nothing right and I felt them mocking me when my back was turned. It brought to the surface my barren and childless state – I couldn't have children of my own, and I couldn't relate to other people's children either. That hurt. But I was crazy about Rod and finally understood what falling in love was about. He proposed and I accepted – with some trepidation, I must confess.

It was at this point that the children had a sort of pow-wow in deciding how to treat this woman who was to become their stepmother and an integral part of their family. They voted in my favour and wrote me a long letter (unprompted by their father), welcoming me into their lives.

They were true to their word and I am now a fulfilled stepmother. We have been through so much together – good and bad: exams, sporting competitions, teenage crushes, a dalliance with drugs, plus all their young adult achievements. I am their mother – they call me Row, but I *am* their mother.

When I look back over my own life, and the inevitability of my child-lessness, this is an outcome that I could barely have dared to wish for.'

Jayne, 46

Rummaging through an old storage box at my mother's house, I came across a photograph of me, taken when I was about three. I was standing outside a Wendy house in our garden with the little boy from next door – Jeremy, I think he was called. I was holding my favourite dolly, Polly. We looked like a miniature married couple proudly showing off our new baby.

The photograph triggered in my mind a recollection that as a child I always wanted to have a family. Right up to adulthood, this recollection became an assumption. So, from an early age I aspired to have a family, yet decades later I had failed to live up to this blueprint for life. Although there has been a man in my life most of the time, this is always a transient arrangement. A permanent fixture is the house and car, but somewhere down the line I missed my chance to acquire the husband and the children – and love.

I wasn't a bad person. I wasn't unstable or selfish. I didn't look or act weird – I was just nice and normal. And passive.

I didn't miss out on having a family because I was infertile (although I will never actually know), nor because I postponed pregnancy to concentrate on my career. Along my romantic journeys I never actually met anyone who mutually agreed that we should make babies together. I just navigated the maze of serial monogamy, each boyfriend buying a few years of my fertility timeframe. We had fun, some great holidays and everyday companionship, but each relationship eventually hit a dead end and I would start the unbreakable pattern all over again.

Because I was 'nice', I was never the sort of person to trick a man into making me pregnant, nor was it in my nature to bludgeon a man into becoming a parent with me. I wasn't brave or selfish enough to seek sperm donation, so I just waited in vain for my dreams to come true, and looked on as my friends hitched and hatched.

I am so angry with myself that I didn't dump the ditherers and wasted my most precious years. I indulged myself for the moment and hoped that the future would work out fine. I yearned for a nuclear family, quietly and to myself. I lived in fear of a relationship breaking up – I couldn't bear the prospect of being alone, and I hoped that things would change. But they didn't.

Looking back, my life was completely without drama – no ultimatum-fuelled rows, no fraught Christmases, no probing fertility specialists, no mourned miscarriages. And without defining moments – no breath-catching declarations of love, no blushing bride, no shared ownership, no screaming labour pains or trials of motherhood. It was a kind of neutral, joyless, middle-of-the-road existence. I wasn't prepared to say what I wanted, or to go after the things I desired most. I didn't even get angry. At night, lying awake and alone in the darkness, I imagined that I could hear my unborn children in the distance, crying, 'Come and get us, Mummy, come and get us!' And as the years rolled by, their cries became quieter and quieter. And now there is just silence.

Yes, it is a kind of bereavement and a regret. I try not to make judgements on cigarette-smoking teenage mothers as they stroll past me in the street, pushing a buggy, a phone clamped over an ear with a bawling toddler in tow. I do get a pang when I see older mothers with babies or small children in a clutch at the school gates. How did they manage to cross the line when their time was almost up and I didn't? And I do wonder how fate conspires to ignore some people's dreams and lavish on others things that, by rights we're all entitled to.

I have made my bed and I must lie on it. There are no children in my life, but I have my health and my (modest) wealth. I have resolved to find passion, colour, interest and opinion in many new fields and to shake off the beige passivity that has hung over me like a cloud for so long. I will find a new vibrancy, purpose and happiness and will stop wallowing in the 'what might have been'. My horizon is already looking brighter.

35.

Motherhood: the over-forty perspective

So many women are now embracing late motherhood for a variety of reasons. But is being an older mother any easier, or is it more demanding? We know that from a certain age the biological options diminish, but what's having children like for those who succeed after 40?

I married Will at 36 and we waited about a year before we started trying for a baby. Becoming a mother is my obsession, and I have been knocked back three times – first by not being able to conceive naturally, and then by the failed IVF. It is heartbreaking for both of us. I had an abortion when I was 17, and although I have been assured this has nothing to do with my infertility, I regard it as a kind of taunt. I fear that, like my mother, I may be experiencing an early menopause. All my friends are having babies and I feel such a failure. This is an emotionally fraught time for both of us and we're under a lot of strain, mentally, physically and financially. I had taken my fertility for granted; I had assumed having a child was a right to which I was entitled. I am praying that this time will be lucky for us.'

Jasmin, 41, and about to embark upon her third round of IVF

'I didn't plan to have my daughters so late, but I didn't actually meet my partner until I was 40. For some reason, I assumed that I wouldn't be able to conceive or that, because of my great age, I would have a child with

Down's. I was also very happy managing my own small business and spending time with Clive at weekends. For those reasons, becoming a mother wasn't really on my agenda. My first daughter was a happy accident – I honestly cannot remember her conception and it was a complete shock when I found out I was pregnant. As soon as Lucy was born (perfect), fired up with sheer joy we got down to work to have another. We love our role as parents. Tiring it may be, but I feel I am better able to cope with children in my late forties. However, I do worry about being menopausal and having to deal with adolescent girls at the same time. When hot flushes and hot dates clash, that will be a real test.'

Maggie, who had her daughters when she was 42 and 44

'Having been a European vice president for a software company, my lifestyle changed dramatically about a year after we married. When motherhood became my full-time job I traded in my £150,000 salary for £50 per month child benefit. Instead of managing strategic brand awareness and a 30-strong sales force, I juggled nappies, sleep times, feeding times, playgroups, bath times and story times. My brand awareness became focused on Thomas the Tank Engine and Bob the Builder. Glitzy corporate launch parties in Paris were swapped for Mr Marvel the magician performing a show in our living room, followed by pass-the-parcel and slices of Scooby-Doo cake. And you know what? Running the lives of a husband, babies and toddlers while keeping everyone happy, 24/7 with no days off, is far, far more demanding than running the corporate show!

'I had the option to buy into the services of a nanny or outsource my children to nursery care and continue to work. But the reality would have meant never seeing the children except when they were asleep at night and missing all those incredible milestones like first words and first steps.

'I married late in life and wanted children so much. It just didn't seem right to forfeit narrowly missed motherhood once I had been blessed with three beautiful boys.'

Henrietta, who had one son at 38, her second at 39 and her third at 41

'Jake and I had actually been married for ten years, but the much yearned for children didn't materialise. I had IVF – which worked first time – and I gave birth to triplet boys. And then I became pregnant naturally, unbelievably quickly, raising quite a few eyebrows. Apparently, IVF or being pregnant can kick-start a rather reluctant fertility system into action. Having four children under two was absolutely horrendous. We had to move house because I couldn't park outside and I couldn't carry four children and all the groceries down the road in London at the same time.

'Time has flown and the boys are now doing A-levels. We are bracing ourselves for the financial and logistical impact of (as is likely) three different universities. I love them to bits and would recommend IVF to anyone. Never give up hope, and be prepared for everything!'

Tasmin, who had triplet boys at 39 and a daughter at 40

'Having a husband and children was all I ever wanted and they came along in rapid succession. I was absolutely elated and felt I had achieved my life's ambition. But what I hadn't bargained for was the drudge and relentless chores involved in looking after two very young children. I was on duty day and night without a break. While villa holidays were relaxing for my husband, I found being away from home and all its conveniences even more of a challenge – laundry, shopping, preparing meals, changing nappies, tidying, etc.

'Motherhood was really hard after such a long time working at a publishing house, independent and single. I don't think my age had anything to do with it – it is just the same for everyone else, whatever their age. But after an extended period of liberty, when I could do anything, go anywhere, live in an organised house and spar with people on an intellectual level, it was a shock. However, I believe I am a better mother now than if I'd had them in my twenties.

'My boys are now seven and six, and we have established a family rhythm. The drudgery has eased a bit. We have a lot of fun as a family. I love my life and we get so much pleasure from seeing them develop and prosper as little individuals. They are making so much headway at school and with their swimming, football and friendships. Having children was the best thing I ever did – I just think I wasn't particularly prepared or coping when they were babies.'

Laura, 39 when she had her first son and 41 when she had her second

'We met and married when we were both 37 and agreed from the outset that absolutely, categorically we didn't want children. We both had demanding careers in local government, enjoyed an active social life and our passion, sailing our yacht at weekends. When I fell pregnant, I was in complete shock. How could we have allowed an accident like this to happen?

'Although I had expected my world to crumble, I confess to feeling excited with a rush of maternal instincts and hormones. Connor took longer to embrace the idea of parenthood, but as soon as we saw the first scan, he too was smitten. We now find it hard to believe how our earlier, selfish approach to marriage could so easily have denied us this wonderful opportunity. Our daughter is a true princess and an unexpected gift. No longer our main passion in life, we've sold the yacht.'

Fennella and Connor, 45, parents to five-year-old Savannah

'I won't go into the details about Joe's father, suffice to say he is absent and I am happy about that. I desperately wanted a child, but the realities of life meant that I had to continue with my job as a teacher. Joe went to nursery full time and when he was two, attended the nursery at the independent school, where I teach. I'm fortunate in that with teaching the holidays mean we can spend large chunks of time together.

'I have no regrets about being a single parent – many of my friends are single parents through divorce – but I wish that I had met more of the mothers and experienced the toddler-mums-playtime-birthday party thing when Joe was a tot. Having a young son has made me feel much younger and I am no longer panicked or indeed concerned that I don't have a partner. I am fulfilled with my job and in my role as mother, and it's great to see him every day at school – other mothers don't get to do that.'

Helena was 41 when she had her son Joseph as a single mother

36.

Women who conceive 'accidentally on purpose'

Clover Stroud

Katya's entire adult life has been characterised by driving ambition, which has seen her achieve a first-class degree in classics from Cambridge and a six-figure salary as a barrister. Now approaching 37, she hasn't let singledom get in the way of her next goal: motherhood. And because she is accustomed to taking the initiative, she was less than careful when she had a two-week affair with Phil, her cousin's friend, earlier this year. Of course, he wasn't consulted about whether he wanted to become a father, but when a man sleeps with a woman without using contraception . . .

'Most men I've been out with have been pretty disappointing,' she says, one hand on her pregnant tummy. 'I'm not making any demands on Phil, and I'm not expecting him to be involved. I'm financially independent, so I know I can give this baby an amazing life. I will be able to offer a more stable life than some of my girlfriends, who gave up their jobs a decade ago to have children, and who are now in failing marriages and have no independent income.'

Katya's attitude might seem blunt, reducing it to nothing more than a biological transaction between herself and a suitable stud but as a fiercely independent and financially secure woman, she is not alone. Former French justice minister, Rachida Dati's pregnancy at 42 was greeted with feverish speculation about the identity of the father and she remained resolute in not naming him, stating simply that her private life is 'complicated'. 'I've always said that having a child was fundamental to me,' was as far as she would go.

Actress Minnie Driver has a young son whose father she refuses to name, while Geri Halliwell has been bringing up Bluebell independent of the child's scriptwriter father. Figures indicating the number of women who choose to have a baby this way don't exist, of course, but fertility clinics report growing numbers choose donor insemination (DI) as a form of conception. And then there is the overwhelming anecdotal evidence: we all know someone who has done it. For example, the 35-year-old record producer and mother of a three-year-old son, who dines out on the account of how she knocked herself up with the help of a turkey baster and a good-natured male friend, or the society girl who, at 38, was so desperate for a baby, she resorted to a quick fumble with the plumber.

Unsurprisingly, few women will admit to having actively stolen a man's sperm. It's still one of the last sexual taboos in an age when almost anything goes — sleep around as much as you like, but don't do that.

'People have a real problem with the fact that I positively chose this course,' says Sarah, 35, a script editor. Her daughter is now five – she found herself pregnant as her relationship of three months was breaking up. 'I have only spoken to my closest friends about this, because most people find it totally unacceptable. In the past, with other boyfriends, I had been much more careful, but I was in my early thirties and my biological clock was in overdrive. I really, really wanted a baby, and I didn't have any time to waste. My daughter's father was clever and good-looking, and I suppose it seemed safer to have an affair with him than a one-night stand. And it was cheaper and a lot more fun than doing it in a clinic.' He, perhaps understandably, was less than delighted to find out that he was going to be a father. 'He put pressure on me not to have the baby, but for me, it wasn't an accident,' she says.

There is something courageous about women who choose to have a baby via DI. It's a decision they make alone, and you will find plenty of websites and support groups devoted to the subject. But it's quite another matter when a girl finds herself pregnant but doesn't get the support she might expect. Actor Eddie Murphy and Steve Bing expressed disbelief at whether they were the fathers after Mel B. and Elizabeth Hurley respectively announced their pregnancies. Faith, a music scout, has muddled through an arrangement with Sam, a sexy, but struggling musician, who she was sleeping with on and off for nearly a year when she became pregnant. They were open with each other about the fact that it was not what Sam might have called an 'exclusive relationship', and although he initially didn't want to have contact after she told him the news, he now sees his five-year-old daughter, Maya, 'about once a month'.

'I don't feel guilty about having his baby,' says Faith. 'He was happy enough to have a lot of sex with me without using a rubber, and as soon as I was pregnant, I told him that I wouldn't expect anything from him financially. It is quite nice having the odd Saturday off when Sam takes Maya out, but I really wouldn't want him to have much more access than that, and I think it suits us both. She's my daughter.'

What about the children? For many, it's not an ideal upbringing. Dan, 31, and his twin sister were born as a result of a fling between his mother and a young academic, who she had decided would be perfect father material. She lost contact with him soon after she conceived. He doesn't feel his life has been dramatically overshadowed, but 'I resent the fact that, on a basic level, you don't and can't ever know half of your own background,' he says. 'There'll always be a void. In my case, do I have siblings? What about genetic diseases?

'Imagine not having an explanation for certain things you do, and not being able to find them, ever. At least with sperm donation or adoption you might be able to trace some answers. But when a woman decides to go it alone, she is ultimately trying to eliminate the father. What gives her the right to make that decision? It's selfish, and I don't see a difference between these women and the 16-year-old who has a baby because she wants someone to love her.'

However, when even an eminent fertility expert points out that there is 'a shortage of men in their thirties and forties who seem capable of real commitment', what's a girl to do? Katya, for one, wouldn't have it any other way: 'I'm looking forward to bringing up my baby alone. Much better that than being in a second-rate relationship,' she says. 'And anyway, I've never relied on anyone else for anything in my life, so why should I start now?'

As she marches down the street by herself, on her way to her next scan, the inevitable question hanging over her isn't how long she should have gone on waiting for Mr Right, but whether she ever really wanted him in the first place.

. . . *And the man who tried it*

Joe Kurtzer, 45: 'By the time I got to my late thirties, I'd had several long relationships that hadn't resulted in marriage, and I became more and more concerned about my ability to have a child with a wife or girlfriend. Although men don't have a traditional biological clock, we do have our own version of it, and I didn't want to be a father at 50. So I decided to go to a surrogacy agency (Circle, in Boston). Most people's reactions to my decision were positive, though some questioned whether a man has the same nurturing emotions as a woman. But you dismiss those people.

'My son, Anthony, was born to a surrogate mother in Missouri on Boxing Day, 2003, and I took him home three days later. I took a couple of months off to care for him, then he went to nursery and I went back to work — like millions of other parents. I never really missed a woman being there, because you can't miss something you never had. I just concentrated on bonding with my child. I didn't start dating again straightaway, but when I did, I found women were impressed and, in some cases, attracted to a man capable of caring for a child on his own. Now I'm in a relationship and Anthony loves having a mum. My girlfriend and I also have a three-month-old daughter, Catherine, and it's wonderful. But before she came along, having a child with someone just wasn't on the horizon, and if it hadn't happened, I'd still have Anthony. If people out there are thinking about it as an option, they should know it's a very real one. You need a very supportive family, employer and friends, but you need that if you are a woman, too.'

Reflecting part of a growing trend in the USA, at 36, the singer Ricky Martin became the father of twins by surrogacy. He is the sole parent.

Clover Stroud is a freelance journalist who writes regularly for the Saturday and Sunday Telegraph *and the* Sunday Times, *among other publications. She lives in Oxford with her two children, and has a weakness for country music.*

Overcoming a single state of mind

It can, and is, being done. Draw from the collective wisdom of those who emerged from the fear of being alone to lead happy and fulfilled lives.

'And here comes Suzy . . . She's perpetually single. There's people all over the church! She thinks it's all over . . . It is now!'
>   Football mad Ron Pearson, father of the bride,
>   Suzy Meadows (39), on her wedding day

37.

Ultimatums — when and where they work

Just about every agony aunt advises *against* women dishing out ultimatums to get what they want from their men. Ultimatums are seen as a manipulative way to behave and often toll the death knell for a partnership based on trust. Once used, where do you draw the line? And how would you like it if your partner used an ultimatum on you? In this chapter, I have plundered the sources of experts to find out exactly how women can kick-start or bail out of relationships beginning to stagnate.

Picture the scenario: Mike and Kate are both in their mid-thirties and for almost two years, they have been a happy couple. They spend a lot of time together, including holidays, share common interests and enjoy each other's company. There might even be a bit of love lurking in the background, although this isn't referred to. They're also independent types and have their own circles of friends and pursuits to keep themselves amused whenever they are apart. This couple talk about everything, but avoid the following: commitment, engagement, marriage, babies, living together, joint bank accounts, the future, shared ownership (of anything) and they rarely make plans much further than a month in advance. Mike seems content with the present arrangement, but Kate feels she needs to know if this is going somewhere because after 20 years, her fertility window is starting to close. Sounds familiar?

Kate has a number of options:

1. She can maintain the status quo and continue with the relationship, waiting for Mike to decide and make the next move. The problem is how much more time does she want to invest? Simmering resentments will build up, and he might surprise her by terminating the relationship if he feels it isn't going anywhere or he can sense unwanted pressure from Kate.

2. Kate can suggest a number of options to Mike to bring commitment a little closer, such as moving in together. The problem might be that he could just laugh this off, defer the decision to a later date or refuse altogether.

3. Kate could end the relationship and resolve to find someone else. Not such a bad idea. This might be the wake-up call Mike needs to encourage him to think about the next step. If his feelings are sincere, he will come rushing after Kate. If not, better she knows now than a few more years down the line. Here, the problems in Kate's mind will be: 'Why did I finish with such a wonderful guy?' or 'What if I can't find someone else? There could never be another man as nice as Mike', even 'I couldn't bear to be apart from him' or 'OK, so I could cope with being on my own for a while but what if Mike meets someone else, they have a whirlwind romance and then get hitched? How would I ever get over that?'

4. Or, she can give him an ultimatum – a reasonable one, such as 'Make up your mind within four months or I'm out of here.'

Though I'm no agony aunt, I do believe an ultimatum is the only viable way forward for Kate. In making her feelings known, she needs to be clear what she is asking for, to have a firm deadline and stick to it. She shouldn't have to remind Mike of the deadline – he will *know*. It wouldn't harm Kate's cause if she also acknowledged that she understands the distasteful nature of ultimatums. If Mike shows no outward sign of changing or making plans, he is sticking his head in the sand and ignoring her deadline. But an ultimatum that affects two people's lives should not be taken lightly, so don't wait till the final day to decide the outcome. With an ultimatum, the recipient should indicate one way or another what the likely outcome might be. From Kate's point of view, why would she want Mike to fulfil her wishes if his feelings don't come straight from the heart?

In some cases, an ultimatum may serve to unmask the reality of a relationship. The two parties may be deluding themselves that they are a couple; an uncomplicated co-existence might be all their relationship aspires to. The sudden presentation of a 'list' of objectives within a given timeframe will reveal a hollow arrangement in which both parties want different things. In this case, the ultimatum serves its purpose and although negative, the outcome will be the right one.

Let's face it, no one wants to get dumped and a man such as Mike may try to instigate a compromise in place of terminating the relationship. Ultimately this would prove detrimental with both parties in the relationship feeling new strains.

Psychologist Melissa Kampf says, 'An ultimatum only works if the person to whom it is being given really has an investment in the relationship. And the person has to believe that the one giving the ultimatum will follow through.' It might be a sweeping generalisation, but in most marriages or co-habiting relationships, it's the woman who makes the majority of managerial decisions and domestically she is often the chief organiser. How many couples do you know where the man organised the wedding ceremony and now coordinates the weekly grocery shopping? Mostly it's women who make sure the loo roll is replaced, that they don't run out of milk, that great aunt Hilda receives a birthday card and the car tax is renewed. And it's usually women who push for change – redecorating the hall, switching utility suppliers, fundraising through the PTA at school, choosing where to go on holiday, extending the loft. The role of each partner within the running of a home and family tends to become segregated. Although both may be working, a significant proportion of men prefer the day-to-day and family-enhancing decisions to be taken by the woman.

So it stands to reason that in a relationship where none of these everyday matters is going on that the woman should raise the stakes. Let's not forget, time is of the essence here. Unless she is a mistress and perfectly happy with the deal, no woman wants to invest in a relationship which coasts along in neutral, heading nowhere. If she is to be released, either by her partner or of her own free will, she needs time to start anew. She must also factor in time to offload any emotional ties before she meets someone else. She might even be surprised to find that she enjoys her new-found singledom.

This might sound patronising, but it needs to be said: ladies, please allow a respectable amount of time to pass before you contemplate issuing an ultimatum. Let a relationship blossom and find out if you are compatible first before asking for a more formal commitment. Ultimatums should only be issued when the relationship has been on a plateau basis for some time. Mairead Molloy, of elite dating agency Berkeley International, warns of a high casualty rate in late thirtysomething relationships: 'A relationship can be strangled before it ever gets going because the woman is desperate to move things along too quickly. I've known women who have issued marriage ultimatums after just a month. What kind of guy needs that sort of pressure? This desperate urgency on the part of women is the single biggest relationship killer. Don't do it!'

Equally, don't feel bad about giving your man an ultimatum after a reasonable amount of time. You have the right to know where things are leading. As the saying goes, it's your life and it's not a dress rehearsal. No man is entitled to indulge himself in your precious prime without an ultimate goal, but you have a duty too. So, take responsibility for your own life and make sure that if you choose to be in a relationship with a particular man, it's what you both want – or else!

38.

Are you a quirkyalone?

Sasha Cagen

A quirkyalone is a neologism, referring to someone who enjoys being single (but is not opposed to being in a relationship) and generally prefers to be alone rather than dating for the sake of being in a couple. The quirkyalone has come to appreciate singledom as a natural state and a way to live a fulfilling life. Quirkyalones are romantic and would rather spend time in the company of good friends and people with whom they share a meaningful relationship, rather than someone with whom there is no connection. The quirkyalone possesses unique traits and an optimistic spirit, and they have a sensibility that transcends relationship status.

Among the celebrated quirkyalones are: Ally McBeal, Cher, Cleopatra, Joan of Arc, Katharine Hepburn, Liza Tarbuck, Oprah Winfrey, Oscar Wilde, Ann Widdecombe, Morrissey, Eddie Izzard, George Clooney, Elizabeth I, Wonder Woman, Whoopee Goldberg, Selina Scott and Freddie Mercury . . . there are many more.

I am, perhaps, what you might call deeply single – almost never, ever in a relationship. Until recently, I wondered whether there might be something weird about me but then lonely romantics began to grace the covers of *TV Guide* and *Mademoiselle*. From *Ally McBeal* to *Sex and the City*, a spotlight came to shine on the forever single. If these shows had touched such a nerve in our culture, I began to think, perhaps I was not so alone after all.

The morning after New Year's Eve (another kiss-less one, of course), a certain jumble of syllables came to me. When I told my friends about my idea, their faces lit up with instant recognition: the quirkyalone.

If Carl Jung was right in his view that people are different in fundamental ways that drive them from within, then the quirkyalone is simply to be added to the pantheon of personality types assembled over the 20th century. Only now, when the idea of marrying at the age of 20 has become thoroughly passé, are we quirkyalones emerging in greater numbers.

We are the puzzle pieces who seldom fit with other puzzle pieces. Romantics, idealists, eccentrics, we inhabit singledom as our natural resting state. In a world where proms and marriage define the social order, we are, by force of our personalities and inner strength, rebels.

For the quirkyalone, there is no point in dating just for the sake of not being alone. We want a miracle. Out of millions, we have to find the one who will understand. Better to be untethered and open to possibility: living for the exhilaration of meeting someone new, of not knowing what the night will bring. We quirkyalones seek momentous meetings.

By the same token, being alone is understood as a wellspring of feeling and experience. There is a bittersweet fondness for silence. All those nights alone – they bring insight. Sometimes, though, we wonder whether we have painted ourselves into a corner. Standards that started out high only become higher once you realise the contours of this existence. When we do find a match, we verge on obsessive – or we resist.

And so, a community of like-minded souls is essential. Since fellow quirkyalones are not abundant (we are probably less than five per cent of the population), I recommend reading the patron saint of solitude: German poet Rainer Maria Rilke. Even 100 years after its publication, *Letters to a Young Poet* still feels like it was written for us: 'You should not let yourself be confused in your solitude by the fact that there is something in you that wants to break out of it,' Rilke writes. 'People have (with the help of conventions) oriented all their solutions toward the easy and toward the easiest side of easy, but it is clear that we must hold to that which is difficult.'

Rilke is right. Being quirkyalone can be difficult. Everyone else is part of a couple. Still, there are advantages. No one can take our lives away by breaking up with us. Instead of sacrificing our social constellation for the one all-consuming individual, we seek empathy from friends. We have significant *others*.

And so, when my friend asks me whether being quirkyalone is a life sentence, I say, yes, at the core, one is always quirkyalone. But when one quirkyalone finds another, oooh la la! The earth quakes.

Sasha Cagen is the author of Quirkyalone: A Manifesto for Uncompromising Romantics *and founder of the quirkyalone movement: www.quirkyalone.net*

39.

When does a man want to get married?

*I*n compiling this book I researched an abundance of literature, trawled the Internet and continuously interviewed. I have also gleaned snippets and vital pieces of information from many helpful people encountered along the way.

Throughout my research, I have become, almost to the point of obsession, fascinated by how men and women who marry select each other. Today, a microscopically small proportion marry the first person they meet: most play the dating field to a greater or lesser extent, and when the time is right, settle down with one person. OK, not everyone makes the right choice when they marry, and divorce statistics bear this out, but generally, there is an acknowledgement that 'this person is the one for me' and the question is popped.

For those women who have never been on the receiving end of a marriage proposal or who may have turned one or more down and are now unhappy about their single status, there are inevitable questions. As she lies alone, blinking into the darkness, the single woman audits the status of all close friends: who's married, who's engaged or co-habiting? Who's got children or has a baby on the way? Invariably this is closely followed by 'but what about me?' moments.

Even in the 21st century, chivalry still decrees it is the man who asks and the woman who accepts. Through discussions with married men and a little help from the Internet, I have gleaned the following reasons why men choose their life partners. These observations aren't based on any formal research on my part, but are backed up by the findings in John T. Molloy's fascinating work, *Why Men Marry Some Women And Not Others*.

Fundamental to a woman's quest to find a husband is that she seeks out and gets close to the marrying kind. So what is the marrying kind of man? Study the findings below:

* Many men in their early twenties adopt a promiscuous and peripatetic approach to women. There is a gradual transition to monogamy and stability as they progress into, and through, their thirtysomething years.

* This nomadic relationship life phase wears off after a few years when men tire of the single life and their friends begin to stabilise in their relationships. The influence of peers is strong.

* Men working in the professional sector between the ages of 30 and 38 are the age group most likely to settle down, either through co-habiting or marrying. Before such a timeframe, men in this category rarely consider permanency in their relationships.

* After 38, male levels of commitment diminish, plummeting after 43.

* When a man's friends, colleagues and siblings start to get married, this triggers a domino effect. He doesn't want to be left behind and is more likely to leap onto the marriage bandwagon than watch it roll past.

* Men's lives are also governed by biological clocks that start to tick in their late thirties and early forties. They aren't worried about being able to father a child, but they do want to be young enough to play actively with their children and encourage sport, adventure and fun. Men invariably imagine having sons with whom they can bond as fellow males, play football, go camping, ride bikes, etc. Therefore, men in this age bracket who say they want a family are ideal candidates for marriage.

* His own family life as child has a bearing on a man's attitude to marriage later in life. A happy, stable childhood provides a firm foundation. If his parents fought, bickered and divorced when he was young, then he may hesitate before formalising commitment.

* It's obviously true that opposites attract, but statistically, marriages have a better chance of survival if the man and woman have similar backgrounds (socio-economic, religious and political) and are matched psychologically, professionally and spiritually with shared personal tastes and values.

* Don't dismiss a good man out of court if he doesn't initially impress you with his physical presence or mannerisms. You might not notice

him at first because he has been dismissed by women many times in the past for his perceived failings. He might well be hiding a number of good points or they might get overlooked because you are not seeing him as he is. Many women I've interviewed have 'discovered' wonderful things about their partners as their relationships progressed. Be open-minded because these unpolished jewels are usually keeping the most attractive aspects of their personalities under wraps. Such men are often strong candidates for marriage. How many of your married friends' husbands, in your opinion, are beyond perfection?

* Divorcees and widowers over the age of 40 are more likely to marry than their 40-year-old single counterparts.

So, to enhance your chances of finding a life partner, seek and flirt with the marrying type. Meanwhile, steer well clear of the following:

Stringers or serial monogamists

Check out his track record and examine his state of independence. Does he value his own space too much and apart from the sex, how close does he get to the real you? Does he give off any commitment signals? Take his emotional temperature and if it's cold, find someone else to warm the cockles of your heart.

Married men

If you are dating a married man, who still lives with his wife and family but promises to leave them, then you are being lied to: he *won't* leave and he *won't* set up home with you. If you do manage to marry him, beware. The excitement from the days of your clandestine assignations is likely to vanish because the chase and the secrecy will be over. How long will it be before he eschews monogamy and seeks sexual comfort elsewhere?

Mummies' boys

It probably goes without saying, but try and avoid a man who still lives at home with mum. Men who have their own homes and have lived as self-supporting, independent adults are more likely to marry. And you wouldn't want a mother-in-law moving in as part of the marriage deal, would you? Avoid a man with an Oedipus complex. No matter how wonderful you are, you'll never come close to receiving the level of adulation he has for his mother.

Misers

Men who regard the institution of marriage as some kind of financial coup for women and a fiscal disaster for themselves are unlikely to marry, and don't make good prospects either. Meanness is an unpleasant streak in anyone and marrying someone who regards his hard-earned fortune as 'all mine', protected with a lengthy pre-nup is unlikely to mellow or start to share. Run!

40.

Exploiting the second relationship window — a dating expert explains

At the back of most single people's minds is the hope that one day soon they will meet someone special. Perhaps they have never met the right person. Maybe they married the wrong person. Perhaps they want to start a family or find a suitable partner to be parent to their own children. Whatever the reasons, there is a plethora of single people out there scouring the country in search of love. Not surprisingly, the singles business has capitalised on this demand for partners and there is a burgeoning market of websites, advertisements, singles clubs and introduction agencies all promising to find true love for their clients, in exchange for money.

But is it possible to click on your perfect life partner in cyber space and meet in your email Inbox? Or is the personal touch more effective? However easy it is to join social networks and line up a string of dates online, in the end it's all going to boil down to chemistry and one's approach to relationships. And as some women who are getting older start to panic, they must surely overcome their fears and learn not to prejudice or jeopardise an encounter with a potential Mr Right.

I got married and had my children in what I thought then was the nick of time. Casting my mind back, I remember those feelings of urgency, desperation and despair. I recall doing the sums – checking to see how old someone was when she'd had a baby, exhaling with relief when I read how a 45-year-old celebrity had just given birth, and mentally doing everything I could to buy myself a few more years. If I could just meet 'the one' and have babies. And hey, 37 isn't really that old, is it? What if there isn't a man on the planet who wants to be with me? How empty will my life be if I never have children? It must be a volume thing. If I can meet 100 'suitable' men, then one of them must be OK, mustn't he? I'm an ideal prospect and I'll be spoilt for choice . . . Won't I?

Unfortunately, the metronome ticking of biological clocks is symptomatic of the ageing process in childless women over 35. For some women, the emotions surrounding the desire to have a child can be extremely powerful, overwhelming even. And if they aren't kicked into touch, they can prove destructive. It was much easier for our mothers' and grandmothers' generations: Women then didn't have the same career aspirations as women today; feminism hadn't yet decreed that we could have it all; the Pill hadn't been invented and married women couldn't even pay tax or have a mortgage without the intervention of their husbands. I can remember as a child family jibes about an aunt 'who nearly missed the boat as she didn't get married until she was 28'. I also resolved that I would get married at 21, just like my mother, and have my first baby when I was 25. Little did I imagine I would have to add around 18 years to both those figures in order to aspire to the status of 'married with children'.

When I was about 12, my mother told me that the best time in a woman's life is when she reaches 30. By then, she has a husband, children and a family home. She is still young at heart, but also worldly wise and she still has her looks and energy. When she reaches 30, a woman has reached her personal zenith.

That rather saccharine image may well have been possible for some women in the 1960s and 70s, but today, things seem to have been shunted on another ten years. Forty is indeed the new 30. It now takes a bit more than an additional decade to assemble the whole package. But it can, and is being done. You only need to look at the statistics to see that in the UK women are marrying later and the ages at which they are giving birth are continuously setting new boundaries.

So I arranged a meeting with personal dating agent and relationship expert Mairead Molloy. A fresh-faced late thirtysomething herself, for the last five years she has run Berkeley International, an elite intro-duction agency. I wanted to find out about relationship prospects for this burgeoning demographic of single women and uncover the secrets to success.

Mairead is a guerrilla dating agent. Armed with her mobile phone and an encyclopaedic knowledge of her clients, she juggles the needs and aspirations of everyone. She consoles the disconsolate, sends flowers to the disappointed and eggs on the romantically cautious. For those who need it, she'll demand a diet and exercise programme to get them in shape. And Mairead is upfront and personal with anyone with bad hair, urging them to get an appointment at Michaeljohn and 'sort it out, for God's sake!' But it's her mix of agony aunt intuition and empathy coupled with perspicacity and passion that enables her to connect with everyone she meets. Her phenomenal success at linking people to their life partners ensures a home mantelpiece chock-full with wedding invitations.

Although it costs thousands of pounds to have your name in Mairead's little black book, her reputation for zoning in on the perfect partner guarantees a steady line of hopefuls at her door. For many years Berkeley International has boasted an extraordinary record of introducing successful and intelligent people to equally discerning life partners. The agency has almost 2,000, mainly professional, people on its books – 50:50 men and women – spanning all ages, but with the majority between 30 and 45.

Having married into an Irish family myself, I am well accustomed to the frank, say-it-as-it-is approach of the Irish, so over afternoon tea in her exclusive Mayfair club, Mairead from County Wexford gave it to me straight.

Mairead says that all her clients want to settle down and live happily ever after. 'Isn't that what everyone wants deep down, if they are honest? That's what I aim to do – get people married. But this is a two-way thing: I have to work with people who have the right attitude to the opposite sex as well as to themselves.

'I know within the first two minutes whether or not a person is going to be successful at finding love. It isn't about how attractive or successful they are, how developed their sense of humour or about the expanse of their bank balance: it's all about how happy they are within themselves. That's the key. It doesn't matter how much a woman's got to offer, if she is desperate because time is running out, this will show and it will scupper her chances – not just with us, but through any other means too. I have seen it happen literally hundreds of times.' Harsh words, perhaps, but Mairead speaks with first-hand experience of having met more people seeking a life partner than the rest of us.

'Our success rate at finding partners for women in their late thirties or early forties is defined by certain factors. If she's normal, if she's content with her life, if she's unburdened by emotional clutter from previous relationships and if she's not coming across as desperate, then we have little trouble creating a near perfect match. But there are a lot of ifs to consider, and it's sad that so many content, happy, well-adjusted women seem to self-destruct when they hit their late thirties.'

I had read somewhere that Mairead referred to 'relationship windows' in defining optimum timeframes for people to meet and settle down. In response she says: 'Your twenties are for having fun. Some people settle down then, but I don't get many 23-year-old ladies asking me to find them a husband. However, by the time they are around 28, subconsciously, single women become aware about relationship windows. In their minds, they have about seven years to meet someone, settle down and have a family, as there is a perception that this relationship window slams shut at 35, drastically affecting their chances of finding love and a life partner. I see a stream of highly organised, focused women in their early thirties who don't want to miss out, so they come to me to help them.

'Typically, they're educated, overworked, high-achieving and financially independent. They imagine that they'll settle for anyone and walk into our offices professing to have an open mind. But often the reality is that they are on a precarious fulcrum, and the slightest setback could tip them into mainstream desperation. Peer pressure and our media-obsessed society require them to conform to acquiring the ideal husband: someone of a similar age who is tall, rich, hilariously funny, popular and handsome. They choose to overlook the reality that most men have one or maybe two of these attributes, but for every upside, there's a downside. Whatever happened to finding someone who is fun, kind, gentle and loving and can prepare a decent Sunday roast, or who has the potential to be a lifelong soul mate?'

I asked Mairead why, if women are aware of the relationship window, they miss out on it. 'There are two main reasons: first, some women become consumed by their personal and financial independence and are simply too busy for commitment. At 37 they suddenly look up from their BlackBerrys and ask, "Hey, where's the man in my life?" And second, they're having affairs with married men – and we do get a lot of these. Believe me when I say that married men, when they promise to leave their wives, never do. It is a case of "always the mistress, never the wife". Don't go there if you want to settle down with someone and have kids. It just isn't going to happen. Married men want their sex on the side – they don't want a costly divorce, a downgraded lifestyle and everlasting monogamy.'

Like a beacon of hope to the woman reaching the end of her thirties, Mairead has identified a second relationship window, which opens up roughly between 38 and 44: 'We have on our books, a host of women within this age group who are divorced, with or without children, who have come out of long affairs or are single and looking for a husband. I match them with a whole band of fortysomething men who might also be divorced and don't want more kids, or with guys ready to do it all over again.'

However, Mairead's biggest placement challenge is for the woman of 45 who has missed her second relationship window. She says: 'A 45-year-old woman wants to date a man who is around 47, or perhaps a good-looking 50-year-old. But the sad fact is that a 47-year-old man wants to find a 40-year-old woman. Stalemate is reached when the 45-year-old woman doesn't want to date the sixtysomething man who wants to go out with her. And yet she's terrified of facing 50 alone – and that comes across big time.'

This all seems very ageist. Why is everyone so hung up on age when the rules of attraction are based on looks, personality and chemistry? Mairead says: 'People are *obsessed* with their age. Just about everyone I interview lies about their age too. The saddest thing is I see so many lonely people. I hear, "I just can't go to weddings and parties by myself anymore." All they want is to have someone to love and be loved and for companionship – age is actually irrelevant.'

Today, finding love through dating agencies, online dating and by placing lonely-hearts advertisements is widely acceptable. The desire to meet someone is there, it just seems that huge numbers of people just don't know how to settle down. Maybe with all this choice, they are always searching for someone better – they don't know when to stop. Also, it would appear this epidemic of loneliness has made women so paranoid that they are segmenting their lives into windows of opportunity. If finding love is paramount, why is everyone failing?

In response, Mairead says, 'We do have a lot of success with women in their late thirties, but as I said earlier, this mostly boils down to their attitude to men and themselves. It is worth highlighting what men want: men like confident women who are not in any rush. They like a bit of mystery and want to experience the thrill of the chase. They don't want someone with screaming ovaries handed to them on a plate demanding a wedding and instant procreation.

'So, as we evolve socially to seek fulfilment a decade later than our mothers' generation, we have to re-adjust to make our lives meaningful. Scary and impossible as it sounds, relationship success is about slowing down. Not giving up, but letting go of all that self-imposed pressure. Your life won't end if you don't meet someone, but to be happy, you have to fulfil yourself.'

I asked Mairead about success. What, in dating agency speak constitutes success, and what is her success rate? 'We consider an introduction to be successful when a relationship goes beyond six months. Eighty-nine per cent of our introductions for people under the age of 34 are successful. In the age bracket 35–50 we currently have a 72 per cent success rate.

'I'm very selective about who we take on as clients. Our fee levels generate high expectations from our clients and our business thrives on successful introductions. Our success rates are high because we are discerning. Regretfully, I do have to turn away some people, both men and women, because I don't believe I can help them.'

I wanted to end my interview with Mairead on a positive note, so I asked her what advice she would give to a woman in her late thirties who is angling to fill her second relationship window. 'Just be happy within yourself. Do this by distracting yourself away from the gnawing worry about meeting "the one". Take up some new interests, travel, or do something daring or caring. Smile, laugh more, be optimistic and open-minded about *everything*. If you can create an aura about you that is positive, confident and content, everything else will fall into place.'

www.berkeley-international.com

41.

New beginnings

Rhona Mackie

Do not stand at my grave and weep
I am not there; I do not sleep.°

I was married to Jeff, a good, kind, funny and loving man: my husband, my rock, my soul mate, my best friend. I was so, so fortunate – I had it all.

And then he was gone. Jeff left this world quickly and painlessly, without saying goodbye. He breathed his last breath lying on our bed, one hot Sunday afternoon, while I vacuumed downstairs.

I am a thousand winds that blow,
I am the diamond glints on snow,
I am the sun on ripened grain,
I am the gentle autumn rain.°

Hypertrophic Cardiomyopathy (HCM) was the hidden killer, which lurked deep within Jeff's heart. No one knew it was there and no doctor could ever have diagnosed it. It was genetically heritable and lethal.

He had returned early from playing cricket at our neighbouring village, feeling unwell. 'Probably a virus,' he said. Jeff drew the curtains in our room, took off his shoes and lay down in his whites for the last time.

When you awaken in the morning's hush
I am the swift uplifting rush
Of quiet birds in circled flight.
I am the soft stars that shine at night.°

After a couple of hours, I brought him up a cup of tea. The room was dark and still, and I couldn't hear him breathing. He was cold and damp. I tried to wake him, but I was too late. My dear husband, aged just 37, had died 13 months after our May blossom wedding.

After World War I, someone wrote:

Grief has no wings.
She is the unwelcome lodger that squats on the hearthstone between us and the fire and will not move or be dislodged.

Grief stayed with me for a full year. All around me were spaces he had once occupied, but had now vacated, plus all the memories. His suits hung in the wardrobe for months. His cricket whites, Wellingtons, tools, shaving kit, CDs, whisky decanter, contact lenses, laptop and his car just stayed there. His polo shirts, his underwear, his shoes, his cufflinks, his briefcase, his mobile and his eclectic library were all immovable. I wanted to smell him and envelop myself in his lingering presence. I wanted to feel his broad shoulders, run my hands through his blond curls, see his generous smile and hear him shut the front door and drop his keys in the bowl. Who would make me laugh and smile? Who would tell me I was pretty? Who would tell me every day that he loved me? I could feel him near me. In my dreams at night I could hear his whispered regrets for having left so suddenly. I wanted him to stay. Why did he have to go?

I am in the flowers that bloom,
I am in a quiet room.
I am in the birds that sing,
I am in each lovely thing.°

Till death us do part. My family and friends were there for me, wholeheartedly, but I just felt empty – trapped in a void. Before he died, we had been making plans to start a family, so my grief was compounded for my departed husband and the children that we would never have.

I was at a critical stage in my own life, with just a few years available to me whereby I might be able to have a child. With that thought uppermost in my mind, and with the certain knowledge that Jeff would have hated me to 'mope about', I initiated closure. He wasn't coming back. I couldn't go on living in the past and wallowing in misery. Time does heal, not completely but slowly, piece by piece.

And so, after a year, having 'talked this through' in my flickering dreams with Jeff, I got rid of his things and cleared his physical presence from our home. But I kept our wedding photograph, the one with the cherry blossom blowing on our laughing faces like confetti. I could, and would never forget that I married my rock, my soul mate and my best friend.

Hasna is my bereavement counsellor. She has been visiting me for a few months now and we sit in the living room, sipping coffee, and talking. She is helping me set myself straight, as I am emotionally out of kilter. How could I love someone else? How do I stop comparing everyone with Jeff? Would Jeff be watching if I embraced another man? Who would ever want such a battered wreck as me?

I have so many questions and there is a constant knot of pain in my solar plexus, but I am working through it. I am learning to look to the future and to brighten the flame within. I had three very happy years with Jeff, for which I am grateful. He has gone now, but there is more happiness out there, if I wish to find it.

> Do not stand at my grave and cry,
> I am not there; I did not die. °

With grateful thanks to Rhona Mackie, a nursery teacher, who was widowed at 39.

°'Do not stand at my grave and weep' by Mary Elizabeth Frye (1905–2004).

42.

Picking up the pieces after divorce

The popular perception of single women in their thirties and forties is that, for whatever reasons, they have never married. Divorced women are regarded somewhat differently. They did get married but it didn't work out. Bizarrely, society is more accepting of single people who are divorcees. 'They've been there, done that, so they're OK.' This is strange because in most cases, the lives of divorcees are more complex than people who have never married. Although legally no longer married, there may still be links through children, property and financial arrangements. And they may carry with them a whole gamut of emotions and attitudes from a bad marriage into the next phase of their lives.

Catherine, 37

I was blinded by love when I met Neil and we epitomised the perfect couple. The envy of my friends, I had bagged a corker when we got married. My hen party was four days' pony trekking in Iceland, and Neil and his buddies hit the golf circuits in Spain. We were both 32 and our wedding for 200 represented an extravagant and hedonistic public display of our love for each other. As soon as I had tossed my bouquet to the upstretched hands of my closest single friends, we were wafted away for an idyllic honeymoon in the Seychelles.

But four years on, I have to say that, in my opinion, marriage is over-rated. Getting married is the ultimate target of so many women, who believe a ring on their finger and the title of Mrs will somehow transform them into a happier person. The reality can be somewhat different.

I don't know of any woman who looks forward to emptying the dishwasher every day or scooping up wet towels from the floor, but after the high octane rush of the marriage ceremony and honeymoon, everyday life was much the same as before. Neil and I certainly came crashing down to reality after our nuptials, and although we settled at his house, while mine was rented out, we seemed to lack permanence. Yes, we were married, yes, we were happy at first, but we were co-existing alongside each other in his house. I began to feel I had compromised my life, while his was enhanced. I quickly put on hold all thoughts I'd hitherto had regarding babies.

Nineteen months after we married, Neil woke up next to me one morning and said, 'Cath, I'm sorry, but I just don't love you any more.' I was stunned that he'd said it, but I understood what he meant and the feeling on my part was mutual. I just wish I'd said it first.

We got divorced, and it was easy to split the proceeds, as I just moved back into my house. I didn't feel anything about the collapse of our marriage – I was completely inert. But I did feel terrible for my parents who had been so generous and financially pushed in funding our lavish wedding. As Neil and I divvied up the wedding gifts and our short life together I felt as if I had cheated all our guests by not continuing with the marriage dream.

Marriage had been a costly and foolish exercise for both of us. Like a tempting window display, we had been lured in without thinking things through.

I am now far more reserved in my attitudes to men. I don't need commitment, and I'm not sure that I want to remarry; I think I would prefer to keep the door slightly ajar. Oddly, I think that this attitude is something that men actually like. They don't want a woman who comes on strong, or is planning her imaginary life in cosy co-habitation. I would like to have children, but I am prepared to sit this one out for as long as it takes. Only fools rush in, and I have learned my lesson.

Patty, 41

I was 39 when my decree absolute plopped onto the doormat. After 19 years of marriage, I was for the first time in my life living as an adult alone. I am so grateful to have my two beautiful daughters, but as A-levels loom and university beckons, I know that they will flee the nest in a few years and it will just be me, rattling around in this house of memories.

For most of our marriage, Tod and I were happy, but he was never content – he always wanted something new, bigger or better. He was never satisfied with anything – his job, our home, his car, or any of his numerous gadgets. He always wanted the next best thing so I shouldn't have been surprised when he decided to trade me in for a younger model.

I must have been the last person on the planet to discover his affair with a divorced mother from our daughters' school: it wasn't just his deception that was so hurtful, but the fact that so many other 'friends', who I'd sat next to at school concerts and rubbed shoulders with at social events over the years, chose to say nothing. I just couldn't get over it. And the very same people came rallying their support when they heard that we had split up; I couldn't believe the insincerity. So I am now divorced from my husband *and* a significant part of my peer group.

While my self-esteem hit rock bottom a year or so ago, I have regarded 'being divorced' as a positive thing – I am free to do things that interest me, and now the girls are gaining their independence, I can explore the world and take on new challenges. I may have been a meek little wife, but I didn't take divorce lying down. With the very best legal representation I could afford, Tod got an absolute pasting in the courts, so I am financially secure and no longer have to share my life with a complete tit!

I have taken up line dancing and fencing, I read voraciously and my only promiscuity is in reading books (anything). I've also started to travel. I've been solo across India on a train and will be learning scuba diving in the Red Sea later this year. Divorce has given me a new lease of life, prompting me to give up my career in marketing. I am now a freelance journalist, with a novel in the pipeline. I have a new network of friends (most of them divorced) and have found a more meaningful, purposeful existence being in command of my own destiny.

If I wasn't already a mother, I think my outlook at this late age would have been completely different. But with regards to a 'love interest', although I am fully occupied in my life, I would like to meet someone else, for the companionship. I'm worried about my ability to present myself and flirt. Having been married for so long I have forgotten how to be attractive, and I hardly ever make the most of my appearance. I have met interesting people on my travels and am discovering the real me – it's a revelation. I don't want any more babies, but someone content with his life with whom to share my new experiences and maybe even grow old alongside does appeal.

Sarah, 38

With marriage, what you see is not always what you get. Marriage is an investment and you are buying into a promise. The marriage package promises a lot: a lifetime of love, fidelity, security, friendship, growing old together, sharing responsibilities as well as worldly goods. I went into marriage believing I was buying the dream. In reality I was just renting it – I got the reverse of the deal on offer.

There is nothing new about divorce and nothing shameful either. It happens to lots of people, but for me it left a bitter legacy.

I married at 34 and we divorced when I was 37. Although we had fallen out of love, we started trying for a baby in the final six months of our marriage. It could have been a lifesaver, but conception just didn't happen. We discovered that I had fertility problems, which although not insurmountable, would take time and money to fix. So rather than hang around in a miserable, barren union, Sean decided to ship out and shack up with someone else.

Seeing your former husband have children with another woman hurts (especially as we were still legally married at that point). I didn't want him, but I didn't want anyone else to have him either. I was the one who yearned for children and now he was having them and I was isolated, infertile and alone.

I wish with all my heart I could shrug off the state of emotional melancholia, which enveloped me when he'd gone. Divorce papers put an end to everything in a legal sense, but it's impossible to quell the flood of bitterness that slops around me.

I have some serious work to do before I can contemplate my future. I am seeing a wonderful therapist, who, in me as a patient, has her work cut out. I have issues I need to get over, including the prospect of never being a biological mother. I need to learn to like myself and to laugh again. Only then can my legacy of divorce slip into the past and be forgotten. Only then, can I contemplate the kind of future I want.

Claire, 38

Divorce is similar to splitting from a long-term boyfriend, only much, much bigger. The emotional fallout is just the same, but more turmoil lies ahead in the form of protracted legal wrangling. With a boyfriend, providing you aren't linked through shared property, you split and hopefully, you'll never see him again. This helps you get over the tumultuous upheaval. If you have a child and you get divorced as I did, it's bad – bad for you, and bad for the child. The shakedown was devastating for my three-year-old son, Fin, who suddenly lost his dad and only gets to see him at weekends.

It was bad for me, in that the acrimony on both sides never went away. Jon will always be involved in our son's upbringing (and I wouldn't want this any other way for Fin), so he'll be around for a long time. We will witness each other's relationships. In Jon's case, I already have to endure his girlfriend reading my son bedtime stories, preparing his lunch and driving him about in her sports car. She has no maternal instincts and I can tell that she resents his presence and demands when he stays at weekends.

I work myself up into a complete state when Fin is late being brought home after the weekend, worrying what could possibly have happened. Jon does it deliberately – not all the time, but often enough.

Would I want to marry again? Oddly enough, yes, I think I would. Ideally, I would like to end up with someone who already has children. My life ticks along, but it's complicated at weekends, during holidays and at Christmas. Now that Fin is about to start at an independent school, I can envisage more disputes and pettiness as me and my ex-husband beg to differ on how he is to be raised and educated. I couldn't therefore see myself with a partner who leads an organised, uncomplicated existence; it just wouldn't work. No, bring on a divorced guy with kids, who has to juggle his life around his ex, and let him join the party! This is normal life in the 21st century – a complex mishmash of arrangements, finances, exchanges, acrimony, children and love long gone.

K., 46

I have just got divorced from J. Nobody else was involved. To the outside world we were the perfect couple, but behind closed doors we were both nasty and snarling. I was his third wife. I got married at 41, and I knew I was letting myself in for trouble. J. is a chef, who had cut his teeth on the top New York restaurant scene. Over the last ten years he has worked for two multi-millionaires, so our lifestyle has been on the periphery of the jet-set highlife in the world's capitals and on yachts in the Caribbean. We have two young daughters. J. has a 20-year-old son from his first marriage.

A chef is a volatile, demanding perfectionist. He works under immense pressure, in great heat and unsociable hours, all the while seeking ever-greater culinary achievements. His reputation is constantly at stake and he doesn't suffer fools or shirkers. Hardly surprising then that he doesn't have the resources, time or energy to make marriages work.

I knew what I was letting myself in for when we married. I married late, for the first time and took a chance. J. is rakishly handsome, charming and popular. I saw him as a real catch. How could two previous wives have walked away from this? They must be mad! We were happy for a while, oddly enough when we were peripatetic and had no base. As soon as we became grounded and lived together in our own house, our marriage disintegrated. Like thousands of other women, I tried to pick up the pieces and maintain seamless normality for the girls. My marriage failed – there was no one else involved. We just didn't like each other any more. It happens to lots of people and it's hard, painful and life altering, but I'm getting through it. I have my lovely daughters, a good job and half-shares in our houses in Long Island and Hampstead. We will share everything out, including a Transatlantic existence bringing up of the girls.

What irks me is that J. has done it all before – twice. He's an old hand at divorce and has passed across the threshold with barely an emotional blemish. I, on the other hand, am weary and battle-scarred from the breakdown. I'm braving all the anguish and upheaval while trying to hold down a job, a jolly façade at school and a 'normal' family life.

I would urge any woman in my position – marrying late because there are no other options to someone with a poor relationship history – to brace themselves for failure. It will be easier when this eventually happens, and you will be pleasantly surprised if it doesn't. One failed marriage is forgivable, two or more is asking for trouble!

43.

Finding love on a shoestring

When I first began to compile this book, things were definitely good out there. Business was booming and for most of us, lifestyle and career opportunities were there for the taking. For those with a sense of adventure or seeking new horizons, the zeitgeist was about riding the crest of the boom wave and having access to it all. We could have our cake and eat it – and take another slice for later too.

But by the time this book went forward for publication, the feel-good factor had evaporated, and events had taken a dramatic turn downward – in some cases, backward. Like many other countries in the world, we find ourselves immersed in a deep and long-forecasted recession. Some authors and journalists have been quick off the mark to produce copy on frugal living, cheap travel, economic recipes and ways to hang on to our diminishing assets, but I have yet to see anything on cutting costs for lonely hearts. Dating, whatever your age, tends to be an expensive business for men and women alike. So how do you cut back financially, while moving forward romantically?

In 1997, in the build-up to the dot.com bubble, there was prosperity and opportunity. For most people, times weren't particularly hard. That was the year I met my husband, Stephen. At the time, I was living and working in London, while he did the same about 100 miles away in Gloucestershire. We saw each other at weekends, but circumstances dictated the majority of our courtship was conducted over the phone.

Today, with free phone and video connections through organisations like Skype, the phone can be an effective and economical assistant in the dating process. You don't need to be all dressed up in order to have a good conversation; you have access to someone at odd times of the day and night, and you can just talk and be yourself. And you can dispense with all the preoccupation about having lipstick or spinach stuck on your teeth and slob out in your dressing gown sporting greasy hair. During hours of conversation you can ask all sorts of questions more tricky to approach on a contrived dinner date and debate politics, the economy, make confessions, explore fantasies and make each other laugh. And it's fairly low cost too. All this fun, just by staying in.

Over 18 months, Steve and I notched up hundreds of hours of calls and we discussed everything. In many ways, we had more to say on the phone than we did when we were surrounded by other distractions. Our conversations digressed and pinged off at different tangents; they were quirky, funny and fascinating. Email had just hit the mainstream, so we augmented our calls with electronic quips, anecdotes, observations and jokes. By talking every day, it over-rode the long-distance weekend relationship arrangement and helped bring us even closer together.

In the not too distant past, it was possible to rack up quite a lot of expenditure in the initial stages of a potential relationship – dressing to impress, eating out, a taxi home. It all added up, and for some meeting a series of new men regularly (through Internet dating, for instance), the costs could be high. Spending good money on a first date without actually getting as far as 'I'd really like to see you again,' was wasteful and potentially financially limiting for the next night out.

With the dramatic downturn in the economy, money is tighter than ever before while thrift has forced most of us to downplay our aspirations. However, this era of prudence also ushers in new challenges without removing our ability to be impressed. It is possible to dispense with rampant materialism and embrace a culture of simplicity and invention in our wooing.

So, where to go on a cheap first date? Walking with a potential beau offers a perfect excuse to escape the rat race and get out and about. An adventurous weekend stroll in a part of the countryside or city unfamiliar to you both, armed with a map and some sturdy boots is fun, challenging, invigorating plus a good way to put the world to rights and be the real you. All those ions wafting about on the sea breezes at the coast will charge you with vitality. Views from the tops of hills, wide horizons or cities at sunset provide great talking points and eliminate awkward silences. Instead of a lavish dinner with a new outfit to match, why not head for a cheap noodle house to enjoy delicious food in an informal, bustling environment, while saving money in the process? You will learn far more about each other in these less contrived, more spontaneous encounters.

What's wrong with enjoying just a cup of coffee with a new man, rather than committing time and money to the formality of a restaurant, particularly if you feel a second date is unlikely? If you meet for a flirt over a cappuccino and things go well, you can always move on to somewhere more intimate and special. Museums and public art galleries also tend to be free (or inexpensive), as well as cultural. Thrift can be a great motivator, and many people are triumphant when they succeed in getting cheap, 2 for 1 or free tickets for the theatre, the cinema, the ballet or radio and TV show recordings. Then there's cooking a simple supper at home and/or opening a bottle of wine and just talking. Or going for a picnic in the park or hiring a rowing boat; perhaps playing cards or Scrabble, or maybe getting physical and competitive over Wii. On a second date, how about staying in and watching a hired DVD or listening to music?

All these things are ice-breakers and they don't need to cost the earth. Spending less on personal presentation is no bad thing either. Magazines and newspapers are full of examples of minted versus skinted fashion items. In that traditionally British way, it's far from taboo to boast about amazing bargains and discounts picked up on eBay or at fashionable charity shops.

If you are single and currently jobless, this doesn't necessarily mean that you won't be able to meet someone. By being proactive, through retraining, travelling out of your area to find new work and using your time to pursue your interests, you will come into contact with others, and who knows where that will lead?

I was made redundant in an earlier recession during the autumn of 1992. After the initial shock, I remember finding empathy and new friendships among the vast numbers of other people who also suddenly found they were jobless. This became a kind of club with a growing membership as redundant people gravitated towards each other. With their day jobs now defunct, erstwhile musicians, artists and hobbyists found time to cultivate and improve their talents and develop their artistry alongside other kindred spirits. Away from the stress of working and between trying to find other jobs, there was time to make new friends and explore other interests.

The quest for love will go on, as it has for thousands of years, undaunted by financial challenges. Our parents' generation grew up in post-war austerity and survived. And as frugal children of the Sixties and 'Seventies, my peer group made the most of what it had – we simply didn't know any better. I was happy with a single pair of platform shoes, a tank top, two pairs of bell bottoms, a cheesecloth shirt and some love beads. My wardrobe didn't extend much beyond that. Today's teens have been fired by rampant consumerism and a culture of acceptable debt, and we have all embraced the spending culture.

Materialism took a while to enter the everyday lexicon. Back then, we were blissfully unaware of the material excesses and indulgent lifestyles we would enjoy decades later . . . or the protracted payback to follow.

I'm sure that by focusing less on wealth and its trappings, we will come to learn more about each other and ourselves. Instead of shopping, there will be more time for talking; having less may give us a better sense of values and encourage sharing. We will see people for who they really are and not judge them on their net worth or the value of their property. The world will still keep turning, people will still fall in love, babies will continue to be born and friends will always be there for us . . . Unburdening our need to compete, impress and flaunt our success may ultimately be a good thing.

44.

Lonely heart ends up saying 'I do!'

OK, OK, throughout this book there have been several pieces in which women are positively encouraged to chill out, calm down and look the other way so they absolutely, definitely won't come across as desperate. And yes, it's true that up-front desperation is off-putting, even downright scary sometimes, but in researching this book, I have come across one true story in which this stance proved to be successful.

Anna Welles from Barnes in London (then 36) had split with her boyfriend of four years and was wallowing in self-pity. She felt washed-up, washed-out and with limited prospects on the love front: 'I wanted to go to sleep and wake up in the morning with a husband and a baby. I couldn't bear the prospect of looking, finding, courting and waiting in order to reach that conclusion – I wanted it all straightaway!' Jenny, a single friend, suggested they each place an advert in the *Daily Telegraph*'s 'Kindred Spirits' section for lonely hearts to see what would happen.

Feeling reckless, Anna decided to be bold and chose the following wording for her advert:

Pretty, witty, bright and keen as mustard. Naturally gorgeous, London-based 36-year-old seeks husband for love and procreation with whom to share fun times, mutual child rearing and fulfilling family life. If you're happy, solvent and ready for a challenge, let's meet up. Box 1524

She went on to leave a voicemail message as part of the advertisement, emphasising her good points, being positive about herself and her outlook, while clarifying the fact that she was looking for a husband and wanted to have children. Soon. She explained, 'Why is it that when a woman is bold enough to be direct everyone goes into paroxysms of "Oh my God, you can't do that. All the men will run a mile!" Well, the ad was only £95 and I thought I would cut to the chase early on.'

But she was stunned by the response: her friend Jenny received 173 replies by post and on the voicemail, while Anna had just 34. (This was in 1997 before Internet dating took off.) Jenny whittled down her selection to about seven men, while Anna struggled to refine her list.

'There were one or two obvious circulars in my mailbag – guys who had photocopied or written the same boring letter to everyone, plus a couple of cranks left messages on the voicemail. But most of the replies were genuine and many said the same thing – they too wanted to reach a quick dating conclusion. A lot of men were tired of being 'set upon' after a few dates by desperate women who were unable to keep up the pretence of being cool. My in-your-face approach was, apparently, refreshing. They all wanted to meet and, like me, were open-minded. At least we wouldn't have to tiptoe around each other, avoiding the c, m and b words (commitment, marriage and babies).

'So I corresponded with the 15 who were geographically closest. I had to draw the line somewhere as I didn't fancy trekking off to Switzerland or the Highlands on a blind date. We talked at length on the phone and I had never felt so popular. A few proved to be a bit weird or desperate themselves so my filtration process continued. I arranged a series of dates with six of them, but only got around to meeting three: Angus, Rory and Laurie.

'They were all lovely, but I ended up marrying Angus. We met at a wine bar on the river and both knew instantly that "this was it". We both had similar jobs and wanted to move out to the country. We shared common interests, had followed almost identical patterns romantically and held mutual values and aspirations. He had a quick, sharp and intelligent sense of humour and in a flash we both felt a kind of immediate joy in each other's company. Marriage wasn't instantaneous, but we tied the knot 14 months after meeting. We now have two boys and live in rural Wiltshire.

'Happily married? Yes, indeed! But nothing ventured, nothing gained. If you are upfront in an advert about what you want, you have nothing to lose. If men are put off, they won't contact you and you'll avoid pussyfooting around with someone who has uncertain intentions and "never realised what it was that you really wanted".

'Most of the men you attract from an ad *will* be unsuitable, but if my or Jenny's experiences are anything to go by, assuming you're not a complete oddball yourself, you will definitely meet someone. Go for it!'

Anna told me she has an unusual montage on the wall inside their downstairs bathroom. It's a series of cuttings from the *Daily Telegraph*. The first is her 'Kindred Spirits' advertisement, followed by the announcement of Anna and Angus's engagement. Underneath are the birth announcements in the newspaper for each of their boys. So, a potted history of their life together hangs on the wall, all as a result of being upfront, honest and running out of time.

Jenny went on to have a string of dates from her advertisement, but nothing 'conclusive'. However, she placed another advertisement after attending Anna and Angus's wedding and has been living with Tony ever since. They now have a three-year-old daughter.

Of course technology has moved on since Anna found Angus. The following are some tips for Internet dating novices:

* **Write something original so you stand out from the crowd.** If you read through other people's profiles you will be amazed how many like 'cinema, eating out, log fires and country walks'. Fine, you might enjoy them too, but add something different to your profile. Who remembers the Pina Colada song?

* **Include a photo.** With digital photo editing software it is possible to 'retouch yourself' slightly, but avoid using a photograph taken twenty years ago. Again, pick something a little different to the usual mug shot. Janine, 34, met her husband through a dating site. She had a picture of her laughing, with sunglasses perched on her head, her hair streaming back, driving a convertible. Bruno, her large shaggy dog was next to her, hanging out of the window, mouth open in a huge grin, his ears also blowing back behind him. It was a wonderful, happy, fun, picture which spoke volumes about Janine's personality – and it found her a husband.

* **Be proactive.** Trawl the site for people who interest and attract you. Contact them first, don't wait for them to track you down. It may take a long time and you will undoubtedly receive interest from people who don't take your fancy, but like eBay, the good ones will be snapped up quickly and you'll want to be in the running.

* **Don't despair.** The frog-to-prince ratio is high in the hit-and-miss world of Internet dating. As with any kind of dating, or sifting through job applications at work, you'll have to work your way through a lot of dross before someone good catches your eye.

* **Don't be dejected if your perfect prospect doesn't write back.** There are lots of reasons for not getting a reply – he could have found himself an early bird, he might be swamped with hopefuls, you may not suit . . . Whatever you do, don't take it personally.

* **Avoid writing essays.** Introduce yourself with a short, intriguing email and just ask one or two questions. He will be compelled to reply. If you unleash two whole pages about how wonderful you are, like a guy on a first date getting a full-on blast of 'me, me, me', he might not feel the urge to reply.

* **Safety.** Whenever you meet someone who is not known to you or anyone who knows you, remember to take various steps to ensure that you are safe and can make a quick escape, if necessary. Avoid divulging too much information which could potentially compromise you later on.

45.

Meditations whilst flying a kite

Nadine Starr, 86

ritten by a woman in her twilight years, her poem looks back on her life and how she limited herself and conformed. Here, she speculates on how she would live her life again, had she the chance. I feel this poem is important because it underlines the fact that our lives are the real thing: if we don't live life to the full, exploit opportunities or be happy in ourselves, we will miss out. Although Nadine Starr was 86 when she wrote this, I believe it applies to all of us, whatever our age. Go seize the day!

Meditations whilst flying a kite

If I had my life to do over, I'd make more mistakes next time.

I would relax. I would limber up.

I would be sillier than I have been this trip.

I know of very few things that I would take seriously.

I would laugh more and cry less. I would be crazier.

I would worry less about what others thought of me and I would accept myself as I am.

I would climb more mountains, swim more rivers, and watch more sunsets.

I would watch less TV and have more picnics.

I would have only actual troubles and very few imaginary ones.

I would feel only sad, not depressed. I would be concerned, not anxious.

I would be annoyed, not angry.

I would regret my mistakes, but not feel guilty about them.

I would tell people that I like them. I would touch my friends.

I would forgive others for being human and I would hold no grudges.

I would play with more children and listen to more old people.

I would go after what I wanted without believing I needed it and I wouldn't place such a great value on money.

You see, I am one of those people who live life cautiously and sensibly and sanely, hour after hour, day after day.

Oh! I've had my moments, and if I had it to do over again, I'd have more of them. In fact I'd have nothing else.

Just moments, one after another, instead of living so many years ahead of each day.

I have been one of these people who has never gone anywhere without a thermometer, a hot water bottle, a gargle, a raincoat and a parachute.

If I had it to do over again, I'd go to places and do things travelling lighter than I have. I would plant seeds and make the world more beautiful. I would express my feelings of life without fear.

If I had my life to do over, I would start barefoot early in the spring and stay that way late into the autumn.

I would play hooky more and eat more ice cream.

I wouldn't make such good grades except by accident.

I would ride more merry-go-rounds. I'd pick more daisies . . . and I'd smile.

46.

The elusive life partner

This is not a book about dating. In fact, a trawl through Amazon identifies nearly 1,500 books under the search for 'dating', each of them promising to unlock the secrets to attracting and capturing the heart of a potential lover. Invariably these books are aimed at women and are stuffed full of rules, checklists, body language interpretations, makeover tips plus do's and don'ts.

There's no doubt that a businesslike approach to getting into dating shape might help, but I'm not offering that sort of information here. However, I feel this book would be incomplete if I didn't include reference to where people meet. The vast majority of the couples interviewed for this book met in a non-contrived way, through happenstance, serendipity or purely by chance. The special person you end up with is not some kind of wild animal to be stalked, tracked and ensnared. Love is elusive and it will find you when and where you least expect it. But if you don't want to wait and see what happens and prefer to help your chances of finding a life partner along, then I am happy to share with you the places and events where contributors to this book and others found success. In no particular order and with some overlap:

* **Travelling**: it's a volume thing. Trains, ferries, planes . . . all modes of transport carrying large numbers of people. Then there's the places themselves – wherever you travel in the world, you will meet people. So get yourself out and about.
* **Activity holidays** likely to attract men include cultural pursuits, cookery, hiking, climbing, trekking, walking, windsurfing, skiing, scuba

diving, sailing, tennis, golf, kayaking, mountain biking, diving, wildlife watching, creative writing and photography. Are you up for caving or pot holing, or taking flying lessons – almost exclusively male pursuits? What about dogsledding in Lapland, another manly exploit?

* **Recreational pursuits**: anything that involves being with people with common interests such as amateur dramatics, a cycling club or a walking group, hang-gliding, gliding, sailing, horseracing, off-roading or playing in a squash or tennis league. How about a book group, regatta, choir, cricket matches, hockey team, wine appreciation, ballroom or Latin dancing? Can you sing or play a musical instrument well? Find out about auditions.

* **Quirky**. Sometimes the right man is there when you least expect him – playing a film extra, in the checkout queue at the supermarket, during a prolonged motorway hold-up, at a fun run, in the dentist's waiting room, garden centre, airport lounge or book signing. Anywhere. And of course, when you're looking your absolute worst that's the most likely time you'll meet someone special. Or join associations or discussion groups, round tables or livery companies to come across people who share your interests.

* **Courses.** Whatever you are passionate about. Again, you will be united by similar experiences or understanding. This could be an evening class, course, university or independently run classes or courses, business courses or attending college as a mature student.

* **Events.** The numbers thing crops up again, combined with common interests: TV audience, classical music concerts, exhibitions, country shows and festivals (arts, literary, pop and film).

* **Parties.** In these credit crunch times, people might be partying less, but try and get yourself on the invitation list to any of the following: house parties, dinner parties, drinks parties, Christmas parties, office parties, charity balls, launch parties, fundraising parties, barbecues, weddings, christenings and bar mitzvahs.

* **The Arts.** Attend book groups and launches, wine tastings, gallery private views, museums, previews and premières, art galleries, open-air concerts/theatre and poetry readings.

* **Divorced dads.** Remember, a lot of divorced fathers take their kids to the zoo or swimming at weekends.

* **Friends.** For blind dates, set-ups, straightforward introductions, friends of friends, friends of colleagues and brothers/cousins of friends. Tell people (discreetly – don't use a megaphone) that you're looking to meet someone – you never know from where the help might come.

* **Work.** A significant number of relationships germinate at, or through, work. This is hardly surprising as it takes up so much of our lives and brings us into continuous contact with people in the working environment, on courses and at social and corporate events. You can get to know someone quite well at work before your crush turns to romance, although they might distract you from your work. Jealous or disapproving colleagues or management may suddenly spring from nowhere to foil a discreet fledgling relationship. But the most obvious reason for treading carefully regarding a work-related romance is coping with the emotional turmoil if it doesn't work out.
* **Dating ads.** On-line dating, dating agencies or lonely-hearts advertisements).
* **Apparent misfortune**. At a funeral, during a rail strike or missed flight, when bookings become muddled up, in A&E . . . Cally Lowe crashed her car into one driven by Michael Brice: the ensuing legal, insurance and garage visits eventually led to marriage.
* **Steering clear.** I am told by British 'women of a certain age' who have tried cruises, speed dating, bar pick-ups and singles holidays that the chances of finding your perfect life partner are virtually zero. Avoid!

Holidays

From the hundreds of communications I have received from women who did meet their life partner during their late thirties and early forties, a significant proportion first set eyes on each other while on holiday. Two overwhelming factors became apparent here: a) the type of holiday and b) absolutely not taking a vacation with the intention of meeting someone.

For the single woman, there's a wealth of holidays out there but you need to be completely open-minded, prepared to enjoy your freedom and have fun, not dwell on the angst of being single. Things are more likely to happen as a result of avoiding family resorts or activity holidays aimed predominantly at women (yoga, for example) or singles.

Katy was 38 when she went on a charity trek in Peru. She met another single woman, Cindy, there and they became firm friends. Although Cindy lived two hundred miles away, they met up a few months after the trip. Cindy introduced Katy to her divorced brother Vince and they made an immediate impression on each other. A year later, they were married and they now have two children.

Claudia, then 40 (and in her own words 'horribly single'), met her husband Andrew, then 38, on a sailing holiday in Turkey. After trying and failing to book a flotilla yacht in Greece and then Croatia, she accepted a place with a group of people (even older than herself), none of whom she had met before, on a chartered yacht in Turkey. They sailed to towns and remote areas along the Anatoylian coastline. Claudia had an inspiring holiday although she had little in common with the people on the yacht. On the penultimate day of the voyage, they found a tiny cove on a small island, where just one yacht was moored. Claudia met Andrew sitting on a rock. They talked, swam, laughed and exchanged email addresses before departing on their separate yachts . . . they are now married.

Internet dating

Everything can be found on the Internet and the opportunity to trawl for cyber flirtations is vast. Dating websites have burgeoned to cater for a culturally diverse and geographically spread client base and sites exist for every interest and taste. Away from the larger, conventional dating sites is a plethora of sites targeting specific and wide-ranging love interests from millionaires to large people, wine lovers, dog lovers and music lovers. There are sites catering for people from particular faiths or ethnic origins, with a common purpose politically, ethically, or culturally; also for people within certain age brackets, for widowers, gays and lesbians, and for single parents. If on-line dating is the route you select, then there should be something or somebody to suit you, but go cautiously.

Alternatively respond or reply to a lonely-hearts ad in your preferred newspaper. Remember, you are more likely to find someone with a similar outlook to yourself if you start from common ground.

Singles organisations

From what I have gleaned in compiling this book, singles clubs, organisations and groups are not really the best places to meet a significant other. Carol-Anne, 44, is a member of a singles club in Wiltshire. She says: 'Our club has about 100 members and we undertake many activities and adventures as a group. The purpose of the group is not primarily to meet a soul mate, lover or potential spouse, but to have fun as a group.

'We are single for a variety of reasons – widowed, divorced, unmarried or out of a long-term relationship. The club provides friendship, companionship, laughter and a network of people to do a range of activities with, either on a one-to-one basis, or as a group. We might yomp ten miles across the Downs, ending up at a pub for dinner, or go to the theatre in London or play poker at someone's house late into the night. We've had picnics at the races, visited Barcelona for the weekend and been go-karting. All terrific fun. We're not a bunch of lovelorn, lonely misfits. Being single actually suits most of us and the club provides a close network of supportive friends. If you were married or in a close committed relationship, you'd be hard pressed to have as much variety in your life as we do!'

Dating/introduction agencies

You might use an estate agent to find a house and a recruitment consultant to find the perfect job, so why not employ the best people in the business to find you the perfect partner? Adverts for dating or introduction agencies are listed aplenty in the national and regional press. If your budget permits, take a closer look.

This book includes the advice of two dating gurus from the elite end of the introduction agency world, Mary Balfour and Mairead Molloy. Pay attention to their combined wisdom for they have met hundreds of hopefuls. Over the years they have witnessed many, many successes, but they have also seen dreams crushed through misadventure. A good match-maker is never off-duty: she attends exclusive events, private members' clubs and charity balls, scouring the room for exact matches for her client list. 'Are you single? Great! Here's my card. Give me a call because I know someone you must meet.' Their rigorous selection criteria and commitment to success means the calibre of candidates on their books is high, thus ensuring an excellent strike rate and lots of happy clients.

In conclusion

Speak to an adventurer or someone who travels and he or she will always be able to regale you with so many stories about things that happened to them on their way and the people they met. I think it's true to say that no one returning from a voyage of discovery would ever complain that they had not come across interesting people on their travels (unless they were trekking solo across the Arctic). It's human nature to socialise and interact; we like to feel some kind of connection with a place, usually through its history, culture or the people living there.

So, while it's easy to bemoan the fact that 'all the decent men have been snapped up', the reality is actually the opposite. There are plenty of good and interesting men out there. It's down to you to find or stumble across them, wherever they might be hiding. Being proactive, plus having a sense of adventure and serendipity all have their roles to play, and you must be the catalyst. If romance isn't happening in your life, tinker with your routine and focus your interests on a new project or revive former interests. Make the time too – don't let commuting, long hours or domestic routines stand in your way. Get out and start doing something you enjoy, something that brings you into contact with other people. You'll be pleasantly surprised by the new connections and opportunities you can discover or create.

47.

What am I like? A self-assessment questionnaire

If relationships aren't working out for you, what's going wrong? Perhaps you're repeating negative patterns that hinder your progress? It's now time to hold a metaphorical mirror up to yourself: take a long, hard look at who you really are. What are people's first impressions of you? How do you come across to men? Who is the real person behind the veneer? How have you changed in recent years? Who do you want to be, and what do you really want?

Over the next few pages, you'll find some positive and negative character assessments to complete, but first, you may need to clarify your attitudes to men and relationships. There are no scores or 'categorised types', but these prompts may help you to identify some of your attitudes and belief systems. Do any of the following apply?

Learning from the past

I'm an idealist with an exact idea of what I do and don't want.
I'm always attracted to the wrong kind of men.
My career and my life have been very successful. I think men are put off by this and feel threatened.
I'm way too hasty – I try to plan our future together at the start and move things along quickly.

Too much work, no play and not enough hours in the day scupper my chances of starting and continuing relationships.

Negative patterns – something inside me wells up to destroy or sabotage relationships before they get underway. I don't seem to possess the necessary skills to develop relationships.

I probably come across as too overbearing or controlling.

I try to be what I think he will want, and am not really being myself.

I may project a kind of desperation.

I possess a low personal sense of esteem.

I'm shy and lack confidence.

My need to have children is intense and off-putting.

I have fabricated pieces of my personal history in order to be attractive.

I confuse sex with love and I'm too eager to jump into bed.

I have issues/problems of which I'm aware, but I haven't done anything about overcoming them.

Other _____

So, what do I want from a relationship?

Love leading to marriage or co-habitation.

Closeness to one person, but gregarious and hectic social life too.

A committed and permanent lover, but retaining independence.

No man, just a child.

Just a man and to be child-free.

Financial security.

Friend and lover – open-ended and no pressure.

A soul mate.

Someone who shares the same interests and outlooks as me.

The complete opposite of me.

Togetherness, family life and children.

Other _____

Why I never even begin to find a partner

I'm nervous of rejection or being hurt, so I resist opportunities for meeting potential life partners.

Confusion about 'love'. What if I don't fall in love? What if *he* does? How does love affect commitment?

Pressure of work and long hours has sapped my energy and erased any potential opportunities.

I don't feel I have enough to offer – I'm not a good catch.

Incompatibility: I'm never attracted to men who are attracted to me.

I don't want to lose control or make sacrifices with my lifestyle.

I can't contemplate a new relationship until my children are grown up/I can stop caring for my mother/I stop travelling at work, etc., etc.

I don't want to waste valuable time dating the wrong kind of men.

All the decent, single men have already been snapped up.

I'm physically less attractive than I was when I was younger.

I have extremely high standards and won't give men a chance to win me over. I won't lower my standards.

Reasons why I don't meet available, single men

1. Circumstantial

I live in a remote place.

My job dominates my time.

I'm financially restricted.

My circle of friends has moved on.

2. Psychological

I'm shy.

I lack confidence.

I feel lonely.

I'm too inexperienced.

I'm too picky – I want perfection.

I attract the wrong kind of men.

I'm stuck in a rut.

There are no single men out there.

I try too early to get commitment.

I'm terrified of ageing.

What will I be like if I never have children?

3. Physical

I'm concerned about my appearance.

I'm concerned about my weight.

I'm aware that I am ageing.

I smoke/drink/take drugs to excess.

I need a make-over.

4. Habits
         I surround myself with my own set of friends.
         I lead an insular life.
         I don't make any effort to meet men.
         I'm too committed to other things _____

5. Things I would like to change
         My approach – I frighten men off.
         My tendency to meet the wrong kind of men.
         I would like to get beyond the first date.

There now follows a number of assessments that are to be done by you, *for* you. These are not tests and there are no scores, but they should help you to identify your strengths and weaknesses, your assets and your shortcomings. The assessments will allow you to establish certain targets and identify negative traits. Do the assessments again in a few months' time to make sure you are keeping on track. PDF versions may be downloaded from the links section on www.findingmrrightthebook.com

My best qualities

This is to be completed by you. Be absolutely honest with yourself – this doesn't have to be seen by anyone. Keep it somewhere safe and do the exercise again in a few months' time. Compare the results.

Date _____

My name is _____

My real age is ___ but I actually feel ___

Select from the following positive descriptive traits, those that you consider apply to you the most. Be careful about your selections and tick only those of which you are 100 per cent sure. Remember, this is you *now*, not what you want to be. Tick all that apply and complete any requiring a written response:

Positive traits

Adventurous
Affectionate
Appreciative
Attractive
Attractive to men
Beautiful: face, hair,
voice, legs, other _____
Bright
Capable
Caring
Charismatic
Cheerful
Classy
Clear thinker
Clever
Committed
Communicative
Compassionate
Confidante
Confident
Contemplative
Content
Cool
Creative
Curious
Dedicated
Deep-thinking
Diplomatic
Discerning
Disciplined
Domestic goddess
Efficient
Elegant
Empathetic
Energetic
Enigmatic
Extroverted
Faithful

Feel young
Feminine
Friendly
Fun
Funny
Generous
Gentle
Genuine
Get things done
Good company
Good dress sense
Good figure
Good flirt
Good mother
Good-natured
Gregarious
Happy personality
Happy with oneself
Healthy
Helpful
Honest
Idealistic
Imaginative
Independent
Insightful
Intelligent
Interested
Interesting
Intuitive
Joyful
Kind
Laid-back
Lateral thinker
Liberated
Light-hearted
Loving
Loyal
Magnetic personality
Maternal
Modest

Mysterious	Soft
Nurturing	Sophisticated
Open to new ideas	Strong
Optimistic	Stylish
Physical	Successful
Playful	Supportive
Popular	Sweet
Pretty	Sympathetic
Pure	Talented
Quirky	Tender
Reflective	Thoughtful
Relaxed	Tolerant
Self-respecting	Unconcerned about ageing
Sense of humour	Warm
Sensual	Wholesome
Sexy	Witty
Sharing	Younger-looking
Sincere	Zestful
Smart	Zany
Smiling	Other
Sociable	_____

My worst qualities

Don't be put off by the length of this list. There are far more negative traits listed here because single traits have been broken down into specifics. Once again, this is to be completed by you and you need to be absolutely honest. Keep the list somewhere safe and do the exercise again in a few months' time. Compare the results.

There is no restriction on the number of boxes you can check, but be as honest with yourself as you possibly can. Some traits, such as 'independent', appear on both the positive and negative lists – they will depend on your interpretation of the words.

Date _____

My name is _____

A moaner
A put-down artist
Addictive personality
Age – look older than actual age
Alcoholic
Always needs approval
Always right
Angry (prone to be)
Antisocial
Apathetic
Arrogant
Avoid commitments
Babies – unable to hear
   about/discuss/meet/hold
Bad driver
Bad eye contact
Bad hairstyle/bad skin/breath
Bad lover
Bad-mannered
Bad mother
Bad posture
Badly groomed
Bitchy
Bites nails
Biological clock (governed by)
Bitter about the past
Blind to _____
Boastful
Body odour
Boring
Brusque
Can't keep secrets
Can't relax
Career-dominated
Chaotic
Chemically dependent
Cold
Come over as too
   religious/political/alternative
Completely absorbed by

interests/hobbies/own life
   other _____
Conceited
Conformist (explain) _____
Controlling
Deprecating of men
Desperate (come over as)
Determined
Discontented
Dishonest
Disinterested
Disloyal
Dismissive
Disorganised
Distant
Doesn't ask questions
Doesn't listen
Doesn't pamper self
Dogmatic
Dominated by mother, father,
   brother, sister or another
   _____
Domineering
Dresses inappropriately
Driven
Easily offended
Emotionally bereaved by
   childlessness
Emotionally immature
Emotionally inhibited
Emotionally linked to ex-partner
Exaggeration (prone to)
Extroverted
Fall out with people easily/often
Feel intellectually inferior
Feel old
Feel rejected
Financial management (poor)
Flirt too much
Fitness – unfit/obsesssive

Frigid
Gloomy
Guilt tripper
Hormonal
Hung up by/on _____
Hypercritical
Immature
Impatient
Inconsiderate
Independent
Inefficient
Ingenuous
Inhibited
Insensitive
Insincere
Intellectually superior
Intense
Intolerant of _____
Intransigent
Introverted
Irritating _____
Jealous
Judgemental
Lacking commitment/
    creativity/dedication/energy/
    insight/intuition/other

    _____

Lacking interests/hobbies/other

    _____

Lacking self-respect/originality/
    spontaneity
Lazy
Lethargic
Liar
Likes to shock
Looks older than actual age
Manipulative
Martyr
Mean-spirited
Miserable

Morbid
Needing make-over/to be
    loved/to be needed/to impress
Negative attitude
Negative body language
Neurotic
No get up and go
No sense of fun
No sense of style
Not very bright
Obsessed by _____
Obsessed with success
Offensive
Older in outlook/attitudes than
    actual age
One dimensional
Out of touch
Over-confident
Over-emotional
Over-enthusiastic
Over-indulgent: food, drink,
    drugs
Over-organiser
Over-perfectionist
Panicky
Poor communicator
Possessive
Predatory
Preoccupied
Profligate with money
Promiscuous
Prudish
Quirky
Racist
Resigned to failure
Rivalrous
Sarcastic
Scary _____
Scatterbrained
Selfish

Self-deprecating
Self-obsessed
Sense of failure
Sexually deviant
Sexually inhibited
Shallow
Show-off
Showing signs of ageing in
    attitude
Showing signs of ageing
    physically
Slave to routines
Slutty dresser
Smothering
Snobbish
Socially inhibited
Stalker
Stereotypical _____
Stressed
Stick-in-the-mud
Stuck – in house, job, the past,
    emotionally, other

_____

Supercilious
Sycophantic
Talks too much
Talks with mouth full
Tense
Threatened by others because

_____

Threatening to others because

_____

Too intellectual/intense/loud/
    quiet/radical/serious/feminist

Too wrapped up in own physical
    attributes – height, weight,
    breasts, legs, nose, teeth other

_____

Traumatised
Tries too hard
Two-faced
Unable to flirt
Unable to hold drink
Unable to share
Unadventurous
Unappreciative
Uncaring
Unconformist (explain) ____
Unconfident
Un-cool
Under-emotional
Undermining
Undiscerning
Unfaithful
Unfeeling
Unfit (physically)
Unfriendly
Ungenerous
Uninhibited
Un-sexy
Unsophisticated
Unsympathetic
Untrustworthy
Violent
Volatile
Weak
Weight – overweight/too thin
Worried

Positive traits to which I aspire

Now tick the achievable traits to which you aspire. This is who you want to be. Be realistic – don't tick everything on the list, just enough so you can focus on working towards this. When you have done this, in your own handwriting (not typed) write down a list of these traits and add in the positive ones from the first list. Keep this list somewhere at home where you can see it every day – by your make-up mirror, on the fridge, by your computer . . . Now work towards it.

Date _____

My name is _____

Positive traits to which I aspire

Adventurous
Affectionate
Appreciative
Attractive
Attractive to men
Beautiful: face, hair,
    voice, legs, other _____
Bright
Capable _____
Caring
Charismatic
Cheerful
Classy
Clear thinker
Clever
Committed
Communicative
Compassionate
Confidante
Confident
Contemplative
Content
Cool

Creative
Curious
Dedicated
Deep-thinking
Diplomatic
Discerning
Disciplined
Domestic goddess
Efficient
Elegant
Empathetic
Energetic
Enigmatic
Extroverted
Faithful
Feel young
Feminine
Friendly
Fun
Funny
Generous
Gentle
Genuine
Get things done
Good company
Good dress sense

Good figure
Good flirt
Good mother
Good-natured
Gregarious
Happy personality
Happy with oneself
Healthy
Helpful
Honest
Idealistic
Imaginative
Independent
Insightful
Intelligent
Interested
Interesting
Intuitive
Joyful
Kind
Laid-back
Lateral thinker
Liberated
Light-hearted
Loving
Loyal
Magnetic personality
Modest
Mysterious
Nurturing
Open to new ideas
Optimistic
Physical
Playful
Popular

Pretty
Pure
Quirky
Relaxed
Self-respecting
Sense of humour
Sensual
Sexy
Sincere
Sharing
Smart
Smiling
Sociable
Soft
Sophisticated
Strong
Stylish
Successful
Supportive
Sweet
Sympathetic
Talented
Tender
Thoughtful
Tolerant
Unconcerned about ageing
Warm
Wholesome
Witty
Younger-looking
Zestful
Zany
Other

_____

48.

Single, thirties and anxious?

Mary Balfour, dating coach

I have always enjoyed interfering with other people's lives. First, it was getting my friends fixed up with flats, jobs, kittens and dates. Then it was setting up courses for educationally deprived adults in a run-down inner city neighbourhood.

In 1986, I thought it was time to move on, so I bought an introduction agency called Drawing Down the Moon. I hardly paused for thought – I knew it was exactly what I wanted to do. I had a vision of languishing in a sort of fin de siècle salon sipping delicious coffee with fascinating people telling me all about their lives and loves. Of course, I would be able to add that finishing touch they all yearned for by introducing them to their equally fascinating other half.

The dream turned out to be the reality for about 30 per cent of the time. The other 70 per cent was an extraordinary mixture of rapid learning about what makes people fall in and out of love, fending off those I couldn't help and lurching between financial famine and feast. The learning curve was both enjoyable and intense. I became obsessed with the urge to find out more and I gained a huge amount from studying the approaches that work and comparing them with those that didn't.

I saw thousands of individuals succeed in the love stakes and noted certain formulae emerging as the winners. I also discovered that I could spot the recipes for failure a mile off. So much so, that at the agencies which I run, my staff and I can often predict within a couple of minutes who will get into a good relationship quickly. The others, who will have to learn new strategies first, we call the 'blossomers'.

From years of experience, we know what guidance to give people and what advice is the most constructive. In particular, for women in their late thirties and early forties, we can help them create and make the most of dating opportunities. We can help them take control of their chances of love in spite of the apparent dearth of commitment-minded men and the chances to meet them in society today.

We have a high degree of success with women within this age group, but many newly signed-up women need to draw upon a number of basic lessons before they can go find and captivate Mr Right.

Over the years I have heard variations on the following phrases, many times from new women members who are hearing the ticking of their biological clocks:

'I am 38 years old. I simply don't have time to test drive lots of different men. I want you to match me with my perfect partner really quickly.'

'Let's cut to the chase here. I'll tell you what I *don't* want: I don't like men who are not as intelligent or as successful as me, who aren't wealthy, or are not good-looking. I don't want to meet anyone who lives outside south-west London, and I am only interested in men in their 30s, not older. They should have a degree and their success should be evidenced by where they live and the car they drive. By narrowing these things down, I believe I will have greater success in finding the right man.'

In that quote above, I may be exaggerating a little, but today's quest for a perfect life means our relationship wish list is far longer today than previously. This makes us much fussier and far pickier than ever before. Some people are so particular that they will keep picking and never find anybody. They need to take a long look at themselves and become more open-minded. If they close themselves off from the world of opportunities out there, love will pass them by.

But for men, the image of the sassy, successful, thirty-something female executive, who is completely in charge of her own life and wants a man only marginally more than she wants another garment from Voyage, is also pretty daunting. For all the macho posturing the world expects from men of almost any age, rejection still hurts, and nobody brags to his mates about joining a introduction agency for fear of being seen as a failure.

On the positive side, I do find a great many women of all ages say roughly the same sort of thing. They all want to meet someone who is independent, who's curious, who's playful, who shares the same values and outlook, and who's seeking a permanent relationship.

I find that people nowadays seem to be looking much more for the quality of the emotional connection than they would have done, say twenty years ago. Many women 'of a certain age', look for qualities in a man that are romantic in the sense of a relationship being about tenderness, emotional tenderness and being a best friend and a lover. But I have also found that in some cases, both men and women have developed ideas about relationships, which are becoming increasingly impossible to meet.

Sometimes, being single or unsuccessful in love, coupled with a fertility time line actually exudes from women a state of singleness. They have an aura about them, which can be interpreted as saying, 'If you are not perfect in every way I imagine, then I will not waste my time with you.' A man who is a potential date need not be a mind reader to be able to pick up on these negative vibes.

It's also worth remembering that a significant proportion of people in their late thirties or early forties are actually fairly inexperienced players in the dating game. Many have emerged from long relationships or marriages and are completely 'out-of-practice' when it comes to dating.

If I had to give just one piece of advice, based on all my years of match-making experience, it would be, 'Relax and stop trying to manipulate the future.' If you can just slow down and stop searching and trawling as if your life depended on it, if you can look the other way and discover the real you, then love will track you down. It will. I have seen this happen hundreds of times.

I would also urge women looking for their perfect partner to enlist help. With the career demands and today's hectic lifestyles, it is becoming increasingly difficult to meet suitable partners. Ask your friends or colleagues to matchmake for you. Why not take up an unusual hobby or activity, which engages the chaps (if you can bear to go shark fishing, hang gliding or rock climbing), or go on a cultural or adventure holiday? Wine tastings and private viewings at art galleries are enlightening, non-threatening meeting grounds too. Market yourself through various dating channels, but choose who you use with great care.

Today, the dating industry is big business. National and regional newspapers and magazines have thousands of lonely hearts advertisements; the Internet has opened up a vast array of on-line dating services; there are dating event organisers, speed dating, dating TV channels, singles holidays and many other things in between. In most cases, you pay your money and go about the dating process single-handedly. Of course, there are many successes, but there can also be a lot of time wasted, expense and disappointment, especially if you have gone through the processes all by yourself.

Some people prefer to use an introduction agency because of the personal support and encouragement it can offer. Joining an introduction agency is an investment – an investment in your future happiness. It shouldn't offer a quick fix, which will guarantee to have you lined up with your perfect date within a week. A good agency needs time to help you narrow your search, and give you help in learning or relearning certain dating skills. A good agency will have its members' best interests at heart and will thrive on their success. Furthermore, a good agency will greatly cut down on the heartache, time and expense of numerous unsuccessful or bad dates.

An introduction agency is the perfect way to meet someone who is right for you. In turn, that person is also someone committed to finding the perfect partner. You are matched by your interests, beliefs, character and aspirations and if you require some metaphorical handholding or support in choosing your partner, then there are people there to do just that.

So to summarise, I would urge any woman in her late thirties or early forties, who has so far been eluded by love to broaden her outlook and horizons, to stop clock watching and relax, enlist support and help in her search and get back into circulation. If you can do all those things, the path that fate has divined for you will cross with that of the man with whom you are meant to be, I promise.

When I met Mary Balfour to discuss this book, she made a really startling comment about particular older women who literally try to pinpoint their potential partner. She said, 'Think about your friends. Maybe they are friends you have had from school, or university or from somewhere you worked. Perhaps some of your friends were former neighbours or you met them on holiday or on a course. Whoever your friends are, whether they are old friends or new acquaintances, I bet you didn't have a wish list about their attributes and tick them off. Your friends didn't need to qualify in order to win your friendship; they didn't need to meet certain criteria.

'Yes, you probably found that you had a lot in common and shared similar outlooks, or maybe they are very different to you – that's what makes them interesting. We don't choose our best friends and we don't go out and hunt for them either. "Right, it's the New Year and I am jolly well going to find myself some new friends. I've drawn up a list of the kinds of friends I want and I am going to be very particular – no compromising or making do. Anyone who doesn't meet my stringent standards will be rejected!"

49.

My epiphany

Annie Harrison

The failure of my early romantic life is here within these pages. It's a mixed pallet of several of the recounted experiences, which left me feeling isolated and single at the age of 37. I was emotionally battered and fearful of the future.

Like many women I have interviewed, I couldn't understand what my problem was. I was a good person, popular, attractive, kind and successful. I wanted a family so much and knew I was a perfect candidate for this role. And yet, for a variety of reasons, every romantic relationship I had eventually faltered after a promising start. I started to become desultory and daunted by the magnitude of the quest to find Mr Right.

In August 1997, I resolved to put 'finding the one' on hold, and escaped, alone, to the Greek island of Skyros to sort out my head on a yoga holiday. It gave me time to think about and evaluate my life. I was able to expunge negative thoughts and cut emotional ties to departed love. I cultivated a positive and optimistic mindset; I started to see opportunities and good things when previously I'd been blind to them. Now my glass was half-full instead of always half-empty. And being single and happy wasn't such a bad thing either.

Afterwards, I immersed myself in work and spent weekends in the company of good (mostly married) friends, out of London in the fresh air. In the autumn of that year by pure chance I met Stephen, who is now my husband.

One of my friends had invited me to join a large party at Cheltenham races. Since I am passionate about horseracing, I accepted without hesitation. On the big day, I researched the racing form and went along with the intention of having a good time and picking some winners. I had no idea that I would meet my future husband in the mêlée and jubilation of the racecourse on that bright November day.

I first became aware of Steve shortly after our party arrived at our restaurant table. He was in a different group, but we had some mutual overlaps in friendships. Steve was introduced to our table as 'someone in the know' and he began to tell us which horses would win that day. And he was right.

During that race meeting, Steve and I left our respective parties and buddied up. We scrutinised the horses in the paddock and cheered on our winners from the stands. We'd only just met, but we both felt a comfortable familiarity with each other and a powerful attraction. He made me laugh and I was drawn to his crooked grin, his smiley eyes with long lashes and his mercurial, clever mind.

A few months younger than me, Steve was a doctor of genetics – an equine geneticist working in the thoroughbred breeding industry. He had an ambitious idea to identify the genes linked to performance in thoroughbreds and make a fortune; he was also an accomplished horseman, rode out horses-in-training and horse whispered problem animals. My new friend had learned carriage driving from an antique book and had broken in Finbar, a Shetland-Welsh cob cross stallion. Locally, he was well known for charging like Ben Hur across the Cotswolds, standing in his chariot. He was also an accomplished sportsman, plays the saxophone and is a great host.

At the end of our race day, we exchanged phone numbers, he gave me a big bear hug and we promised to be in touch. I left for London feeling elated. We talked for hours every night and sent funny emails to each other. The following week he invited me to a ball at the Royal Agricultural College in Cirencester, where he also lectured on equine science. We partied all night and I observed that I was old enough to be the mother of many of the younger ball-goers. Not wishing to feel too old, at dawn we saddled up in the first light of morning and sprinted across the gallops on two flighty racehorses.

The rest, as they say, is history. We spent as much time as we could together between the Cotswolds and London, and love blossomed. After so much unhappiness and emptiness in both our previous relationships, we found a deep, companionable and respectful love. A year later he proposed to me on a tiny island off Singapore and we were married in the College chapel just before the Millennium.

During our wedding ceremony we had to stifle giggles when Steve was asked to declare '. . . and all that I have I share with you.' We both knew this amounted to some rugby trophies, a collection of old LPs, a stereo, a 24-year-old Land Rover Defender, a box of tack and some musical instruments. Making this pledge in front of our more affluent friends was quite bizarre and for the first couple of years I was known affectionately as 'the gold-digger'. Steve's young spaniels, Pogue and Rus, 'sang' at our wedding reception, howling their accompaniment to his saxophone with a rendition of Madness' 'House of Fun'. Now geriatrics, the two dogs have been at the core of the family throughout our marriage.

Together we set up a business using DNA analyses to fine-tune the breeding of the perfect racehorse and Steve embarked upon his mission to discover the speed gene combinations in mitochondrial DNA in racehorses. I sold my London flat and shares in a public relations company that I had co-founded to fund our business. Steve developed the science and I obtained as much global media coverage as I could for our fledgling operation. We began married life living in a rented house and drew no income for three years while the research, scientific paper publication and patenting process ate into our resources.

Our two boys were born in quick succession. Not quite a honeymoon baby, Daniel arrived just before my 40th birthday and Louis entered the world a few months before I turned 42. Steve is really a seven-year-old boy at heart and consequently a wonderful father. Our lives are filled with Romans, tanks, archery, yetis, guns, canoes, bikes, kites, robots, rockets, pirates, sword fights, wrestling, fossils, football and rugby. The house is mud, mess and testosterone-filled most of the time – in stark contrast to my quiet, tidy single existence of the past. Both of us have been fulfilled in our late roles as parents to two crazy boys and belonging to the circle of friends that being a parent brings.

After several tough years financially, our business took off and we now provide genetic advice and DNA data to owners, breeders, trainers and betting syndicates around the world. Steve has identified and patented the gene combinations that help elite horses to win. After years where we risked everything we had, even in these difficult times we are bucking the trend. It's taken a long time and the ride was quite scary at times, but it's been worth it.

Now it's nearly 12 years since we first met. Family life came to us comparatively late, but that was good. We have slowed down and filled out a bit around the girth. Steve didn't have much hair anyway, but the spread of grey for both of us is increasing. Being settled with each other's company, we no longer crave such hectic social lives and making the most of every minute; there's no more waiting and wondering if 'the one' will arrive. For both of us, 'the one' is right here. From the safety and reassurance of a happy marriage, we have reflected on our adult lives and have had time to examine mistakes, missed opportunities and past poor judgements. They all happened for a reason and in the patterns of destiny, we wouldn't have arrived where we are now without some of the pitfalls along the way.

Nor do we mourn the passing of all the good times and the vitality of youth. In having my children in my forties, I have finally learned to let go of the past – the good, the bad and the what-might-have been. Instead, we are focusing on the present and channelling our energies into enriching the lives of our two sons. Marriage has killed my previous obsession with age and hanging onto the past. With 50 just around the corner, my attitude now is 'bring it on, and let's enjoy it! Life is for living'.

Steve was not how I imagined my husband would be: he is far more. But I'm not going to sit here and gloat about how brilliant he is and how happy we are together – that's not what this book is about. What I will say is this: if you want to find your life partner and be fulfilled as a person, by making some fundamental changes within yourself, these and other good things will come to you. Rhonda Byrne's new age bestseller, *The Secret*, extols the values of attracting the things you want most in life. To me, it makes perfect sense. When I read it last year, I realised that I had already adopted many of the lessons in making my dreams come true

Take note of the cautionary tales in this book and draw on the positive experiences of those women who beat a path through the dark state of singledom to emerge the other side into sunlight. Expect the unexpected, be prepared to take risks and allow yourself to be surprised. If you have a hunch that something is good, follow it. Whenever you have misgivings about something or someone, trust your instincts but maintain optimism and positivity throughout.

My life has been, and continues to be an adventure. I'm just so grateful that I now have three others to share it.

50.

Finding Mr Right: the sum total

So now you've read the book. Hopefully, there will be a few chapters to which you can relate. I hope too that you will be able to draw on some of the stories, testimonies, experiences and thoughts of the contributors. Collective experience is always a good thing. Far more than men, women tend to share their thoughts, feelings and life episodes – it's very much the Mars and Venus thing.

When we reach a certain age, however worldly wise we may have become, we can begin to feel isolated by our own existence. Friends move on to new pastures, we remain consumed by our work and life-changing events seem to be less spontaneous and more infrequent. It's no longer so easy to tap in to a mine of female knowledge relating to this particular phase in our lives – married friends are occupied with their own lives, single women can be widely dispersed and kindred spirits may now be in short supply. Whatever happened to the female intuition we're supposed to possess in abundance? Facing the future single-handedly at this critical stage in one's life can be scary, so I wanted to distil from the pages of this book the quintessence that could change your life.

What, then, is the secret? How does an unattached, worried single woman in her late thirties suddenly morph into a smug-married with babies? How does she get from being one to becoming two, and possibly more all within a short timeframe? It's a tall order, but it can – and is – being done. Even with my fairly disastrous dating history, I'm living proof and the experience prompted me to compile this book. There's no magic formula, but some broad-brush guidelines may just add the clarity you seek. In summing up, I've taken the informed wisdom of the contributors and set it out, succinctly:

✳ **Let go.** Cut yourself off from your past. Let go of lost loves, might-have-beens, former loves of your life, complete bastards, timewasters, the best times, the worst times. In the laundry of life, throw out those old photographs, letters, mementoes and keepsakes from your dating history. Start anew, fresh and uncluttered. Close past chapters and begin your life on a new page.

✳ **Develop a positive mental attitude.** Find ways that are right for you in coping with your emotional baggage. In your head, rid yourself of negative or hurt feelings. If you think you need it, get professional help, even if it's just for a few sessions. Read books on letting go. Being free of your emotional past is critical to success in making a fresh start. Try to develop a positive mental attitude to all aspects of your life. Take up some new interests, travel, or do something daring or caring. Smile and laugh more. An optimistic demeanour will bring good things to you in abundance. Be open-minded about *everything*. If you can create an aura about you that is positive, can-do, confident and content everything else will fall into place. Avoid proactively meeting anyone until you are unburdened from the things that are pulling you down.

✳ **Get unstuck and go and do something.** If you feel stuck or trapped by your current lifestyle and it appears to be hampering your progress, make changes. Move house, change jobs or careers, take up new pastimes or hobbies, go travelling or indulge in some adventure. If you can't do something big, try changing smaller things in your life. Do something different, challenging or charitable. Take your mind off your existing worries and instead do something for you – not for your friends, your peers, your parents, siblings or a potential lover. You don't need to impress anyone – you just have to be comfortable with who you are. But get on and do something.

 Take a decision about your way forward, and be open-minded. EXPECT THE UNEXPECTED. If you decide to join a dating agency, place a lonely-heart advertisement, go paragliding in the Alps, learn to tango or open a guest house in Marrakesh, do it! Whatever you choose to do will change your life, but don't try to predict or engineer the future to suit you. And view any setbacks or disappointments as positives. Remember the Buddhists' mantra about cause and effect: everything happens for a reason. Who knows what will happen? Things always change when you start a new project.

* **Personal tinkering.** If you are unhappy about certain aspects of your physical appearance or personality, take steps to change them. You don't need to undergo a radical make-over or character replacement, but just a few tweaks here and there. A new look or a slight change in style will make you feel better about yourself. This personal feel-good factor permeates through into the wider world.

* **Babies.** This is a tough one, but temporarily forget about babies in an emotional sense. If everyone around you seems to be pregnant or having babies, face up to it. Take an interest in their pregnancies, hold babies and smile at them. Get practical and offer to change a nappy or push the buggy. Fact: men who want to have children are attracted to maternal types. At social events, if you can demonstrate that you enjoy the company of little ones, your desirability will be boosted hugely. OK, the pain might all come out when you arrive home alone – this is aversion therapy at its absolute worst. But remember, a new man won't take pity on you because past lovers forgot or refused to give you children. He won't give you a handkerchief and a cuddle, or offer to give you a baby to make you happy. He's going to run a mile!

  There's a real possibility that you might meet a man in the future who already has children, so having a child-friendly attitude would prove an asset. Take pleasure from the children around you – nephews, nieces, godchildren, friends' children, or sponsor a child overseas. This might help ease some of the angst. Think very hard about any decisions you might take to have a baby as a single person – through adoption, IVF or any other means. Involve friends and family in your decision-making, particularly if you think you will need their support and help in the future.

* **Change your environment.** This means 'get out more' or if you are already in a social whirl, try mixing in new circles. You won't meet a potential love interest if you continue to socialise in the same groups or stay in every night. If your social life has taken a nosedive, pep it up with activities and functions where you will come into contact with new people and prospects.

* **Understand what men like.** Remember, they prefer to do the chasing and asking and they always want something they can't have. As a generalisation, the qualities they prefer in women are mystery, femininity, individuality, humour, intelligence, creativity and practicability. They like women to show them kindness, gentleness, nurturing and feminine assertiveness.

* **Understand what they don't like.** Men don't enjoy being hunted, stalked or presented with the whole deal. Being too keen, intense, available or pushy is a real turn-off. Men are just as bored, as any woman might be, by people who talk about themselves, their work or money the whole time. A man is not attracted to a woman who is resentful or angry about her past – it's not his fault you spent five years with a serial monogamist. And contrary to popular belief, most men want to have children – not with anyone – with someone they love, who is permanent in their lives and shows maternal instincts, at a time when he's ready. If a man doesn't want to have children, he will make that very clear from the outset, so don't try and sell parenthood to a man you have recently met. Whether or not he wants children, he just won't be forced into buying.

* **Take a risk and open your mind to new possibilities.** Play hard-to-get, not just at the beginning, but as he is drawn in. A bit of mystique is very alluring. Throw out all your fixed ideas and wish lists, and instead see what happens. You don't know everything and you might just be surprised by something (or someone) new. As we get older, we tend to become more one-dimensional in our ideas and tastes (look at your mother!). Ease up a bit on your outlook and attitudes, look around and notice all the things you haven't seen before. Dispense with timeframes, too. Stop measuring time and calculating how much you've got left.

* **Be feminine and womanly.** Rarely are men look for a woman who is 'just one of the boys' and enjoys doing all the things they like doing – only with their mates. They can do all that macho strutting and competitive posturing with male colleagues, their friends and at the gym. However, try as much as possible to understand how men think and act as you would wish anyone to treat you. Treat them with respect and honesty; discover who you really are and be yourself. Find an inner generosity – of spirit, thought and attitude. The attributes of sincerity and kindness will enhance your attractiveness.

* **Make the most of it.** Each of our lives pans out in a certain way. In some cases we can influence how things turn out, but the hand of fate ultimately pushes us towards whatever destiny awaits us. Along the way there will be surprises and disappointments, joy and regrets. Some things will be achieved almost undeservedly, while other things might elude us. What we all need, and women possess this, is an ability to deal with everything thrown at us and to remain positive. We should never allow ourselves to be defeated just because we didn't get what we wanted. There is still work to be done, opportunities to exploit and happiness to seize.

Thank you for reading *Finding Mr Right*. I hope that you have found it empathetic and helpful. I understand what you are or have been going through – I've been there myself. This book of shared experiences and knowledge has been compiled from the heart. May it help you in your quest to find happiness and fulfilment in the future.

Further reading

Balfour, Mary, *Smart Dating*, Mary Balfour Publications, 2008.

Black, Rachel and Louise Saul, *Beyond Childlessness: For Every Woman Who Ever Wanted to Have a Child*, Rodale International, 2005.

Byrne, Rhonda, *The Secret*, Simon & Schuster, 2006.

Cagen, Sasha, *Quirkyalone: A Manifesto for Uncompromising Romantics*, HarperSanFrancisco, 2006.

Clover, Andrew, *Dad Rules*, Fig Tree, 2008.

Defago, Nicki, *Child Free and Loving It!*, Vision Paperbacks, 2005.

Fielding, Helen, *Bridget Jones's Diary*, Picador, 2001.

Fisher, Bruce, *When Your Relationship Ends*, Impact Publishers Inc, 2005.

Gray, John, *Men are from Mars, Women are from Venus: How to Get What you Want in Your Relationship*, Thorsons, 2002.

Gregory, Elizabeth, *Ready: Why Women are Embracing the New Later Motherhood: Inside the Lives of the New Later Mothers*, Basic Books, 2008.

Hewlett, Sylvia Ann, *Baby Hunger: The New Battle for Motherhood*, Atlantic Books, 2003.

— *Creating a Life: What Every Woman Needs to Know about Having a Baby and a Career*, Hyperion Books, 2004.

Ironside, Virginia, *You'll Get Over It: The Rage of Bereavement*, Penguin, 1997.

Krystal, Phyllis, *Cutting the Ties That Bind: Growing up and Moving on*, Red Wheel/Weiser, 1993.

McKenna, Paul and Willbourn, Hugh, *I Can Mend Your Broken Heart*, Bantam Press, 2006.

Molloy, John T., *Why Men Marry Some Women and Not Others*, Element Books, 2004.

Quilliam, Susan, *Positive Thinking*, Dorling Kindersley, 2008.

Sweet, Corinne, *Birth Begins at Forty*, Hodder & Stoughton, 2001.

Young, Toby, *How to Lose Friends & Alienate People*, Abacus, 2002

Watson, Shane, *How to Meet a Man After Forty and Other Midlife Dilemmas Solved*, Penguin, 2009.

Contact Annie Harrison at: www.findingmrrightthebook.com

Acknowledgements

First, a big thank you to my husband, Stephen, for his patience and for putting up with my obsessive behaviour while researching this book. When we married and had our boys, both Stephen and I thought I had left thirtysomething angst behind. Obviously I hadn't, although the emphasis has shifted from me onto others. The fruition of this book has made it all worthwhile. Second, I wouldn't have been able to assimilate all the experiences without the help and support of so many friends, acquaintances and contributors, some of whom I have never even met. Many, many thanks to all those men and women who emailed me and to those I nabbed for information.

Thank you to Lorice Lazarus, who serendipitously introduced me to JR Books, and to Jeremy Robson of JR Books for taking me on. I am humbled to debut alongside such esteemed company in the publisher's catalogue.

Because my experiences in relation to 'meeting the one' are limited, I am indebted for the time, honesty, encouragement, knowledge, invaluable opinions, quotes, anecdotes, contributions, edits and introductions from the following:

Sam Abdalla, Alison Baldwin, Mary Balfour, Kate Battersby, Dr Peter Bowen-Simpkins, Sasha Cagen, Louise Chatwyn, Andrew Clover, Caroline Davies, Professor Robin Dunbar, Mariella Frostrup, Professor Elizabeth Gregory, Donna Grieg, Steve Hampson, Dr Sylvia Ann Hewlett, Fiona Higgins, Tom J., Jacqueline J., Melissa Kampf, Dillie Keane, Joe Kurtzer, Professor Ian Lancashire, Jeremy Laurance, Dr Gillian Lockwood, Rhona Mackie, Frances Manwaring, John Mirowski, John T. Molloy, Mairead

Molloy, Nick O., Darshna Patel, Amanda Platell, Susan Quilliam, Dr Janet Reibstein, Mona Saleh, Mandy Saligari, Nadine Starr, Clover Stroud, Sarah Symonds, Hugh & Emma S., James T., Tom Tomaszewski, Shane Watson, Daisy Waugh, Anna Welles, Lesley Wilson and Catherine Bailey at JR Books, Toby Young, Elizabeth Williams and her friends, the 'ladies who know' for their pearls of wisdom, all the guys who contributed opinions to 'being the ideal woman', all those who pondered the single life, those who settled for less, three generations of the Tennant family, the mistresses and wives, serial monogamists and tail-enders, all those who commented on 'creeping nonchoice', the health professionals, the agony aunts, the 'birth mothers not' ladies, the motherhood over-40 brigade, the divorcees, the women who found their elusive life partners, the happily single, the unhappily single, the quirkyalones, the parents, the childless and the child-free.

In addition, I would like to thank the following organisations for their assistance:

Berkeley International

The British Association for Adoption and Fostering

The British Association for Counselling and Psychotherapy

The British Association for Sex and Relationship Therapy

Cruse Bereavement Care

the *Daily Mail*

the *Daily Telegraph*

Divorceaid

Drawing Down the Moon

growupdating.co.uk

The *Guardian*

Harvard Business Review

The Human Fertilisation & Embryology Authority

The *Independent*

Marie Claire

IPC Syndication

Midland Fertility Services

NI Syndication

The National Council for Hypnotherapy

The National Gamete Donation Trust

The *Observer*

Office for National Statistics

quirkyalone.net

Solo Syndication

the *Sunday Times*
Thoroughbred Genetics
The Times

The following articles, extracts and advice have been reproduced with kind permission:

'An older girl's guide to husband hunting' by Shane Watson, © NI Syndication, 8 July 2007.

'Finding love in your forties' by Mariella Frostrup, © Mariella Frostrup/*Marie Claire*/IPC+ Syndication, February 2007.

'If I could change one thing in my life . . .' All quotations remain the intellectual property of their respective originators. I do not assert any claim of copyright for individual quotations. All use of quotations is done under the fair use copyright principle.

'Free again' by Frances Manwaring, © Frances Manwaring, July 2007.

'Striving to be happy' by Mandy Saligari, © Mandy Saligari, August 2008.

'Singledom and the great media myth' by Mariella Frostrup, © Guardian News & Media Ltd, 2007.

'Pondering the single life': Licence to quote extract from *Notes on a Scandal* by Zoe Heller, March 2004, granted by Penguin Books.

All other quotations remain the intellectual property of their respective originators. I do not assert any claim of copyright for individual quotations. Use of previously published quotations is done under the fair use copyright principal.

'Looking For Mrs Goodbar' by Toby Young, © Toby Young, March 2009.

'Is your man Mr Right or Mr Write-off?' by Amanda Platell, © *Daily Mail*. This is an edited version of a longer article published in the *Daily Mail*, 28 July 2006.

'Always the mistress, never the wife' with grateful thanks to the mistresses and wives for their frankness. Section contributed by Sarah Symonds, © Sarah J. Symonds, January 2009.

'Settle for less in love' with grateful thanks to Elizabeth Williams.

'Where have all the men gone?', © Professor Robin Dunbar.

'Try this instead' by Andrew Clover © NI Syndication, 1 February 2008.

'Motherhood, to be or not to be?' Grateful thanks to Jeremy Laurance, health editor of the *Independent*, the *Independent* newspaper and all the health professionals quoted, January 2008.

'Pregnant and single – am I brave or selfish?' by Mariella Frostrup, © Guardian News & Media Ltd, 2007.

'Creeping nonchoice' extracted with the kind permission of *Harvard Business Review*, April 2002.

'Child-free – I'm not ill or nasty, I just don't want to be a mum' by Kate Battersby/the *Daily Telegraph*, 31 May 2005.

'Women who conceive accidentally on purpose' by Clover Stroud, © NI Syndication, 5 October 2008.

'Are you a quirkyalone?' © Sasha Cagen, January 2004.

'New beginnings' with grateful thanks to Rhona Mackie. 'Do not stand at my grave and weep', © Mary Elizabeth Frye 1932.

'Meditations whilst flying a kite' by Nadine Starr – Note: This poem has been printed in a number of publications and versions through the years showing the author as Don Herold, Nadine Starr, Jorge Luis Borges, and many others.

'Single, thirties and anxious?' with grateful thanks to Mary Balfour.